THE BATTLE OF NEW ORLEANS
IN HISTORY AND MEMORY

THE BATTLE OF NEW ORLEANS IN HISTORY AND MEMORY

EDITED BY
LAURA LYONS McLEMORE

Louisiana State University Press Baton Rouge

Published with the assistance of the Noel Foundation

Published by Louisiana State University Press

Manufactured in the United States of America
First printing

DESIGNER: Michelle A. Neustrom
TYPEFACES: Tribute, diplay; Adobe Minion Pro, text
PRINTER AND BINDER: McNaughton & Gunn, Inc.

LIBRARY OF CONGRESS CATALOGING-IN-PUBLICATION DATA

Names: McLemore, Laura Lyons, 1950– editor.
Title: The Battle of New Orleans in history and memory / edited by Laura Lyons McLemore.
Description: Baton Rouge : Louisiana State University Press, 2016. | Includes bibliographical references and index.
Identifiers: LCCN 2016017096| ISBN 978-0-8071-6465-5 (cloth : alk. paper) | ISBN 978-0-8071-6466-2 (pdf) | ISBN 978-0-8071-6467-9 (epub) | ISBN 978-0-8071-6468-6 (mobi)
Subjects: LCSH: New Orleans, Battle of, New Orleans, La., 1815.
Classification: LCC E356.N5 B229 2017 | DDC 973.5/239—dc23
LC record available at https://lccn.loc.gov/2016017096

The paper in this book meets the guidelines for permanence and durability of the Committee on Production Guidelines for Book Longevity of the Council on Library Resources. ♾

In Memory of James S. and Ruth Herring Noel

Contents

Preface and Acknowledgments

LAURA LYONS McLEMORE

Americans sing the "Star-Spangled Banner" with gusto at all sorts of events, from commencement ceremonies to baseball games. Phrases like "our country right or wrong," "Don't give up the ship!," and "We have met the enemy and they are ours" have become standards in American culture. The iconic figure of General Jackson on his steed in front of St. Louis Cathedral in New Orleans adorns countless postcards and often provides the backdrop for political photo opportunities. These have become so ingrained in American life that few Americans ever think about their origins, and fewer still know the real history behind them. For others, who may know about the War of 1812 connection, these phrases and images and the lore attached to them may represent the entire story. The War of 1812 is a "forgotten conflict" for most Americans, or, more accurately, a conflict many twenty-first-century Americans outside academia never knew enough about to forget. The myths are far better known than the actual battles. But the War of 1812 was an important milestone in our nation's history. The occasion of the bicentennial of that war seems appropriate for bringing that history to light. The essays that follow attempt to do just that by exploring aspects of the war, specifically the Battle of New Orleans, and how events such as this make their way into our "memory." In November 2014 a symposium commemorating the bicentennial of the Battle of New Orleans was held at Louisiana State University in Shreveport. These essays are the product of that meeting.

We are indebted to the board of the Noel Foundation for its support of the bicentennial symposium on the Battle of New Orleans and for helping to make the publication of this volume possible. I am also grateful to LSU Shreveport and to Dr. Alan Gabehart, Dean of Noel Library, for supporting this project. Margaret Lovecraft, Acquisitions Editor at the LSU Press, enthusiastically embraced the proposal and ushered it through the approval process. Most especially, I thank the nine contributors to the volume, who so generously devoted their time, scholarship, and expertise to its completion.

THE BATTLE OF NEW ORLEANS
IN HISTORY AND MEMORY

Introduction

LAURA LYONS McLEMORE

The summer of 1811 found US President James Madison between a rock, Great Britain, and a hard place, France. War between the two European powers had reignited in 1803 and caught the neutral United States in the middle. The most critical problems were commercial and maritime. The United States was the world's largest neutral shipper. A fortune was at stake, but only if the neutral rights of the fledgling nation were respected. Through a barrage of orders and decrees, Britain and France made neutral shipping impossible. Both belligerents seized US shipping. In addition, Britain made a habit of confiscating sailors as well as cargo, pressing them into British service. It was an act of disrespect, a direct violation of the sovereignty of the United States and a mark of Britain's refusal to recognize that the American flag protected people sailing under it. Madison's predecessor, Thomas Jefferson, had tried "peaceable coercion" in the form of an embargo that, by the end of Jefferson's administration in March 1809, proved a demonstrable failure and was repealed. Several complicated measures of economic coercion were tried in 1809 and 1810, but each measure was weaker than the previous one. Neither Britain nor France made any concessions. Madison was pushed one way and another by the two powers. In 1811 the situation was such that the American minister to Britain returned home, in effect breaking off diplomatic relations.

That same year, some remarkable new leaders joined the Twelfth Congress. They were young Republicans from the South and West, led by John C. Calhoun and Henry Clay. Soon called the War Hawks, they led in persuading Congress that while there were dangers in war (the republic was barely two decades old and still very weak militarily), there were even greater dangers in continued submission. The War Hawks were concerned about the continued presence of the British in the old Northwest, where they were believed to be stirring up Indians to oppose American settlers. These new congressmen were also concerned about the agricultural depression in the South and West, which they blamed on American efforts at economic coercion. At the same time, Spain continued to occupy Florida and to support the Creek and Seminole Indians there as a barrier to US expansion. Though British and Spanish rivalry made it difficult for the two to cooperate, they shared a desire to see a weaker United States. Spain had been actively engaged in opposition to US intrusions for some time.[1] The machinations of Aaron Burr and General James Wilkinson in collaboration with Spain to detach the western states and the Louisiana Territory, along with the West Florida revolt of 1810, left the United States nervous about the Spanish presence in the South, in addition to being concerned about the British in the Northwest.[2] The War Hawks' overriding concern, however, seemed to be the independence and honor of the United States, the security of the republic. As the War Hawks saw it, the sovereign independence and honor of the United States were at stake. Not surprisingly, politics were involved too.[3]

The Republicans had been in control of government since 1801. The failure of the United States to defend its independence and honor was their failure. A national election would occur in 1812. Republican ineptitude might return Federalists to power. The Republicans were well aware that not only the republic but Republican leadership faced an existential threat. In the face of pressure from all sides, Madison asked Congress for a declaration of war in June 1812, and the United States declared war on June 18. Britain repealed its Orders in Council on June 23, but the news arrived too late.[4]

From the outset, the War of 1812 was an unpopular war in New England. It devastated New Englanders' commercial interests; in their view, it threatened the world's last hope for political stability, and in that hotbed of Federalism it was considered a Republican war. Thus, most of New England was at best apathetic and at worst openly hostile. The war was, in general, a fiasco for the United States. There were some notable victories, particularly at sea, but the US Navy, with sixteen ships, hardly presented a serious threat to the British navy, with five hundred. As the fighting wore on, New England Federalism became increasingly associated with opposition to it. New Englanders refused to loan the government money; they sympathized with the British; their congressmen opposed a national draft, and Massachusetts and Rhode Island refused to allow their militias to enter national service in 1814.

This opposition reached a climax in December 1814, when representatives of five New England states met in Hartford, Connecticut, to discuss the war. There was talk of secession and a call for a series of constitutional amendments designed to protect New England shipping. Luck was not with the Federalists, however. Peace negotiations produced the Treaty of Ghent by Christmas Eve, 1814, and the last great British offensive ended in early January 1815, with total victory by US forces under Andrew Jackson at the Battle of New Orleans. The Federalists returned home ridiculed and totally discredited, charged with disloyalty and even treason. The war Republicans probably should not have gotten into and should not have won put an end to their Federalist opposition.[5]

The Battle of New Orleans, then, was a signal victory. It was of great importance for the self-image of the United States. Though the terms of the treaty restored the status quo ante bellum, the Battle of New Orleans enabled a nation very nearly defeated in 1814 to claim a victory. News of the treaty and of Jackson's victory reached the East Coast almost simultaneously. As the historian Reginald Horsman put it, "Americans forgot the reasons the war had been fought, and the humiliations it had brought, and celebrated the successful termination of the 'second war for independence.'"[6]

Volumes have been devoted to the intersection of history and memory and how great events in human experience have been rendered relevant to successive societies. A number of philosophers and historians have observed that every generation writes its own history in search of a "usable past," one that more than simple being relevant, promotes the multiple agendas of that generation. At least one historian has asserted that "history's major contribution to the present may be in promoting an understanding of ourselves in cultural terms."[7] The distinguished historian and essayist Henry Steele Commager noted that societies define themselves by common ideas and historical memories, and he attempted to explain how the founding generations of Americans wrote their own historical narrative. "Nothing," wrote Commager, "is more impressive than the speed and lavishness with which Americans provided themselves with a 'usable past,' manifest in history, legends, and heroes, not to mention such cultural artifacts as paintings and patriotic ballads." These myths and memories, he asserted, act as "cultural adhesive." The War of 1812 is one of those "forgotten conflicts" that has had an ongoing cultural impact even though the war itself is hardly remembered: "Don't give up the ship!"; "Oh say can you see"; "We have met the enemy and they are ours"; the hunters of Kentucky repulsing Pakenham.[8] The farther we get from a historical event, the more we tend to shape the memory of it to make it "usable" and the less we know about the real people and events. This collection of essays examines the real and remembered Battle of New Orleans and War of 1812 and the significance of both two hundred years later.[9]

The Battle of New Orleans, which took place from December 23, 1814 to January 8, 1815, had many consequences: It crystalized the way the United States eventually viewed the War of 1812, as a "glorious victory." It inspired a spirit of nationalism that marked the beginning of America's status as an independent power, set Andrew Jackson on the road to the presidency, made American historians conscious of the nation, and gave Noah Webster's generation the beginnings of cultural independence they had yearned for in the writings of American authors like Washington Irving, James Fenimore Cooper, and William Cullen Bryant. It gave impetus to a school of American painting depicting the romanticism of the Hudson River, the Delaware, "mountain majesties," prairies, and "fruited plains." Whether we in the twentieth century realize it or not, the War of 1812 and the Battle of New Orleans are deeply ingrained in our American collective memory; they have become part of who we are.

Donald R. Hickey acknowledges the significance of this collective memory when he points out that "what we know that ain't so" gives us trouble. Myths are traditional stories of ostensibly historical events that, like history, serve to unfold part of the worldview of a people or explain a culture to itself. Hickey points out that "myths are essentially misconceptions" whose significance varies by degree. When, instead of questioning our national mythology and the evidence we assume supports it, we simply accept it as true, our understanding of history becomes skewed. He examines some of the leading myths that have made their way into the collective memory—some, embellishments on accounts originating with actual participants, and others "invented out of whole cloth" to serve a variety of purposes. Sometimes, he notes, stories become part of the collective memory because of a misinterpretation of the evidence.

Mark Cheathem, in "Assessing Andrew Jackson's Hatred of the British," agrees with Hickey that by reaching larger audiences than the typical academic book or journal article, myths convey lasting ideas about Andrew Jackson's life and career that prove difficult to displace or correct. Cheathem examines how Jackson's sensational reputation derived from contemporary anecdotes and was perpetuated by respected historians. He concludes that though Jackson's intense hatred of the British is a common theme in assessments of Old Hickory, the evidence indicates that Andrew Jackson's anti-British sentiments differed little from those of other Americans who supported colonial independence during the Revolutionary War. Cheathem argues that contrary to the myth that revenge was Jackson's prime motivation for fighting against the British in New Orleans, Jackson did not hold a lifelong hatred of the British but in fact displayed a political maturity and self-control in his later political career that often go unnoticed. He points out that as long as Jackson is dismissed as a man driven by his emotions, the questions that need to be asked about Jackson's influence on the United States and the Atlantic world will go unasked and unanswered.

If myths about Andrew Jackson obscure our understanding of Jackson's real influence on the United States and Atlantic diplomacy, a distinct lack of memory and awareness hamper Americans' appreciation of its significance. Alex Mikaberidze, in his essay "'The Dreams of Empires': The War of 1812 in an International Context," gives us a uniquely European perspective. Like Hickey, Mikaberidze shows that the 1812 conflict between Britain and her former North American colonies may be thought of as a forgotten war, but it was important. He notes that the War of 1812 occurred within a much larger conflict of truly global dimensions. It was the result of friction caused by the Napoleonic Wars, and thus it is necessary to understand the wider, transatlantic context in which this war took place. Mikaberidze provides details of the long-standing conflicts in Europe that were the context for the War of 1812 and the Battle of New Orleans. He also reminds us that even at this early stage in nationhood, America had an important role to play in the European conflict. As one British observer put it, "If it was not for the supplies from America, the army here could not be maintained." The backstory of America's second war with Britain in 1812, Mikaberidze points out, was clearly more complex than most North Americans have ever known or remembered.

By contrast, Gene Allen Smith deals not with what is remembered but rather with what has been forgotten. In doing so, he reminds us how memory serves to promote certain ideas and agendas. He draws attention to the fact that the story of black participation in the War of 1812 and the Battle of New Orleans generally has not been remembered; yet the war represented an important watershed in North American racial relations. African Americans saw the second war with Great Britain as a means for advancing their own agendas. Some joined in hopes of attaining freedom or bettering their material conditions; others sought an opportunity to define their own identity as Americans. Smith argues that instead of marking a favorable change in American racial relations, the War of 1812 marked a worsening of black-white relations, and as new prejudicial racial distinctions arose, public memories of the War of 1812 erased African American contributions.

Paul Gelpi, in his "In Defense of Liberty: The Battalion d'Orleans and Its Battle for New Orleans," provides an example of how memory becomes reality. The Battle of New Orleans, he argues, "Americanized" the New Orleans militia. Gelpi makes the case that the Creole Battalion d'Orleans, in taking up arms to defend New Orleans against the British, became defenders of American liberty.

Blake Dunnavent underscores the relevance of the United States' second major conflict with Great Britain to a number of concepts deemed significant by today's armed forces. Focusing on leadership, Dunnavent shows how Commodore Perry's careful planning, preparation, discipline, flexibility, and inspiring personal courage enabled the United States to attain one of its most decisive victories in the War of 1812 and secure control of Lake Erie. He notes many of the same qualities in Andrew Jackson's leadership at the Battle of New Orleans, enabling the Americans to prevail over a numerically superior and more experienced foe. Dunnavent points out that the War of 1812 altered how the US government viewed America's armed forces and laid the "foundation for the American profession of arms." He concludes that the present-day US military can draw upon and assimilate lessons learned about leadership in the War of 1812 and suggests that that war provided the building blocks for the creation of formal institutions to study the past to develop future war scenarios and leadership.

Returning to examination of the Battle of New Orleans remembered, Joe Stoltz illustrates how commemorations of the battle were employed to create a "usable past" and promote various goals. Stoltz recounts the difficulties of maintaining memorials as society evolves and becomes increasingly distant from an event. He notes that schoolbooks were employed to ensure that children learned the "real" history of the Battle of New Orleans, that is, the version that supported the ideas patriotic associations wished to promote: the romance of the triumphant frontiersman, the importance of the Battle of New Orleans in making the Treaty of Ghent possible, and lessons about the advancement of society that became possible when nations did not go to war. Stoltz points out that among the uses to which commemoration of the Battle of New Orleans was put was recovery by former Confederate veterans of the victory they were denied during the Civil War, recalling Pierre Nora's thesis of memory reconstructing history.[10]

Leslie Gruesbeck illuminates the role of visual images in shaping the contemporary popular perception as well as the public memory of the Battle of New Orleans and its hero, General Andrew Jackson, in "Continually Heroic: Portraying Andrew Jackson through Classical and Contemporary Heroic Devices." She examines both positive and negative depictions that Jackson's personality evoked and their political implications, providing us with insight into the durability of Jackson as an American icon. Jackson remains, in fact, so much of an icon that he has found his way into popular ballads and modern musical drama, which perpetuate his relevance right up to the present day.

In "The Battle of New Orleans in Popular Music and Culture," Tracey Laird deconstructs versions of probably the best-known tune about the battle, "The Battle of New Orleans," to reveal how it has come to epitomize the Battle of New Orleans in the collective memory. It is no accident that the new style of political campaigning, eschewing issues in favor of "personalities and slogans," accompanied Andrew Jackson's first presidential run in 1824. As Laird explains, Andrew Jackson today holds a dual reputation based on two extremes: the competent, skilled military strategist who won the Battle of New Orleans and saved the United States from being retaken by the British and the ruthless ethnocentrist who forced an entire civilization of people to leave their homeland for a doomed Trail of Tears. The Battle of New Orleans, Laird concludes, becomes at once a metaphor for both the best and the worst of American character: the proud battle scars, which represent a uniquely American combination of individualism and communal sacrifice, alongside the shameful scars, which represent the horror and injustices of that same society's history of race-based slavery.

These essays taken together allow us to view the Battle of New Orleans, both the real event and society's memory of it, in ways that it has not often been viewed. My hope is that it will serve as a starting point for considering or reconsidering the part this historical event plays in Louisianans' and Americans' remembrance and understanding of their past.

NOTES

1. Frank L. Owsley Jr., "British and Spanish Activities in West Florida during the War of 1812," *Florida Historical Quarterly* 46, no. 1 (October 1967): 111.

2. James G. Cusick, "Some Thoughts on Spanish East and West Florida as Borderlands," ibid. 90, no. 2 (Fall 2011): 134–35.

3. See Richard Buel Jr., *America on the Brink: How the Political Struggle over the War of 1812 Almost Destroyed the Young Republic* (New York: Palgrave Macmillan, 2005), 61–87.

4. For greater detail on the causes of the War of 1812, see Donald R. Hickey, *The War of 1812: A Forgotten Conflict* (Urbana: University of Illinois Press, 1989); Reginald Horsman, *The New Republic: The United States of America, 1789–1815* (Harlow, UK, and New York: Longman, 2000); Bradford Perkins, *Prologue to War: England and the United States, 1805–1812* (Berkeley: University of California Press, 1968); and J. C. A. Stagg, *Mr. Madison's War: Politics, Diplomacy, and Warfare in the Early American Republic, 1783–1830* (Princeton, NJ: Princeton University Press, 1983).

5. See Buel, *America on the Brink,* 226–41.

6. Horsman, *New Republic,* 253.

7. Walter L. Buenger and Robert A. Calvert, eds., *Texas through Time: Evolving Interpretations* (College Station: Texas A&M University Press, 1991), ix.

8. H. S. Commager, *The Search for a Usable Past, and Other Essays in Historiography* (New York: Knopf, 1967), 13, 15.

9. These essays were originally presented at a symposium commemorating the bicentennial of the Battle of New Orleans at Noel Memorial Library, LSU Shreveport, 13–14 November 2015.

10. The two best-known students of social or collective memory in the twentieth century define the term *collective memory* based on different perspectives. The first contemporary use of the term was in 1925, when Maurice Halbwachs established a connection between social groups and collective memory. In Halbwachs's view, memory and history were antithetical: memory distorted the past, while history tried to correct memory's inaccuracies. In the late twentieth century, the French sociologist Pierre Nora reversed the relationship between memory and history. Nora theorized that instead of being part of a grand narrative, *les lieux de mémoire,* the places of memory, were only loosely connected, if at all, and the task of historians was to reconstruct cultural heritage by tying reference points together, an idea akin to the notion of history explaining a culture to itself. In one view, history shapes memory; in the other, memory reconstructs history. See Patrick Hutton, "Recent Scholarship on Memory and History," *History Teacher* 33, no. 4 (August 2000): 537–38; and Jeffrey K. Olick and Joyce Robbins, "Social Memory Studies: From 'Collective Memory' to the Historical Sociology of Mnemonic Practices," *Annual Review of Sociology* 24 (1998): 112.

1

"What We Know That Ain't So"
Myths of the War of 1812

DONALD R. HICKEY

The title of this essay is taken from a longer quotation that is typically rendered something like this: "It isn't what we don't know that gives us trouble; it's what we know that ain't so." In other words, if we think we know something, we do not question it, and this unquestioning acceptance may cause trouble for us if the "truth" turns out to be false.

This quotation has been variously attributed to Will Rogers, Mark Twain, Artemas Ward (a fictional character created by Charles Farrar Browne), or Josh Billings (another fictional character, created by Henry Wheeler Shaw). Although there is no evidence that anyone in the nineteenth century actually uttered these words, the phrase seems to embody a useful insight and thus has taken on a life of its own.[1] In a broad sense, the phrase seems to apply to the myths of the War of 1812. Instead of carefully examining the myths and the evidence that we assume supports them, we accept them as true, and this can skew our understanding of history.[2]

Overview of the War of 1812

Before examining the mythology of the War of 1812, let us review the highlights of the conflict. This war, after all, is often called our "forgotten conflict," and it is important that everyone understands the basics:

President James Madison issued a proclamation declaring war against Great Britain on June 19, 1812. The purpose of this war was to conquer Canada, but American militia, armed with Kentucky rifles, could not overcome the militiamen of Canada, who were aided by British regulars and by Indians under the command of Tecumseh, the leading native of the period. The US Navy, relying on picked crews that were heavily British, employed large frigates that were actually ships of the line in disguise, whose victories had a profound impact on the war at sea. On January 8, 1815, in the last great battle of the war, American riflemen defeated the British at New Orleans, although this battle was actually fought after the Treaty of Ghent had ended the war on December 24, 1814. The British had planned to sack the city and retain Louisiana if they prevailed at New Orleans, which would have changed the course of American history. Federalists bitterly opposed the contest, which has been aptly called a second war of independence, and their opposition encouraged the enemy and prolonged the war. Had the United States adopted a more focused military strategy, it would have conquered Canada. But even without Canada, the new nation enjoyed enough success on land and at sea to claim victory.

You may not agree with everything in this summary. In fact, I hope you don't agree with anything, because not a single statement in this overview is true. There are more than twenty misstatements. They represent the most common myths of the War of 1812. I will examine the leading myths in more detail, but first let us consider the nature of myths.

What Are Myths?

Myths are essentially misconceptions, and they can vary significantly in importance. The easiest way to envision the scope of myths that exist is to imagine that they range across a spectrum. At one end are the big myths. For the War of 1812 these myths deal with large, overarching questions, such as what caused the war, what role the militia played, who won, or what the war's consequences were. There may be no clear right or wrong position on these issues, and fair-minded scholars may disagree. Nevertheless, the most commonly accepted position is essentially wrong, and thus they qualify as myths.

At the other end of the spectrum are the little myths. These are small misconceptions or factual errors that are widely accepted but are just plain wrong. These myths deal with issues such as whether a woman named Louisa Baker or Lucy Brewer served on the USS *Constitution* in 1812, what flag flew over Fort McHenry during the bombardment in September 1814, whether the war ended when the Treaty of Ghent was signed in December 1814, and what role cotton bales played in Andrew Jackson's line at New Orleans in January 1815. The documentary evidence on these issues is unmistakable, but the myths persist.

Where Do Myths Come From?

Many myths come from those who lived through the war. They misstate, misremember, or misunderstand what they have seen or experienced. This is especially true for those in combat. Such is the fog and friction of war and such is the stress of life-threatening situations that participants in battles may not have a clear or accurate understanding of what has happened. In fact, there is an old saw among military historians that if you ask two participants in a battle to describe it, their descriptions may vary so much that one might think they were in different battles.

Complicating the historical record is the well-known fact that stories can change over time, usually evolving into more coherent and incisive tales, often in response to the reaction of their audiences. This is why we sometimes say that a story improves with the telling. Given the way these stories are likely to evolve, the old military saw might be amended to read as follows: If you ask participants to describe a battle twenty years after the fact, one might think not simply that they were in different battles but that they were in different wars.

Myths come not simply from participants and other contemporaries but also from people later on who write about the war. The nineteenth century was a time when myth and legend often substituted for verifiable history, and assorted patriots and boosters of local, regional, or national history eagerly repeated myths that reflected well on the nation. Sometimes they embellished on old myths that originated with participants. On other occasions, they invented new myths out of whole cloth.

Serious scholars in the nineteenth century also did their part to create and propagate myths. Three stand out. In the immediate aftermath of the war, William James wrote treatises on the Royal Navy in which he repeated a number of myths that he got from British naval officials.[3] James's treatises are still invaluable. He was the first naval historian to rely heavily on primary sources and to try to measure the relative power of opposing ships in an engagement to determine who had the advantage. Many of the details in his works can be found nowhere else. But James, who hoped to secure patronage, was eager to please the British government and did everything he could to make the Royal Navy look good. "I was the champion of the [British] navy on every occasion," he told Viscount Melville, the First Lord of the Admiralty.[4]

Another writer who helped propagate myths of the war was Benson J. Lossing, a gifted American sketch artist and antiquarian. Lossing found a successful model for his talents in the early 1850s, when he published a travelogue and sketchbook featuring Revolutionary War people and sites.[5] He then tackled the War of 1812, traveling some ten thousand miles in the United States and Canada in the 1850s and 1860s, interviewing veterans and other survivors and sketching his subjects as well as the battlefields and other sites that figured in their stories. The result was *The Pictorial Field-Book of the War of 1812,* first published in 1868.[6] Like James's naval history, Lossing's *Pictorial Field-Book* remains a goldmine of information for modern scholars. It is therefore an indispensable reference work. But Lossing was more of an antiquarian than a historian, and he repeated numerous tales that he heard without questioning them. As a result, he unintentionally propagated many myths about the war.

The third writer in the nineteenth century who was responsible for spreading myths was Henry Adams. Arguably the first modern historian of the conflict, Adams belonged to one of America's most distinguished families. His great-grandfather and grandfather were presidents, and his father served as the US ambassador to Great Britain during the Civil War. Adams combed archives on both sides of the Atlantic to produce his masterpiece, a nine-volume history of the United States from 1801 to 1817, first published in 1889–91.[7] Since fully two-thirds of the work is devoted to the War of 1812 and its causes, it is not unreasonable to suggest that this study is mainly about the war. Because of his extensive research, his sharp mind, and his engaging writing style, Adams was long considered the leading student of the war, and his work dominated the historiography on the subject for nearly a century. Although Henry Adams's work is one of the great classics in American historical writing, it is far from unbiased and thus not always reliable. Adams was not a happy man, and he had a flair for irony and seemed to take perverse pleasure in making almost everyone who had a role in the war look bad. There were a few exceptions, most notably his ancestors John and John Quincy Adams and those who Henry Adams assumed agreed with them. Adams's family defense is subtle. His study starts at the end of John Adams's presidency and ends when John Quincy Adams became secretary of state, a post that proved to be his stepping-stone to the presidency. Throughout this lengthy study, Henry Adams generally keeps his illustrious ancestors in the background while heaping scorn on the policy failures and inconsistencies of their enemies.

Adams also had a penchant for presenting his opinions either as fact or as the sort of conventional wisdom that no thoughtful person would dispute. He disguised his opinions by using phrases such as "No one could deny" or "No one could doubt." In truth, many of his views on the people he wrote about were so unfavorable that they could hardly be considered conventional wisdom.

In view of Adams's agenda, it is hardly surprising that three of the figures who fare the worst in his narrative were all family enemies: Thomas Jefferson, who defeated John Adams in his bid for reelection to the presidency in 1800; Andrew Jackson, who defeated John Quincy Adams when he ran for a second term in 1828; and Timothy Pickering, a Massachusetts Federalist who was the nemesis of the two Adamses throughout the early nineteenth century. Whatever its merits, and there are many, Adams's *History* is best seen as a somewhat caustic yet subtle defense of his ancestors.[8]

Why Are Myths So Durable?

Given the role that participants, boosters, and historians played, it is hardly surprising that so many myths proliferated in the nineteenth century. Many of these myths have also proven durable, persisting down to the present day. Why is this so? There are a number of reasons. Myths provide us with heroes and fulfill our need for inspiring stories; they promote local, regional, and national pride; and they put a human face on history and demonstrate that we can indeed influence the course of events. Myths, in other words, help us construct a history that we are comfortable with and that meets certain deep-seated needs. There is another reason for myths' persistence: repeating them does not require any work. Even a careful scholar may find it tempting to use a good story that makes a work more interesting without first determining whether it is actually true.

Because of their appeal to general readers and scholars alike, myths are never easy to knock down. Even when one scholar disproves a story, others are likely to ignore, miss, or forget this study and repeat the myth in their own works. Myths in history are not unlike vampires or zombies in fiction. Quite simply, they are difficult to kill off and thus permanently banish from the accepted narrative.

What Are the Leading Myths?

It is not easy to gauge how many myths the War of 1812 has produced; surely scores, perhaps hundreds. It is even more difficult to rank the importance of myths, that is, to decide which ones we should focus on publicizing and disproving. Scholars may disagree, and their views may change over time. What follows is an arbitrary list of those myths about the War of 1812 that I presently consider most important and pervasive and thus most in need of challenging:

1. *The war began with President Madison's proclamation on June 19, 1812, and ended with the signing of the Treaty of Ghent on December 24, 1814.*

The first series of myths deal with the beginning and end of the war. President Madison issued a proclamation on June 19, 1812, announcing that a state of war existed with Great Britain. This proclamation has been widely reproduced, and as a result some writers have said that Madison declared war on June 19. But the president has no authority to declare war; that power is reserved to Congress. Congress may declare war by a joint resolution or by adopting a bill, which requires a presidential signature to become law. Normally, Congress adopts a bill to give the measure the full force of law, and this is how war was declared in 1812.

The opening sentence in Madison's proclamation makes it clear that the war was declared on June 18 (not June 19) and that the decision was made by Congress: "Whereas the Congress of the United States, by virtue of the constituted authority vested in them, have declared by their act bearing [the] date the 18th day of the present month, that WAR exists between the united Kingdom of Great Britain and Ireland, and the dependencies thereof, and the United States of America and their territories: Now therefore, I, JAMES MADISON, President of the United States of America, do hereby proclaim the same to all whom it may concern."[9] Madison's proclamation, in other words, merely announced that a state of war existed.

The end of the war is even more commonly misstated. Representatives of the two nations signed the Treaty of Ghent (in modern-day Belgium) on December 24, 1814. Had this been a typical European war, signing the treaty would have ended it, because European governments usually gave their peace delegations the power to bind them. But the United States never gives that power to its agents. Any treaty negotiated by a US delegation has to be approved by a two-thirds vote of the Senate and then signed by the president, which completes the ratification process.

On three earlier occasions, in 1794, 1803, and 1806, American agents in London had signed treaties that the US government refused to ratify without changes. The British in 1814 feared that this might happen again. If they agreed to end hostilities immediately and the United States later demanded changes before ratifying the treaty, they would find themselves in the awkward position of having to either agree to those changes or restart a war that everyone assumed was over. Hence, the British insisted that the war end only after both sides had ratified the treaty. The first article of the treaty thus reads: "All hostilities both by sea and land shall cease as soon as this Treaty shall have been ratified by both parties."[10]

The British ratified the treaty on December 27, 1814, but such was the pace of travel in the age of sail that the treaty did not reach the United States until February 11. The truce ship carrying it docked in New York Harbor because there was bad weather in the Chesapeake. The treaty was then raced to Washington, reaching the capital city on February 15. It was unanimously ratified by the Senate the following day, and the president signed it the next day, thus completing the ratification process and ending the war. The War of 1812 thus began on June 18, 1812, and ended on February 17, 1815.

2. The purpose of the war was to conquer and annex Canada.

The United States declared war in 1812 to force the British to give up certain maritime policies, most notably the Orders in Council and impressment. The Orders were executive decrees issued in the name of the Crown that sharply curtailed US trade with the European continent. Under the authority of those decrees the British seized and condemned some four hundred American ships and their cargo between 1807 and 1812. Impressment was the Royal Navy's practice of conscripting seamen from American merchant vessels to fill out the crews of its undermanned warships. Although impressment gangs nominally targeted British tars, between 1803 and 1812 some six thousand to nine thousand American seamen were caught in the British dragnet.

In the language of the day, war was undertaken to secure "Free Trade and Sailors' Rights." Although these were maritime issues, the United States could not seek redress on the high seas, because the Royal Navy had more than five hundred warships in service, compared with the US Navy's seventeen. The only way to pressure Britain was by targeting her North American provinces in Canada. Presumably, any conquered territory would be used to bargain for concessions on the maritime issues, although the Madison administration never explicitly acknowledged this, probably to keep all of its options open.

How do we know that the maritime issues were the real cause of the war and not simply a pretext to seize Canada? The evidence is overwhelming. President Madison focused almost entirely on these issues in his opening message to Congress in November 1811 and in his war message to the same body in June 1812. The House war report echoed the president's message. Moreover, in the runup to the war, the public debate in Congress and the press, as well as comments made in private correspondence, focused almost entirely on the maritime issues.

Even in the West, where there was widespread interest in seizing Canada to put an end to British influence over American Indians, the debate centered on maritime issues. One cannot imagine a more quintessential westerner than Andrew Jackson, and yet here is what he said in an address to his Tennessee militia division several months before the declaration of war:

We are going to fight for the reestablishment of our national character, misunderstood and vilified at home and abroad; for the protection of our maritime citizens, impressed on board British ships of war and compelled to fight the battles of our enemies against ourselves; to vindicate our right to a free trade, and open market for the productions of our soil, now perishing in our hands, because the *mistress of the ocean* has forbid us to carry them to any foreign nation; in fine, to seek some indemnity for past injuries, some security against future aggressions, by the conquest of all the British dominions upon the continent of North America.[11]

Henry Clay, of Kentucky, who as Speaker of the House was as instrumental as anyone in moving the nation toward war, put it this way: "Canada was not the end but the means, the object of the War being the redress of injuries, and Canada being the instrument by which that redress was to be obtained."[12] And President Madison, who had made the case first for war preparations and then for war almost entirely on the basis of the maritime issues, continued to emphasize these issues after war was declared. In peace feelers sent out shortly after the declaration of war, he made it clear that the nation's price for calling off the war was an end to the orders in council and impressment. Canada was not mentioned.

Why, then, do so many people still cling to the Canadian, or land hunger, thesis? For one thing, few people today understand the finer points of neutral rights in the age of sail. Everyone, by contrast, can understand a land grab. For another, the United States *did* covet Canada from 1775 to around 1900. More broadly, the United States was an aggressively expansionist nation throughout the nineteenth century. Targeting Canada thus fits into the broader story of American expansion. But however logical it may be to conclude that the desire for Canada was the real cause of the War of 1812, logic can never trump evidence. In this case, there is plenty of evidence to suggest that the United States went to war in 1812 over neutral rights.

3. The War of 1812 was a second war of American independence.

The War of 1812 is often called a second war of independence, and there is no denying that in a broad sense it vindicated US sovereignty. After the war, Europeans looked upon the young republic with a new-found respect, and during Napoleon's One Hundred Days, the British were careful not to impress any Americans when the Royal Navy returned to a war footing. The British were clearly eager to avoid another war and remain on good terms with the United States.

Because the Treaty of Ghent did not resolve the outstanding maritime issues, few people on either side of the Atlantic thought this would be the last Anglo-American war, and the British still faced the daunting task of providing for the defense of Canada. It did not take British officials long to conclude that the best way to protect Canada was to accommodate the United States, and this became the cornerstone of their North American policy during the nineteenth century.

Still, calling the War of 1812 a second war of independence is problematic. It seems to imply that US independence was at risk in this era or even that the British had designs on that independence. Nothing could be further from the truth. The British in this era were interested in only one thing: defeating France in the Napoleonic Wars. All other foreign-policy objectives were subordinate to this aim. If their maritime practices encroached on US rights, it was not because the British had any designs on American independence but because they thought those policies were vital to their war effort against France. Once the European war ended, any encroachments on American rights would end. The British regarded the American war as nothing more than an annoying sideshow, which explains why they were ultimately willing to agree to peace on the basis of the status quo ante bellum even though they were at the time in the driver's seat in North America.

One of the oddities about calling the War of 1812 a second war of American independence is that the United States was the only belligerent in the contest whose independence was not at risk. If the Indians lost, they would forfeit their independence. Likewise, if Canada were conquered, it might be swallowed by the United States and never gain its independence. Even Britain's independence was at risk, independence not from the United States but from France. If France won the Napoleonic Wars, Britain in all likelihood would survive only as a French dependency.

4. The militias of Canada and the United States played a central role in the war.

The hoary myth that the militia played a central role in the war was popular on both sides of the North American border. Both countries wanted to believe that their militia had done the heavy lifting in the war. For Canadians, it implied that they had saved themselves and did not need the British. It also suggested that later in the nineteenth century there was little need to spend money on a regular army or navy, because their militia could protect the country from any possible threat. For Americans, the argument was similar. If militia had defeated the British, that would vindicate the merits of citizen-soldiers in a republic and also suggest that the new nation did not have to spend an inordinate amount on maintaining a regular army.

The outcome of this war was determined on the Canadian-American frontier, and regulars and Indians had the starring role. Militia did play a part on both sides, but mainly in a supporting role. If militia played a part in combat, it was usually when regulars were present to provide a steadying influence in the heat of battle.

5. The Kentucky rifle was a game-changer and war-winner, especially at New Orleans.

The long rifle enjoyed a good reputation long before the War of 1812. Since it was designed and produced mainly in Pennsylvania, it was commonly referred to as the Pennsylvania rifle. Accurate at 250–300 yards, as opposed to 100–150 yards for the smoothbore musket, it had proven its worth in the American Revolution, when American snipers used it to pick off British officers and sentries. But the American Revolution was waged mainly with muskets, and that was also true of the War of 1812. Although many militiamen and volunteers in the West carried rifles into the field, most battles were determined by muskets or artillery. The musket, not the rifle, was the standard shoulder arm in the war. It was the weapon that most soldiers carried, the weapon that filled state and federal arsenals and armories.

Why didn't the rifle, which had a significantly greater range, supplant the musket? For one thing, the rifle did not use a prepared cartridge and thus was harder to load. For another, the grooves in the barrel, which accounted for the rifle's greater range, were likely to foul over time, rendering the weapon inaccurate if not unusable. Although the governments of the day recognized the value of having some specialized units armed with rifles, they preferred to equip most soldiers with the more reliable musket.

Because the rife was carried by so many westerners, it won an undeserved reputation as a war-winner and game-changer. The Battle of New Orleans helped cement this reputation, although most of the British casualties in that engagement were caused by artillery. "The Hunters of Kentucky," a song that became popular in the 1820s, reinforced the rifle's reputation in the battle and also probably helped change the name of the weapon, completing the transformation of the Pennsylvania rifle into the Kentucky rifle.

6. Tecumseh was the most important Indian leader in the war.

Tecumseh, the Shawnee leader who forged a political and military alliance among Indian bands in the Old Northwest, has always been considered the leading Indian of the period. He certainly was an imposing figure who impressed all who met him. William Henry Harrison considered the respect and obedience that Tecumseh's followers paid him "really astonishing" and concluded that he was "one of those uncommon geniuses, which spring up occasionally to produce revolutions and overturn the established order of things."[13] But Tecumseh's confederacy would not have been possible had not his brother, Tenskwatawa, better known as the Prophet, had a vision in 1805 and then launched a religious movement in the Old Northwest. Tecumseh superimposed his political and military confederacy on his brother's religious movement.

Until 1810 or even 1811, Tecumseh was generally referred to as "the Prophet's brother," a reflection of how much he remained in Tenskwatawa's shadow. It is also misleading to suggest that Tecumseh actually commanded any Indians. No native leader did. Rather he simply headed an ad hoc group of natives who decided to join him on an expedition. They were free to leave at any time. Nor did Tecumseh's star burn brightly for very long. He emerged from his brother's shadow only in late 1811, after the Battle of Tippecanoe (which he did not participate in), and in less than two years, in October 1813, he lay dead on the battlefield of the Thames.

It was not simply Tecumseh's brother who played a more significant role in Indian affairs in this period. So, too, did John Norton, a Scottish-Creek mestizo who was chosen by the Grand River Mohawks to be their leader. Not only did Norton help keep the Grand River tribes loyal to the Crown during the War of 1812 but he also took part, with a small band of followers, in almost every engagement on the Niagara frontier, which, because it was further east, was more significant than the Detroit frontier in the Old Northwest, where Tecumseh was active.

7. American heavy frigates were actually ships of the line in disguise with picked crews that were heavily British, and their victories had a significant impact on the war at sea.

The abovenamed notions, three British and one American, are the leading naval myths of the war. Eager to explain away their defeats in the single-ship naval engagements on the high seas, especially in three frigate-to-frigate duels, the British claimed that American frigates were really ships of the line, that they had their pick of American seamen, and that their crews, especially the tars manning the big guns, were actually British subjects. None of these claims was true.

Although the US frigates were more powerful than their British counterparts, they still fit the definition of a frigate, which was a warship with a single covered gun deck. Moreover, far from having their pick of seamen, US Navy recruiters had to compete with privateers, who offered a shorter tour, laxer discipline, and the prospect of more prize money. The navy also had to compete with the US Army, which offered an ever larger enlistment bounty that by the end of the war was $124 and 320 acres of land. This was a princely sum, more than most unskilled laborers could earn in two years, perhaps equivalent to $30,000 today. By contrast, the US Navy never offered a bounty of more than $30, which it sweetened with three months' advance pay and a 25 percent boost in monthly pay. This never came close to matching the premiums offered by the US Army, and throughout the war navy recruiters bemoaned their inability to attract men.

Nor did British tars constitute a sizable portion of the American crews. At one time they had, but after the *Chesapeake* affair in 1807, the Navy Department ordered an end to the enlistment of British subjects. Some could still be found on board US warships in 1812, but with the beginning of the war most left to avoid fighting against their homeland and risk being hanged as traitors. Theodore Roosevelt estimated that no more than 10–15 percent of any US crew was British, and the average was undoubtedly much lower.[14]

Americans had their own naval myths. They rarely acknowledged that the heavy US frigates were much more powerful than the light British frigates they defeated, and they invariably overestimated the consequences of the US victories, which had little impact on the course of the war. Far more important were the inland naval victories on Lake Erie in 1813 and Lake Champlain in 1814, which changed the course of the land war in those theaters.

In the end, the British gave as good as they got, defeating three US frigates, including the heavy frigate *President*, although in this case some British naval historians have propagated the myth that a British frigate acting alone accomplished the feat, when in truth it was a British squadron.

The most significant use of naval power on the high seas in the War of 1812 had nothing to do with the ship-to-ship duels. Rather it was four larger strategic objectives that the British used the Royal Navy to achieve: (1) the movement of men and matériel to Canada, which ensured that Britain retained control of its North American provinces; (2) the blockade of the US coast, which bottled up many armed American vessels (warships and privateers alike) and had a devastating impact on the US economy and government revenue (forcing the US Treasury to default on the national debt in late 1814); (3) the raids conducted along the Atlantic coast, especially in the Chesapeake Bay, which brought the war home to many Americans and disrupted domestic life; and (4) the protection of British shipping on the high seas by performing convoy duty.

8. The British planned to sack the city and retain Louisiana if they won the Battle of New Orleans.

Shortly after the Battle of New Orleans, George Poindexter, a district federal judge in the Mississippi Territory who was in New Orleans as a volunteer aide but sat out the battle because of what he said was an arm injury, claimed that British prisoners of war had told him that the sign and countersign on the night before the battle were *beauty* and *booty.* This implied that the British planned to sack the city if they won the battle, subjecting its residents to robbery, rape, and murder. British officers vigorously denied this claim, and there is no other evidence to support it. British officers invariably kept their men on a tight leash when in enemy territory, and there is no reason to believe that they would not have done so in New Orleans, just as they had when they occupied Washington, DC, where locals later praised them for their restraint.

Because the British high command carried instructions for setting up a government in Louisiana, the myth took root that Britain planned to retain the territory if it won the battle, the treaty of peace notwithstanding. Again, there is no evidence to support this claim. The Gulf Coast campaign was not even on the radar of British officials in London during the peace negotiations. They were war weary and just wanted to end the conflict, and there is no evidence that they planned to hold on to Louisiana and thus in effect repudiate the peace treaty and risk a renewal of the war. If the British had occupied this territory at the end of the war, they undoubtedly would have returned it, just as they returned Mackinac Island, Prairie du Chen, Fort Niagara, a hundred miles of the coast of Maine, and Cumberland Island in Georgia.

No doubt the *beauty*-and-*booty* and Louisiana-retention myths appealed to Americans because they endowed Jackson's victory at New Orleans with greater meaning. Americans wanted to believe that Jackson not only had saved New Orleans from a grizzly fate but also had ensured that Louisiana remained in American hands after the war, thus guaranteeing the thrust of American expansion into the Southwest.

9. Federalist opposition encouraged the enemy and prolonged the war.

To a man, Federalists in Congress voted against the declaration of war in 1812, and thereafter they voted as a bloc against all bills to raise men and money, to restrict trade with the enemy, or to encourage privateering. The only war measures they supported were those they considered good long-term investments in the nation's defense, namely, bills to expand the navy and build coastal fortifications. In New England, where Federalists won control of all five state governments during the war, there was talk of pulling out of the Union and making a separate peace with Britain. Although nothing came of this talk and it never rose to the level of a serious secessionist movement, Federalists in New England did convene the Hartford Convention near the end of the war to air their grievances.

Republicans claimed that Federalist opposition encouraged the enemy and prolonged the war, but both claims appear to have been untrue. Although the British tried to capitalize on Federalist opposition, exempting New England from their blockade until 1814 and freely trading with all American comers, there is no evidence that this opposition encouraged the British or in any way prolonged the war. In fact, Federalist opposition in the United States, along with Whig opposition in Great Britain, may actually have shortened the war by making both sides more amenable to a compromise peace. Had there been no domestic opposition to their war policy, governments in both countries might have taken a harder line in the peace negotiations, which could have prolonged the war.

10. With a more focused strategy, the United States could have conquered Canada, but it still won the war.

In the two centuries since the end of the War of 1812, armchair generals have criticized American strategy for devoting too many resources to the theater in the West instead of focusing on locations further east, especially Montreal and Quebec, the two cities on the St. Lawrence that anchored Britain's defenses in Canada. Although the criticism is sound, the notion that with a better war plan the United States might actually have conquered

Canada is dubious. It ignores the very real problems that the young republic faced in waging war against British North America in 1812.

The US Army in 1812 had an officer corps that was dominated by political appointees and relics from the Revolution who had lost their taste for battle, and its ranks were filled with raw recruits. In addition, the enemy in Canada was formidable. It was made up of an experienced and disciplined British army aided by Indian allies who were adept at scouting, skirmishing, and tracking and whose reputation for ferocity on the battlefield could panic an inexperienced foe. Finally, the logistical challenges of waging offensive war in the North American wilderness were nearly insuperable. There were few good roads, and mud or snow could make those that existed impassible. Waterways offered a better alternative, but only if they were conveniently located and not subject to enemy interdiction.

Given the state of its army, the quality of its enemy, and the logistical challenges that it faced, it is highly unlikely that the United States could have conquered Canada with any strategy. This means that the war was probably unwinnable, which in turn suggests that the decision to go to war in 1812 was even more ill-advised than contemporary critics or later historians have thought.

Conclusion

Such are the leading myths of the War of 1812. Is this war unique in generating so much mythology? Almost surely not. The other wars from this era, especially the Revolution and the Civil War, lasted much longer and undoubtedly produced many myths. It only remains for historians to uncover those myths and set the record straight.

NOTES

1. For help in seeking the origins of this quotation, I am indebted to Charissa Loftis of the U.S. Conn Library at Wayne State College, Abby Yochelson of the Library of Congress, and John Stagg at the University of Virginia. Abby Yochelson did a particularly broad and thorough search of the resources at her disposal.

2. For more detail on the subject of this essay, see Donald R. Hickey, *Don't Give Up the Ship! Myths of the War of 1812* (Toronto: Robin Brass Studio; Urbana: University of Illinois Press, 2006).

3. James's two naval works are *A Full and Correct Account of the Chief Naval Occurrences of the Late War between Great Britain and the United States of America* (London: T. Egerton, 1817) and *The Naval History of Great Britain, From the Declaration of War by France in 1793 to the Accession of George IV*, rev. ed., 6 vols. (London, 1822–26).

4. William James to Viscount Melville, 4 January 1819, in "How William James Came to Be a Naval Historian," ed. Holden Furber, *American Historical Review* 38, no. 1 (October 1932): 79.

5. Benson J. Lossing, *The Pictorial Field-Book of the Revolution*, 2 vols. (New York: Harper & Bros., 1851–52).

6. Benson J. Lossing, *The Pictorial Field-Book of the War of 1812* (New York: Harper & Bros., 1868). This work has been reprinted at least nine times and is also available in several electronic versions.

7. Henry Adams, *History of the United States during the Administrations of Jefferson and Madison*, 9 vols. (New York: C. Scribner's Sons, 1889–91). Adams put out a slightly revised edition in 1901–4. The authoritative modern edition is Henry Adams, *History of the United States during the Administrations of Thomas Jefferson and James Madison*, ed. Earl N. Harbert, 2 vols. (New York: Viking, 1986).

8. For more on Adams's bias, see Peter Shaw, "The War of 1812 Could Not Take Place: Henry Adams's *History*," *Yale Review* 62, no. 4 (June 1973): 544–56; and Shaw, "Blood Is Thicker than Irony: Henry Adams' *History*," *New England Quarterly* 40, no. 2 (June 1967), 163–87. In *Henry Adams and the Making of America* (Boston: Houghton Mifflin, 2005), Garry Wills rejects the family-defense thesis, but he ignores Shaw's work and fails to make his case. Wills's study is principally a gloss on Adams's *History*, but because he is no expert on the Age of Jefferson, he is at Adams's mercy and repeats many of Adams's myths.

9. Proclamation of James Madison, 19 June 1812, 12th Cong., 1st sess., in US Congress, *Debates and Proceedings in the Congress of the United States, 1789–1824*, 42 vols. (Washington, DC: Gales & Seaton, 1834–56), 2223.

10. Treaty of Ghent, December 24, 1814, article 1, in *Encyclopedia of the War of 1812*, ed. David S. Heidler and Jeanne T. Heidler (Santa Barbara, CA: ABC-CLIO, 1997), 583.

11. Andrew Jackson to the 2nd Division, 7 March 1812, in *The Papers of Andrew Jackson*, ed. Dan Feller, Sam B. Smith, Harriet Fason Chappell Owsley, and Harold D. Moser, 9 vols. to date (Knoxville: University of Tennessee Press, 1980–), 2:291.

12. Henry Clay to Thomas Bodley, 18 December 1813, in *The Papers of Henry Clay*, ed. James F. Hopkins and Mary W. M. Hargreaves, 11 vols. (Lexington: University Press of Kentucky, 1959–92), 1:842.

13. William Henry Harrison to secretary of war, 7 August 1811, in *Messages and Letters of William Henry Harrison*, ed. Logan Esarey, 2 vols. (Indianapolis: Indiana Historical Commission, 1922), 1:549.

14. Theodore Roosevelt, "The War with the United States," in *The Royal Navy: A History*, by William Laird Clowes, 7 vols. (London: S. Lowe Marston, 1897–1903), 6:29.

2

"I Owe to Britain a Debt of Retaliatory Vengeance"

Assessing Andrew Jackson's Hatred of the British

MARK R. CHEATHEM

In the course of researching his biography of Andrew Jackson, James Parton related anecdotes about Old Hickory told to him as he traveled across the country in the late 1850s. Some of the more sensational stories came from residents of the Waxhaws region, the area along the North Carolina–South Carolina border where Jackson spent his childhood and early adolescence. On several occasions, individuals shared with Parton their assessment of Jackson's attitude toward the British. One of Jackson's playmates, a Rev. Dr. Wilson, recalled that his friend often made weapons and pretended to fight the British. According to Wilson, Jackson said, "Oh, if I were a man, how I would sweep down the British with my grass blade!" Another man said that Dr. Wilson's brother had told him that Jackson "*hated* the British. He *longed* to kill them." The most dramatic encounter of Jackson's Revolutionary War experience also came up in the course of Parton's interviews. Parton recorded the commentary of one "aged relative" about a confrontation with the British in 1781 that resulted in a British officer's striking Jackson with his sword: "Paroxysms of contemptuous rage shook his [Jackson's] slender frame when he saw his cousin's wife insulted, her house profaned, his brother gashed; himself as powerless to avenge as to protect. '*I'll warrant Andy thought of it at New Orleans.*'"[1]

That Andrew Jackson's hatred of the British motivated him throughout his life, but particularly during the War of 1812, is a common theme in

FIG. 2.1. *The Brave Boy of the Waxhaws.* Lithograph by Currier & Ives, 1876. From Library of Congress Prints and Photographs Online Catalog, hdl.loc.gov/loc.pnp/cph.3a52022.

assessments of Old Hickory. This theme is prevalent not only in scholarly historical literature but also in nonacademic presentations of Jackson. To date, however, no one has examined this accepted belief in any depth. Taking a fresh look at the ways in which Jackson's relationship with the British has been presented and examining this depiction in light of the historical evidence offers the opportunity to reassess his reputation as a vengeful warrior bent on their destruction.

Biographical and Scholarly Assessments

In biographies from James Parton's initial one, published in the early 1860s, to Pulitzer Prize–winning works written by Marquis James and Jon Meacham, Jackson has been a favorite subject of writers drawn to his dramatic life story and his larger-than-life personality. One of the essential elements addressed in any Jackson biography is his background in the Waxhaws, where he had lost his entire immediate family by the time he was fifteen. Especially emotional were the deaths of his mother and two brothers, all of which were connected in some way to the war with Great Britain. Hugh, Jackson's older brother, died of heat exhaustion during the Battle of Stono Ferry. His other brother, Robert, and his mother, Elizabeth, died as a result of diseases contracted in British prisons. As many biographers have claimed, these losses, along with his permanent scarring by the blade of a British sword, fueled Jackson's desire for revenge, which he achieved on the battlefield at Chalmette Plantation on January 8, 1815.

Parton's biography proved seminal in linking Jackson's hatred of the British to his later actions at New Orleans. During the Revolution, according to Parton, the young South Carolinian came to see the British as evil personified. "In his inflamed imagination," wrote Parton, "the mild Cornwallis figured as a relentless savage, Tarleton as a devil incarnate, and all red-coated sons of Britain as the natural enemies of man." By the end of the Revolution, with his family gone, Jackson "was an orphan; a sick and sorrowful orphan; a homeless and dependent orphan; an orphan of the Revolution, remember. *He* remembered it." The prominent biographer employed recollections of the Battle of New Orleans to drive home his point that Jackson's memory was long. Using the New Orleans resident Vincent Nolte's words, Parton noted that Jackson was "burning with impatience" to fight the British. "He wanted to fight," but not just fight. "'I will smash them,' he would exclaim, 'so help me God!'"[2]

The tone set by Parton continued into the Gilded Age and the interwar periods of the late nineteenth and early twentieth centuries. The sociologist William Graham Sumner, for example, argued that Jackson's injury and loss of family led the adolescent boy "to entertain a vigorous hatred of the English from a very early age." The political scientist Frederick Ogg observed, "Small wonder that Andrew Jackson always hated the British uniform, or that when he sat in the executive chair an anti-British feeling colored all of his dealings with foreign nations!" In his Pulitzer Prize–winning biography of Old Hickory, Marquis James maintained that the "gash on his head left a white scar that profited little to England or any Englishman." The American victory at New Orleans, which resulted in "the

FIG. 2.2. *James Parton.* The Miriam and Ira D. Wallach Division of Art, Prints and Photographs: Photography Collection, The New York Public Library. From New York Public Library Digital Collections, digitalcollections.nypl.org/items/510d47d9-bf16-a3d9-e040-e00a18064a99.

entire destruction of a British army[,] had been an accomplishment for which General Jackson had lived since he was thirteen years old." At the 1928 dedication of the statue of Jackson that was placed in the US Capitol's Statuary Hall, President Calvin Coolidge reminded attendees that "this impetuous warrior took a personal satisfaction in a victory over some of the troops who had humbled Napoleon, especially because of a scar from a British saber which he had received in childhood during the Revolutionary War." In a biographical sketch that accompanied publication of the dedication proceedings, the Tennessee historian John Trotwood Moore reinforced the connection between Jackson's childhood and the Battle of New Orleans by claiming that Jackson had told an officer at New Orleans, "And now we'll give them a taste of Waxhaw!"[3]

One particular writer from this period deserves special attention. The author of several historical books, Augustus Buell proved to be a serial plagiarist and fabricator, and his embellishments and outright lies permeate his biography of Andrew Jackson. For all of the losses, "brutal outrage[,] and cruel outrage" that Jackson suffered during the Revolutionary War, Buell wrote, he

> held the King and his government responsible, and his resentment fell upon every officer and every man, no matter how unimportant or how humble, whom he found wearing the livery of that King and government, no matter where he might find them. At the bottom there may have been the native hatred of the Irishman toward everything English. But in Jackson's case any racial antipathy that might have existed was intensified a hundredfold by his own personal woes and wrongs. He always hated England. And it was a personal, not a national, animosity. He hated England, not simply as a patriotic American, but as an infuriated Andrew Jackson. There were some emergencies in his career when this fierce antipathy wrought vastly and permanently for the public good. There were other emergencies when this implacable animosity created situations of public embarrassment and more than once brought the two countries to the verge of war from which no good could have resulted possibly commensurate with the shock to civilization it must have caused.

In the case of Jackson's hatred of the British, Buell provided the most declarative statement of the Revolutionary War's influence on Old Hickory's relationship with the British, but it is one that fails to stand up to the scrutiny of the evidence. His account of Jackson's wartime experience intermingled a few verifiable facts with numerous instances of invented details, conversations, and correspondence, making his analysis of the war's lifelong effect on the Waxhaws native difficult, if not impossible, to believe.[4]

The turn toward psychohistory in the 1960s and 1970s provided scholars with the opportunity to analyze Jackson's internal world and motivations in a new light. Not surprisingly, some found great import in the disruptiveness of his childhood and the violence that he exhibited in his adult life, and once again Jackson's alleged consuming hatred of the British attracted analysis. The political scientist Michael Paul Rogin saved most of his evisceration of Jackson for his treatment of the Indians, but he argued that Jackson "[blamed] the British" for his mother's death and thought that "turning the army into a family [during the War of 1812] would help avenge the loss of his own family." James C. Curtis also took a psychoanalytical approach, as indicated in his book's title, *Andrew Jackson and the Search for Vindication.* Curtis blamed Jackson's rage on his mother's death and called the War of 1812 "a very personal war" for him. "At New Orleans," Curtis wrote, Jackson "was not the feverish adolescent, helplessly surrendering his family to the British and the ravages of war." On January 8 "he was ready, firmly in control, able to project his fury with devastating accuracy." He was "a man who sought to reestablish his right to survive by violent payment of a longstanding family debt."[5]

Recent historians have continued to emphasize the Revolutionary origins of Jackson's animosity toward the British. The late Robert Remini, the most eminent post–World War II Jackson biographer, was not immune to this claim. In his study of the Battle of New Orleans, Remini argued that Jackson's "hatred of the British lasted for the remainder of his life and no doubt accounted in large measure for his fierce determination to defeat them in battle." John Marszalek's study of the Eaton affair followed Remini's argument. The Revolution left Jackson "angry and frustrated, no doubt developing his lifelong anger." Defeating the British in the War of 1812, Marszalek wrote, "allowed him to rescue his dead mother from the shadow of the once conquering British, who had marched through their neighborhood and created the conditions that had resulted in her death and his orphanhood." H. W. Brands used Parton's anecdote about "Andy" remembering the destruction of his aunt's home while his men slaughtered the British at New Orleans. Sean Wilentz argued that Jackson's rage sprung from his "boyhood tribulations" during the Revolution, which "scorched into his body and soul . . . his hatred of the British and their empire." Wilentz called the British "Jackson's mightiest enemies" and claimed that the victory at New Orleans earned him a measure of "vengeance." Daniel

Walker Howe blamed the Revolution for leaving Jackson with "scars and a bitter hatred of the British." Jon Meacham's Pulitzer Prize–winning study of Jackson's White House referred obliquely to the trauma of the Revolution and its effect on the seventh president. Although Meacham acknowledged the anti-British sentiments that the Scots-Irish Jackson family had brought with them to the American colonies, he also attributed Jackson's familiarity with the Scottish hero William Wallace to the fact that both men had lost loved ones to the British. Lynn Hudson Parsons remarked that the British officer's blow to Jackson's head left "a scar that the future general and president would carry for the rest of his life—along with a hatred of Great Britain." The Rachel Jackson biographer Patricia Brady also believed that Andrew Jackson became "a lifelong enemy of the British" because of the Revolution.[6]

Written Fiction

Fictionalized accounts of Jackson's life treat his attitude toward the British in much the same way as biographers and scholars. Children's books and adult fiction alike tell the same general story. Jeanette Covert Nolan's young-adult biography of Jackson, for example, describes his thoughts on the British upon being struck by the British officer's sword: "'I hate the British'—the feeling was inside him, as it had been when Hugh was killed, as it would always be, ineradicable as the saber scars which he would carry to his grave—'I hate the British!'" Frances Fitzpatrick Wright's *Andrew Jackson: Fighting Frontiersman* notes that the Revolution left him alone, and "the cruel treatment received at the hands of the English would be a bitter memory for a long time." But by the end of the War of 1812, Wright continues, "Andrew Jackson had settled an old score with the English army." In a fictional meeting with Jackson, Ruth Smalley recorded him telling his youthful interviewer, "Even before my capture, I had learned to hate the invaders. My mother and two brothers died as a result of that war."[7]

Adult novels offer similar narratives. Noel B. Gerson's *Old Hickory* opens with the British officer demanding that Jackson clean his boots. Regarding New Orleans, Gerson declares, "One man, with a long memory and a stubborn, unyielding will, was preventing the British from taking

New Orleans." In one scene following the January 8 battle, John Coffee tells Jackson, "You've won, Andy. . . . What more do you want?" The scene continues: "Andrew fingered the long, deep scar on his forehead, and smiled wearily. 'I reckon,' he said, 'that I don't want a blamed thing. It looks like I've set an old score even at last.'" Max Byrd's novel *Jackson* focuses on an author's attempt to write a critical biography of Jackson during the 1828 presidential campaign. This fictional campaign biography presents the American Revolution as a "transformative event" in Jackson's life and reinforces the tie between his Waxhaws experiences and the events of January 8, 1815. "He still carries scars on his head and his hand," it notes. "He would have remembered them at New Orleans." In his *Patriotic Fire: Andrew Jackson and Jean Lafitte at the Battle of New Orleans*, Winston Groom remarks that because of British atrocities in the Waxhaws, Jackson "developed a lifelong loathing of the British practice" of war and offers that he "hated them with an implacable fury that was absolutely devoid of fear." In his presentation of the Battle of New Orleans, Groom argues that Jackson and Americans saw British as "barbarians" and notes that following the battle, Old Hickory's rage burned so brightly that he wanted to hunt down the surviving British soldiers "with hatchets and tomahawks if need be."[8]

Documentaries

Assessments of Jackson's antipathy toward the British extend beyond the written word. In the past two decades, four documentaries that have appeared on public television and are often used in classrooms—three produced by A&E Television and one by KCET Los Angeles, an independent public television station—have centered on Jackson's life or aspects of his military career. Each documentary follows the standard format of mixing historical re-creations of events with narrative voice-overs and interviews with topical experts who offer their analysis of the documentary subject. All four productions emphasize Jackson's relationship with the British in order to explain his life.[9]

Andrew Jackson: A Man for the People (1995) provides a traditional, chronological overview of Old Hickory's life. In the section addressing Jackson's childhood, the narrator notes that "at 15, Andrew Jackson was an orphan with a lifelong hatred of all things British." Sharon MacPherson, then director of research at The Hermitage, expands on this claim. "He never forgot the British," she notes. "Now there were times in his life where he really hates the dons more, as he calls the Spanish, because they're blocking up all that wonderful expansion to the southwest. But the British stay uppermost in his mind."[10]

Andrew Jackson: Conqueror of Florida (2005) examines Jackson's invasion of Florida late in the second decade of the nineteenth century. One of the key incidents of this First Seminole War was his decision to execute Robert Ambrister and Alexander Arbuthnot, British nationalists whom Jackson suspected of assisting the Seminole Indians and their free black allies in attacking and killing white Americans. In discussing the executions of Ambrister and Arbuthnot, the narrator, retired US Marine Captain Dale Dye, remarks, "Jackson may have also felt justified for putting Arbuthnot and Ambrister on trial as a means to exact vengeance on the British. He had a long-standing hatred of them dating back to when the redcoats captured him as a militia boy during the Revolutionary War." Next, the historian Harry Watson recounts the story of Jackson's scar and loss of family and notes, "So, at the end of the American Revolution, Jackson had lost all of his family, and he could blame it on the British. In a child's mind, it's easy to understand that. So, he added the normal hostility to the mother country to this kind of personal hatred."[11]

The 2006 documentary *Andrew Jackson* takes a different approach from its 1995 predecessor. It opens with a re-creation of the Battle of New Orleans. The narrator observes that Jackson's "determination to win was fueled by a deep, personal hatred that went back more than thirty years." The scene then shifts to the Revolutionary War and a discussion of the British officer's assault of Jackson. The narrator emphasizes the importance of this incident: "Three words from a British officer would light a fuse in Jackson that would burn for a lifetime: 'Clean my boots!'"[12]

Of the four documentaries, *Andrew Jackson: Good, Evil, and the Presidency* (2007) offers the most evenhanded analysis. When it comes to Jackson's hatred of the British, however, the refrain sounds familiar. The narrator, Martin Sheen, informs viewers that at the end of the Revolution, "in the boy's eyes, it was the British who were to blame for leaving him suddenly alone in the world." Sean Wilentz reinforces this argument. "For Andrew Jackson," he opines, "the American Revolution was a formative psychic, as well as political, event. For the rest of his life, he would despise the British Empire; he would grow up feeling as if he owed the British a kind of repayment for all that the British had done to him personally, and to his family." Discussing Jackson's military career later, Sheen adds, "Andrew Jackson had been yearning since he was thirteen for another shot at the British. And having been voted commander of the Tennessee militia, his dream had now come true."[13]

It is important to recognize that by reaching larger audiences than the typical academic book or journal article, written fiction and documentaries convey lasting ideas about Jackson's life and career that prove difficult to displace or correct. The narrative that unites all of these accounts of Jackson's life, fictional and nonfictional, is straightforward. During the American Revolution, the British army caused the deaths of Jackson's mother and two brothers, left him with visible scars on his face and hand, and generally wreaked havoc throughout the Waxhaws region of his childhood. As a result, Jackson's hatred of the British motivated him psychologically and emotionally for the rest of his life. According to this narrative, on at least two occasions he was able to exact some form of revenge against the British for his personal losses: the Battle of New Orleans and the execution of Ambrister and Arbuthnot.

The Historical Record

Examining academic and nonacademic perspectives on Jackson's feelings toward the British, however, fails to clarify the validity of these accounts. What did Jackson personally write about his interaction with the British? During his lifetime, what did he authorize or allow others to imply about his attitude toward the British? Finally, what did his actions suggest about the way in which he viewed them?

One place to turn for answers is the biographies of Jackson that were produced during his lifetime. Since Jackson did not record his memoirs, the three biographies that were written with his approval and assistance represent the closest thing to autobiographies that are available.

The first biography was written by John Reid and John Henry Eaton, both of whom served with Jackson during the War of 1812. Reid undertook writing *The Life of Andrew Jackson* shortly after the war ended, completing four chapters before dying in January 1816. Eaton finished the book in late 1816 or early 1817, relying on Jackson's papers and interviews with the General himself to complete the project. According to the editor of the 1974 edition, Frank L. Owsley Jr., the book was "not only the earliest account of Jackson's exploits but can also be considered his official authorized biography." Additionally, Owsley argued, "it is almost certain that Jackson read and approved every line of the manuscript, probably as it was being written," which lends the biography authority.[14]

Reid and Eaton's *Life of Andrew Jackson* recounted that Jackson's mother passed on to her sons "that fixed opposition to British tyranny and oppression, which afterwards so much distinguished them." Regarding the War of 1812, Reid and Eaton observed that at the beginning of the conflict, "General Jackson, ever devoted to the interest of the country, . . . knew no wish so strong as that of entering into her service, against a power, which, independent of public considerations, he had many private reasons for disliking." "In her," they continued, "he could trace the efficient cause, why, in early life, he had been left forlorn and wretched, without a single relation in the world."[15]

Though unpublished at the time, a second biography was written at the peak of the 1828 presidential campaign. Henry Lee, son of "Light Horse Harry" Lee and stepbrother of Robert E. Lee, completed his manuscript at the Hermitage and in consultation with the General. It made similar arguments to those of the Reid and Eaton work. For example, Lee credited Elizabeth Jackson with influencing her son's early impressions of the British. "Remembering the wrongs by England inflicted on her native country, and perceiving a temper of resentment kindling in America at encroachments from the same quarter," Lee wrote, "she instilled into the minds of her sons lessons of early patriotism. The sufferings of their grandfather in resisting the armies of King William, the oppression under which the Irish peasantry groaned and groaned in vain, the lordly desolation which blasted the face of that beautiful country, and seemed to be approaching this, were the subjects of her frequent and fervent recital." The confrontation with the British officer that left the adolescent Andrew scarred, Lee argued, was "supposed to have left a deep impression on the mind of Andrew, and may be referred to as the probable origin of that keen resentment and fearless opposition to the hostility of Britain, which on later occasions he exhibited."[16]

During Jackson's retirement years, his close adviser Amos Kendall undertook yet another biography. While the former president gave him access to his papers, Kendall did not visit the Hermitage. Instead, he sent his nephew James A. McLaughlin to interview Jackson and to copy papers that

FIG. 2.3. *Amos Kendall, Postmaster General,* c. 19 March 1838. From Library of Congress Prints and Photographs Online Catalog, hdl.loc.gov/loc.pnp/pga.06423.

seemed relevant for the book. Kendall published parts of his biography in serial form, but he only got as far as 1814 before abandoning the project.[17]

Kendall followed Reid, Eaton, and Lee in connecting Jackson's ethnic origins to his hatred of the British: "The Jacksons and Crawfords, though of Scotch descent, were natives of Ireland, and felt as keenly the wrongs of their country as the aboriginal race. Antipathy to the English name and dominion had become a part of their nature. Finding the same ruthless power pursuing them into the American wilderness, it was but natural that the spirit of resistance should become desperate and unconquerable." He also cited Elizabeth Jackson's "constant lessons of patriotic devotion" as an additional influence on Andrew. When the Revolutionary War came to the Waxhaws, Jackson "saw the horrors of the war. The mangled bodies of his countrymen presented a sad confirmation of those impressions made upon his youthful mind by the tales of English oppression and cruelty, which he had so often heard from his mother and kindred. The bloody tyranny in Ireland, from which his father fled, had now reached the retreat to which he led his family in the interior of America, and the son saw before him one of its most ferocious displays." Kendall continued, "The father of Andrew Jackson brought his family from Ireland to escape English oppression. Every member of that family which came from Ireland, except himself, perished through the effects of English oppression in America." "Through many perils," he concluded, Jackson "lived to be the avenger of his family and his race."[18]

While none of these biographies explicitly connected Jackson's early years to the Battle of New Orleans, all of them implied that his Scotch-Irish ancestry, his mother's influence, and his Revolutionary War experiences inculcated in him a hatred of the British that led him to seek vengeance later in life. Given Jackson's involvement in the writing of the biographies and the consistency in their presentation, it seems plausible to conclude that the biographies represented an authentic view of his Waxhaws experiences with, and later feelings about, the British.[19]

Another essential source to consider is Jackson's own writings. While not as prolific a writer as some presidents in the early republic, he left enough evidence to draw some conclusions about the development of his opinion about the British. During the 1790s, Jackson's support of Jeffersonian republicanism, not his Revolutionary War experiences, appeared to guide his anti-British sentiments. Letters that he sent from Philadelphia while serving in Congress between December 1796 and March 1798 mention Great Britain on several occasions, but only in relation to broader geopolitical concerns. For example, despite acknowledging the United States' independence in the 1783 Treaty of Paris and agreeing to Jay's Treaty in late 1794, Great Britain continued to violate American neutrality on the oceans. Jackson and other Jeffersonians blamed their political opponents, the Federalists, and Presidents George Washington and John Adams for allowing the British to harm American commerce and sailors. "It is Evident and Every days paper proves the fact that the British are daily capturing our vessels[,] impressing our Seamen[,] and Treating them with the utmost Severity & cruelty," Jackson wrote one of his brothers-in-law, Robert Hays, "but from the presidents [Washington's] speech it would seem that the British were doing us no injury, Committing no Depredations, that all the Depredations on our Commerce was done by the French Nation." He predicted that if France's Napoleon Bonaparte invaded Britain, "Tyranny will be Humbled, a throne crushed and a republick will spring from the wreck—and millions of distressed people restored to [the rights of man by the] conquering arm [of Bonaparte]." The French defeat of Britain would "be a happy circumstance for america," he told the Nashville cofounder James Robertson in 1798.[20]

As the Napoleonic Wars raged in Europe following Bonaparte's rise to power in France in 1799, the United States experienced their effects. In the years immediately preceding the War of 1812, Jackson, like many Americans, began to identify both the British and the French as enemies of the United States. In 1808, for example, he told officers in the Tennessee militia that they needed to prepare to "defend the liberties and independence of our country" from the threat posed by "the great belligerent powers of Europe." He centered most of his criticism on Great Britain, however, blaming the nation's "secrete agents" for inciting Indian "banditti" against white American settlers living in the borderlands. Of specific concern were the Prophet and his Shawnee-chief brother, Tecumseh, who were forming a united Indian confederation to push back against white encroachment on their lands. Jackson speculated that the Prophet was "the tool of England."

FIG. 2.4. William Charles, *A Scene on the FRONTIERS as Practiced by the 'HUMANE' BRITISH and their 'WORTHY' ALLIES,* 1812. From Library of Congress Prints and Photographs Online Catalog, hdl.loc.gov/loc.pnp/ppmsca.31111.

Once the US Congress declared war against Britain in June 1812, Jackson frequently expressed his belief that the Indians were simply pawns in Britain's strategic plan against the United States.[21]

Jackson's denunciation of the British during the War of 1812 hinted at a deeper motivation than simply concern for the Union: revenge. On several occasions during these years, he referenced his Revolutionary War experiences, suggesting that they still held him in their grip. The first mention appeared in a January 1813 letter to the Tennessee governor Willie Blount. "Brought up under the tyrany of Britain," Jackson wrote, "altho young embarked in the struggle for our liberties, in which I lost every thing that was dear to me, *my brothers and my fortune*—for which I have been amply repaid by living under the mild administration of a republican government." He went beyond simply alluding to his personal losses, however. In August of the next year, he explicitly told his wife that he "owe[d] to Britain a debt of retaliatory, Vengeance—should our forces meet I trust I shall pay the debt." These two statements provide the clearest evidence in Jackson's personal writings that he had not forgiven the British for causing the deaths of his two brothers and his mother.[22]

Both letters preceded Jackson's defense of New Orleans, but there are indications that the British treatment of his family and Waxhaw neighbors was at the forefront of his mind during the weeks surrounding the January 8 battle. In public addresses to New Orleans citizens and the troops defending the Crescent City, Jackson frequently referred to the British soldiers' savagery. In his December 15 address he called the British "the common enemy of mankind, the highway robber of the world" and warned listeners to "look to your liberties, your property, the chastity of your wives and daughters," a reference to British looting and raping in Hampton, Virginia, the previous year. Three days later, Jackson reminded the New Orleans militia that they were fighting for "a country blessed with every gift of nature—for property, for life—for those dearer than either, your wives and children—and for liberty" against an enemy that had prosecuted "a war of vengeance and desolation, proclaimed and marked by cruelty, lust, and horrours unknown to civilized nations." Following the battle, he congratulated the corps heads for their victory. Their effort had left "the pride of our arrogant enemy humbled, his forces broken, his leaders killed, his insolent hopes of our disunion frustrated—his expectation of rioting in our spoils and wasting our country changed into ignominious defeat, shameful flight, and a reluctant acknowledgement of the humanity and kindness of those whom he had doomed to all the horrors and humiliation of a conquered state." Other consequences included "your country saved from conquest, your property from pillage, your wives and daughters from insult and violation—the union preserved from dismemberment, and perhaps a period put by this decisive stroke to a bloody and savage war." Even in discussing the return of slave property, Jackson condemned the British. "Would it not be a degradation of that national character of which we boast," he wrote William C. C. Claiborne, "to condescend to solicit the restoration of stolen property from an enemy who avows plunder & burning to be legitimate modes of warfare?"[23]

FIG. 2.5. Charles Severin, *Gl. Jackson—At the Battle of New Orleans.* Lithograph, c. 1856. From Library of Congress Prints and Photographs Online Catalog, hdl.loc.gov/loc.pnp /cph.3a22337.

Jackson's antipathy toward the British continued into his postwar military career. While Jackson was overseeing treaty negotiations with various Indian tribes in 1817, Edmund P. Gaines informed him that he had intercepted a letter written by Alexander Arbuthnot, "one of those *self-styled Philanthropists* who have long infected our neighboring Indian villages, in the character of British Agents—fomenting a spirit of discord." Jackson responded by telling George Graham, the acting secretary of war, that he had ordered British agents posing as traders and helping Indian enemies to be "treated with the greatest rigor known to civilized Warfare." Following his invasion of Florida in March 1818, he arrested Arbuthnot and another British national, Robert Ambrister; after a trial, Jackson ordered both men executed. He told Secretary of War John C. Calhoun that "this Indian War had been excited by some unprincipled Foreign, or private Agents." Britain endorsed the "scenes of wickedness, corruption, and barbarity at which the heart sickens," he continued. "I hope that the execution of these Two unprincipled villains will prove an awfull example to the world, and convince the Government of Great Britain as well as her subjects that certain, if slow retribution awaits those uncristian wretches who by false promises delude & excite a Indian tribe to all the horrid deeds of savage war." Two years later, Jackson was still blaming "British Traders" for inciting Indians and offered his opinion that they should "be hung."[24]

Jackson's Attitude toward the British during His Presidency

Jackson's alleged lifelong contempt for the British appears not to have affected demonstrably his foreign-policy approach as president. The historian John Belohlavek acknowledged that Jackson's "perception of Great Britain has gone largely unchallenged in American historiography" and that his background made him "the quintessential Anglophobe." "It would perhaps then be logical," Belohlavek continued, "to assume that the hot-tempered General would be eminently unsuccessful in his conduct of diplomacy toward Great Britain," appointing diplomats who shared his sentiments and irreparably harming the two nations' diplomatic relationship. "Instead, the opposite came to pass," he noted. Jackson's "attitude toward the English remained calm and dispassionate" during several tense diplomatic negotiations with the Atlantic rival. Belohlavek's final assessment was that Jackson "ushered in a new era of Anglo-American understanding." Likewise, the historian Sam Haynes argued that "Jackson's lifelong antipathy to Great Britain did not prove to be a significant factor in his conduct of American foreign policy."[25]

Jackson's personal writings and public pronouncements reinforce these assessments that he generally sought a good relationship with the British during his presidential years. When faced with circumstances in which he could have lashed out at Great Britain, he either showed restraint or focused on the ways in which the British were helping domestic enemies who threatened the United States and its institutions.

An early example of Jackson's attitude toward the British came in 1831. A dispute with Britain about the Maine-Canada boundary led to the appointment of King William I of the Netherlands as arbiter. His decision to divide the disputed territory met with Jackson's tepid endorsement. Martin Van Buren, who had gone to London while awaiting the Senate's consent to his appointment as secretary of state, conveyed the president's decision in England. The British foreign minister, Lord Palmerston, told Van Buren that the British government had expected "dangers" from Jackson's election but instead "had experienced better treatment at your hands than they had done from any of your predecessors." The president asked Van Buren to reciprocate the "friendly feelings." While the Senate did not accept King William I's arbitration award (the boundary dispute was not resolved until the early 1840s), the American chargé d'affaires in London, Aaron Vail, remarked in 1835 that Jackson was "decidedly the most popular President in England we ever had."[26]

Another opportunity to cast Britain as the enemy came during the Nullification Crisis of 1832–33. Throughout those fall and winter months, South Carolinian Joel R. Poinsett acted as Jackson's agent in the Palmetto State, updating the president on the actions of the South Carolinians who claimed that their states'-rights doctrine regarding tariff legislation trumped the executive branch's enforcement power. Following passage of the Ordinance of Nullification, which pronounced the tariffs of 1828 and 1832 unconstitutional, the former diplomat wrote Jackson about rumors circulating that had the nullifiers hoping to form an alliance with Great Britain, which had allegedly promised them "succor and protection" if they seceded. He even went so far as to accuse William Ogilsby, the British consul stationed in Charleston, of plotting to move his nation's ships into the city's harbor under the pretext of protecting British citizens. Jackson informed Poinsett that Charles Bankhead, Britain's interim chargé d'affaires, had communicated a warning to Ogilsby about interfering in the crisis. If the consul ordered British ships into Charleston harbor, the president told Poinsett, then his credentials would be pulled. Jackson's reaction was hardly as precipitous or as emotional as one might expect from an Anglophobe.[27]

A third case arose during Jackson's fight with Nicholas Biddle and the Second Bank of the United States. The message that accompanied Jackson's Bank veto in July 1832 offered the president the perfect opportunity to lash out at the British. Amos Kendall, the main adviser on the veto message, included multiple references to the British influence over the Bank in his draft. For example, he argued that the Bank would "make the American people debtors to the nobility and gentry of Great Britain" and that it would place a tax on them "for the support and aggrandizement of the enemies of public liberty in the British Isles." The final draft of the veto message, however, was toned down significantly, containing only vague references to foreign influence. These changes suggest that Jackson restrained whatever antipathy he held toward the British. The following year, Jackson read a paper to his cabinet that recommended removing the government's deposits from the Bank to weaken its influence. The draft on which Jackson and Francis P. Blair worked expressed significant criticism of the British government and its use of economic power against its citizens. The draft lambasted the connection between "extensive monied incorporations, with their appendages of exclusive privileges" and "an aristocracy which thro' the influence of riches and talents, insidiously employed, sometimes succeeds in preventing political institutions however well adjusted, from securing the freedom of the citizen, and in establishing the most odious and oppressive Government under the forms of a free constitution." "The history of Great Britain is replete with lessons of instruction upon this point," the draft continued, providing a scathing critique of the British "Kings, Lords, Commons, Fund holders and Bankers" who used "largesses, salaries, pensions and dividends," as well as "bribes," that "[enabled] the higher classes of the community to prey upon the rest and to amass the means of perpetuating their subjection." As with the Bank veto message, however, this anti-British sentiment disappeared in the final draft, and it is not clear whether the views expressed in the earlier draft belonged to Jackson, Blair, or another adviser. Regardless, the sanitized final versions of both papers suggest that Jackson hardly viewed Great Britain as his mortal enemy.[28]

Jackson's Attitude toward the British during His Retirement

During his retirement years, Jackson was more vocal in expressing his suspicions about the British and their influence. This became particularly apparent when the United States' economy took a sharp downturn shortly after his successor, Martin Van Buren, took office. During this so-called Panic of 1837, Jackson highlighted the ways in which Great Britain and the Bank had worked together to create the economic crisis. He encouraged Van Buren to stand firm against the Whigs' attempts to use the depression to destroy the nation. "The great object of the opposition united with Biddle and the Bearings [the British-based Baring Brothers Bank], were to drain us of specie for the benefit of Britain; Bankrupt our Banks; [and] flood our country with depreciated paper [currency]." Jackson insinuated to Amos Kendall that British "foreign agents" were attempting to benefit their nation's merchant class by saturating the American marketplace with their goods, which would place the United States "in debt" to them. He told Francis P. Blair that there was an attempt under way to "form a holy foreign capital allience in america by which, the whole monetary system of Europe and america can be wielded by these Banks, and our country ruled by them." He specifically mentioned to his cotton factor, Maunsel White, that Biddle's Second Bank of the United States, now solely a Pennsylvania state bank, and the Baring Brothers Bank were two of the culprits. They were intent on "bankrupt[ing] their own country and Government by drainings of our metallic currency for the benefit of England." Jackson even blamed Van Buren's loss in the 1840 presidential election to his Whig opponent, William Henry Harrison, partially on the British. "I have viewed with much concern," he wrote Kendall, "the corrupt means employed by the combined opposition to gain their point, which has been hightened by the interference of England with all of her mony power to corrupt our people and elect a President for us, that would unite in her corrupt views, put down our republican system and build upon its ruins a great consolidated Government to be ruled by the corrupt mony power of england and amer-

FIG. 2.6. Edward Williams Clay, *Uncle Sam Sick with la Grippe*, 1837. From Library of Congress Prints and Photographs Online Catalog, hdl.loc.gov/loc.pnp/cph.3a05358.

ica." Any connection to his earlier animosity against the British seemed either ancillary or inconsequential, as Jackson used his Anglophobic rhetoric to make larger arguments about US domestic politics.[29]

The United States' relationship with Texas also provided Jackson with the chance to exhibit his anti-British feelings. In September 1843, he explained to William B. Lewis his concerns that if the United States did not move immediately to annex Texas, then Great Britain might take control of the Lone Star Republic. Before the United States could prepare militarily, the British would send a forty-thousand-man army to "take possession of Memphis and Baton Rough [Rouge], . . . possess herself of Neworleans and reduce all of our fortifications." "It would cost oceans of blood, and millions of mony to regain it," he warned. "Our dearest interests as a nation, the safety of Neworleans, the prosperity of the great vallue of the Mississippi, and our whole union require the annexation of Texas," he reiterated to Lewis a few months later. As with the Second Bank of the United States, Great Britain appeared to serve as a proxy for Jackson's most important concerns, which he revealed in numerous letters to close political friends. To the Tennessee representative Aaron V. Brown, for example, he noted that a British alliance with, or acquisition of, Texas would result in an invasion of the United States, "excite the negroes to insurrection," and produce "a servile war." Jackson made a similar comment to Francis P. Blair, observing that losing Texas and the Oregon Territory to Britain would result in "all the horrors of a servile war and its consequences, aided as it will by great Britain, and the blue light abolitionists of the north and East." If the slaves did not rebel and murder their masters, as Jackson hinted they would, then they would "all run over to Texas, and under British influence, [be] liberated and lost to their owners." Additionally, he told Blair a few days later, annexing Texas would "keep foreign influence from tampering with our Indians." Van Buren's failure to support Texas annexation surprised Jackson and indicated to him the New Yorker's unawareness of the danger to "the safety of the west, our Revenue, and the important interest of the south and west and the safety of Neworleans." Repeatedly, Jackson emphasized that the real concern was not that Britain (or France or Mexico) would annex Texas, but the loss of slave property, capital produced by slave labor, white lives to slave insurrections, and peaceful relations with western Native American groups that would come as a consequence.[30]

Conclusion

Two major conclusions can be drawn from this brief overview of Jackson and the British. First, while Jackson's experiences in the Waxhaws fueled, to some extent, his actions at New Orleans, it would be an overstatement to attribute Jackson's fight against the British in December 1814 and January 1815 solely or even primarily to revenge. As his Creek campaign indicated, his most significant motivation was defeating external enemies, be they Native American or British. In fact, his anti-British sentiments appeared to be little different from those of Americans who supported colonial independence during the Revolutionary period, especially if they had suffered loss at the hands of the British. In that regard, Jackson was exceptional only because his appointment as a military commander provided him with the opportunity to meet the British on the battlefield at a crucial point in the war. Second, Jackson did not hold a lifelong hatred of the British. He expressed suspicions about them during his presidency and during his postpresidential retirement, but they appeared to serve as a convenient substitute for his true fears (e.g., of the Bank and abolitionists), not as the object of his burning rage. Instead, Jackson rejected several opportunities to exact revenge against Great Britain by flexing American diplomatic, economic, or military power. This realization highlights one of the myths about Jackson—that he was a man driven by emotion. While he undoubtedly responded emotionally and violently to circumstances, particularly when he was younger, Jackson usually displayed a mature political prowess and personal self-control during his later political career that often goes unrecognized.

It is safe to say that there is more work to do in understanding the complex relationship between Old Hickory and John Bull. Several important questions remain unanswered. For example, what did the British government and people think about Jackson? Did the Battle of New Orleans figure heavily in their assessment of the War of 1812? Did the execution of Ambrister and Arbuthnot elicit an outcry against Jackson? During his presidency, was there lingering resentment across the Atlantic that influenced British foreign relations with the United States? From the American perspective, is there room to argue that the nation's westward expansion during the antebellum years can be traced back to January 8, 1815? These questions, and many more, offer the opportunity for historians to wrestle more fully with Jackson's influence on the United States and the Atlantic world.

NOTES

1. James Parton, *Life of Andrew Jackson,* 3 vols. (New York: Mason Brothers, 1860), 1:75; research notebook #1, p. 17, James Parton Papers, Houghton Library, Harvard University. My thanks to Tom Coens, research associate professor of history at the University of Tennessee and associate editor of *The Papers of Andrew Jackson,* for graciously supplying his unpublished transcription of this source. The page number refers to Coens's transcription.

2. Parton, *Life of Andrew Jackson,* 1:85, 95; 2:77. The memoirs of Vincent Nolte, an Italian-German merchant who lived in New Orleans during the War of 1812, were published the year

after his death in 1853. See *Fifty Years in Both Hemispheres: or, Reminiscences of the Life of a Former Merchant* (New York: Redfield, 1854).

3. William Graham Sumner, *Andrew Jackson as a Public Man: What He Was, What Chances He Had, and What He Did with Them* (New York: Houghton, Mifflin, 1895), 2; Frederic A. Ogg, *The Reign of Andrew Jackson: A Chronicle of the Frontier in Politics* (New Haven, CT: Yale University Press, 1919), 9; Marquis James, *The Life of Andrew Jackson,* 2 vols. (Indianapolis: Bobbs-Merrill, 1938), 1:27, 268; *Acceptance and Unveiling of the Statue of Andrew Jackson, Seventh President of the United States* (Washington, DC: GPO, 1929), 50, 82.

4. Augustus C. Buell, *History of Andrew Jackson, Pioneer, Patriot, Soldier, Politician, President,* 2 vols. (New York: C. Scribner's Sons, 1904), 1:59–60. For analysis of Buell's fabrications, see Milton W. Hamilton, "Augustus C. Buell: Fraudulent Historian," *Pennsylvania Magazine of History and Biography* 80, no. 4 (October 1956): 478–92, esp. 479, 490–92; and Hendrik Booraem, *Young Hickory: The Making of Andrew Jackson* (Dallas: Taylor, 2001), 201–4. To give one relevant example, Buell is the source of an anecdote relating an alleged conversation that Jackson had with William O. Butler, John H. Eaton, and William B. Lewis in which he gave an extended exposition on the advice his mother had given him as a young man. The anecdote, which has been repeated by Cyrus T. Brady, John Trotwood Moore, Pauline Wilcox Burke, Marquis James, Robert Remini, and Jon Meacham, as well as several children's authors, begins with Jackson's regretful statement, "Gentlemen, how I wish she could have lived to see this day." See Buell, *History of Andrew Jackson,* 1:57; Cyrus T. Brady, *The True Andrew Jackson* (Philadelphia: J. B. Lippincott, 1906), 59; John Trotwood Moore, "Historic Highways of the South," *Taylor-Trotwood Magazine* 5 (May 1907): 143; Pauline Wilcox Burke, *Emily Donelson of Tennessee,* 2 vols. (Richmond, VA: Garrett & Massie, 1941), 1:60; Marquis James, *Andrew Jackson, the Border Captain* (Indianapolis: Bobbs-Merrill, 1933), 284; Robert V. Remini, *Andrew Jackson,* 3 vols. (New York: Harper & Row, 1977–84), 1:11; and Jon Meacham, *American Lion: Andrew Jackson in the White House* (New York: Random House, 2008), 14.

5. Michael Paul Rogin, *Fathers and Children: Andrew Jackson and the Subjugation of the America Indian* (New York: Knopf, 1975; reprint, New Brunswick, NJ: Transaction, 1991), 52, 142; James C. Curtis, *Andrew Jackson and the Search for Vindication* (Boston: HarperCollins, 1976), 10–12, 22–23, 65–66.

6. Robert V. Remini, *The Battle of New Orleans: Andrew Jackson and America's First Military Victory* (New York: Viking, 1999), 12; John F. Marszalek, *The Petticoat Affair: Manners, Mutiny, and Sex in Andrew Jackson's White House* (New York: Free Press, 1997), 3, 12, 238; H. W. Brands, *Andrew Jackson: His Life and Times* (New York: Doubleday, 2005), 26; Sean Wilentz, *Andrew Jackson* (New York: Henry Holt, 2005), 23; Wilentz, *The Rise of American Democracy: Jefferson to Lincoln* (New York: Norton, 2005), 169–70, 171, 175; Wilentz, *The Rise of American Democracy: Jefferson to Lincoln,* abr. ed. (New York: Norton, 2009), 84; Daniel Walker Howe, *What Hath God Wrought: The Transformation of America, 1815–1848* (New York: Oxford University Press, 2007), 10; Meacham, *American Lion,* 11, 19; Lynn Hudson Parsons, *The Birth of Modern Politics: Andrew Jackson, John Quincy Adams, and the Election of 1828* (New York: Oxford University Press, 2009), 5; Patricia Brady, *A Being So Gentle: The Frontier Love Story of Rachel and Andrew Jackson* (New York: Palgrave Macmillan, 2011), 38.

7. Jeanette Covert Nolan, *Andrew Jackson* (New York: Julian Messner, 1949), 31; Frances Fitzpatrick Wright, *Andrew Jackson: Fighting Frontiersman* (New York: Abingdon, 1958), 104; Ruth Smalley, *An Interview with Andrew Jackson* (Johnson City, TN: Overmountain, 2001), 5.

8. Noel B. Gerson, *Old Hickory* (New York: Doubleday, 1964), 3–6, 158, 161; Max Byrd, *Jackson* (New York: Bantam, 1997), 45; Winston Groom, *Patriotic Fire: Andrew Jackson and Jean Lafitte at the Battle of New Orleans* (New York: Knopf, 2006), 36, 100, 214–15.

9. *Andrew Jackson: A Man for the People* (A&E Television, 1995), DVD, ch. 1; *Andrew Jackson: Conqueror of Florida* (A&E Television, 2005), DVD, ch. 3; *Andrew Jackson* (A&E Television, 2006), DVD, ch. 1; *Andrew Jackson: Good, Evil, and the Presidency* (KCET/Los Angeles & Red Hill Productions, 2007), DVD, chs. 2 and 3.

10. *Andrew Jackson: A Man for the People,* ch. 1.

11. *Andrew Jackson: Conqueror of Florida,* ch. 3.

12. *Andrew Jackson,* ch. 1.

13. *Andrew Jackson: Good, Evil, and the Presidency,* chs. 2 and 3.

14. John Reid and John Henry Eaton, *The Life of Andrew Jackson,* ed. Frank L. Owsley Jr. (Tuscaloosa: University of Alabama Press, 1974), v–viii. According to Owsley, later editions were revised significantly and used as campaign propaganda, which lessens their credibility in relation to the original edition (ix–xiv).

15. Ibid., 10, 14, 17–18.

16. Henry Lee, *A Biography of Andrew Jackson, Late Major-General of the Army of the United States,* ed. Mark A. Mastromarino (Knoxville: Tennessee Presidents Trust, 1992), i–iii, 1–3.

17. Amos Kendall, *Life of Andrew Jackson: Private, Military, and Civil* (New York: Harper & Bros., 1843); John McDonough, introduction to *Index to the Andrew Jackson Papers* (Washington, DC: Library of Congress, 1967), xii–xv.

18. Kendall, *Life of Andrew Jackson,* 12–13, 16, 50, 52, 59–61.

19. See, e.g., Jackson's numerous factual corrections sent to Kendall in Andrew Jackson (hereafter AJ) to Amos Kendall, 9 January 1844, in *Correspondence of Andrew Jackson,* ed. John Spencer Bassett and J. Franklin Jameson, 7 vols. (Washington, DC: Carnegie Institute of Washington, 1926–35), 6:253–54 (hereafter *CAJ*).

20. Harry L. Watson, *Andrew Jackson vs. Henry Clay: Democracy and Development in Antebellum America* (Boston: Bedford / St. Martin's, 1998), 28. Stanley Elkins and Eric McKitrick, *The Age of Federalism* (New York: Oxford University Press, 1993), 388–96, 406–31. AJ to Robert Hays, 6 December 1796, 16 December 1796, 25 January 1798, 2 March 1798; AJ to John Sevier, 18 January 1797; and AJ to James Robertson, 11 January 1798, in *The Papers of Andrew Jackson,* ed. Dan Feller, Sam B. Smith, Harriet Fason Chappell Owsley, and Harold D. Moser, 9 vols. to date (Knoxville: University of Tennessee Press, 1980–), 1:101, 103, 173, 185, 117, 165 (hereafter *PAJ*).

21. AJ to Thomas Monteagle Bayly, 27 June 1807; address to the officers of the 2nd Division, 20 April 1808; AJ to Thomas Jefferson, 20 April 1808; address to the brigadier generals of the 2nd Division, 19 December 1808; address to citizens of Nashville, [16 January 1809]; AJ to Willie Blount, [15 February 1810], 4 June 1812, 5 June 1812; AJ to William Henry Harrison, 28

November 1811; AJ to 2nd Division, 7 March 1812, 9 July 1812; and AJ to Tennessee volunteers, 31 July 1812, [14 November 1812], [16 March 1813], *PAJ,* 2:169–70, 190–91, 191–93, 203, 210–11, 236–38, 300–301, 301–2, 270–71, 290–93, 313–15, 317–18, 340–41, 390–92.

22. AJ to Willie Blount, 4 January 1813, in *CAJ,* 1:254–55; AJ to Rachel Jackson, 5 August 1814, in *PAJ,* 3:105.

23. Address to New Orleans citizens and soldiers, 15 December 1814, and AJ to William C. C. Claiborne, 5 February 1815, in *PAJ,* 3:204, 270; address to New Orleans militia, 18 December 1814, in *CAJ,* 2:119; address to corps heads, 21 January 1815, in *Historical Memoir of the War in West Florida and Louisiana in 1814–15, with an Atlas,* by Arsène Lacarrière Latour, ed. Gene Allen Smith, rev. ed. (Gainesville: University Press of Florida and Historic New Orleans Collection, 2008), 339.

24. Edmund P. Gaines to AJ, 2 April 1817; AJ to George Graham, 22 April 1817; AJ to James Monroe, 6 January 1818; AJ to John C. Calhoun, 8 April 1818, 4 May 1818, 10 August 1818; AJ to Rachel Jackson, 10 April 1818; AJ to José Masot, 23 May 1818; and AJ to Henry Atkinson, 15 May 1819, in *PAJ,* 4:106–7, 111–12, 166–68, 190, 197, 199, 232, 191, 207–8, 298. Frank L. Owsley Jr., "Ambrister and Arbuthnot: Adventurers or Martyrs for British Honor?" *Journal of the Early Republic* 5 (Fall 1985): 289–308. Deborah A. Rosen, "Wartime Prisoners and the Rule of Law," ibid. 28 (Winter 2008): 559–95.

25. John M. Belohlavek, *"Let the Eagle Soar!": The Foreign Policy of Andrew Jackson* (Lincoln: University of Nebraska Press, 1985), 54–55, 73; Sam Haynes, *Unfinished Revolution: The Early American Republic in a British World* (Charlottesville: University of Virginia Press, 2010), 115.

26. Belohlavek, *"Let the Eagle Soar!,"* 60–73; editorial note, *PAJ,* 9:24; Martin Van Buren to AJ, 28 September 1831, and AJ to Van Buren, 14 November 1831, in ibid., 9:592–94, 693–94.

27. Joshua Cain, "'We Will Strike at the Head and Demolish the Monster': The Impact of Joel R. Poinsett's Correspondence on President Andrew Jackson during the Nullification Crisis, 1832–1833," *Proceedings of the South Carolina Historical Association, 2011,* http://www.palmettohistory.org/scha/proceedings/proceedings2011.pdf, 13–26; Remini, *Andrew Jackson,* 3:12; Joel R. Poinsett to AJ, 25 November 1832, 9 February 1833, and AJ to Poinsett, 17 February 1833, in *CAJ,* 6:510–12, 5:16–17, 18; Jim Piecuch and Jason Lutz, "Charles Bankhead," in *Encyclopedia of the Mexican-American War: A Political, Social, and Military History,* ed. Spencer C. Tucker, 2 vols. (Santa Barbara, CA: ABC-CLIO, 2013), 49.

28. Draft of Bank veto message, n.d., Andrew Jackson Papers, Library of Congress; Elbert B. Smith, *Francis P. Blair* (New York: Free Press, 1980), 81–82; Donald B. Cole, *A Jackson Man: Amos Kendall and the Rise of American Democracy* (Baton Rouge: Louisiana State University Press, 2004), 165–71, 188; draft of paper read to the cabinet on removal of Bank of the United States deposits, [18 September 1833], in *CAJ,* 5:193–94, 199–200; paper read to the cabinet on removal of Bank of the United States deposits, 18 September 1833, in *A Compilation of the Messages and Papers of the Presidents,* ed. James D. Richardson, 10 vols. (Washington, DC: Library of Congress, 1902), 3:5–19. The *PAJ* editor Dan Feller graciously supplied me with an annotated transcript of Kendall's draft of the Bank veto message.

29. AJ to Martin Van Buren, 6 June 1837; AJ to Amos Kendall, 23 June 1837 and 2 January 1841; AJ to Francis P. Blair, 9 July 1837; and AJ to Maunsel White, 12 July 1837, in *CAJ*, 5:486–89, 489–90, 6:88–89, 5:495–97, 497–99.

30. AJ to Aaron V. Brown, [12] February 1843; AJ to William B. Lewis, 18 September 1843, 31 October 1843, 15 December 1843, 8 April 1844, 12 July 1844, 1 August 1844, 17 September 1844, 1 January 1845, 15 January 1845; AJ to Francis P. Blair, 5 March 1844, 7 May 1844, 11 May 1844, 18 May 1844, 26 July 1844, 15 August 1844, 19 September 1844, 1 January 1845; AJ to the editors of the *Nashville Union*, 13 May 1844; and AJ to Andrew J. Donelson, 2 December 1844, 11 December 1844, in *CAJ*, 6:201–2, 228–30, 238–39, 249, 277–78, 302, 306–8, 318–19, 352, 362–63, 271–72, 283–85, 285–87, 293–94, 304–5, 313–14, 320–22, 350–51, 289–91, 334–36, 338–39.

3

"The Dreams of Empires"
The War of 1812 in an International Context

ALEXANDER MIKABERIDZE

Often labeled a "forgotten war," the War of 1812 has traditionally received little attention in histories of the United States and is largely ignored by historians of Britain and its empire. Yet, the War of 1812, between Britain, the world's leading empire, and its former colonies, the now undefended United States of America, was to be of great importance to the fate of North America. The War of 1812 ensured that the United States was not to conquer Canada and was thus a crucial moment in the destinies of both nations. For Canada, this conflict became the cornerstone of Canadian national identity, or at least of the country's creation myth, and served as the first stage toward the eventual confederation in 1867. For the United States, the failed attempt to "liberate" Canada shaped American understanding of the nature of the American Revolution—the invasion of Canada was often portrayed as unfinished business from the earlier conflict—as well as of Americans' own place and role in the world. Indeed, the history of the United States would have taken a very different path had American invasion of Canada succeeded, not least because the slave states of the South would have been in a decided minority.

By 1812 North America had already witnessed its share of violence, and Anglo-American confrontation was not the sole conflict ravaging the northern regions of the Western Hemisphere. The United States was also engaged in an undeclared quasi war with Spain over the Floridas, supported a rebellion in Texas, and fought a series of wars with American Indians. But more importantly, the origins of the War of 1812, and its subsequent course, lay within a much larger conflict that assumed truly global dimensions. Since 1792, Europe had been locked in an unparalleled struggle that claimed the lives of hundreds of thousands of men and women. These Revolutionary and Napoleonic Wars were not limited to Europe alone. To the contrary, they came to engulf much of the world, precipitating and facilitating innumerable local conflicts in Asia, Africa, and the Americas. In North America it was the War of 1812. Although rooted in larger Anglo-American differences, the immediate causes of the War of 1812 arose from frictions caused by the Napoleonic Wars. Thus, it is of paramount importance to understand the wider, transatlantic context in which this war took place.

The Revolutionary Wars, of which the Napoleonic Wars were a continuation, had begun on April 20, 1792, as a consequence of the revolutionary outbreak in France. From the outset, the French Revolution aroused the hostility of European monarchies that felt threatened by the revolutionary ideas of liberty, equality, and fraternity, which could spread beyond the French frontiers and stir up upheavals in the rest of the continent. Following the execution of King Louis XVI of France in January 1793, the First Coalition (Austria, Prussia, Britain, Naples, Spain, Portugal, Sardinia, and others) was formed. Although France did not fare well in the first year and a half of the war, the French revolutionaries utilized their authority to enact unprecedented political and military measures (e.g., *levée en masse,* which established general conscription) to safeguard the country. Revolutionary France was able not only to protect itself from invasion by Austrian and Prussian armies but also to turn the tide of war and go on the offensive, seizing neighboring territories and spreading its revolutionary ideology.

As the war progressed, a variety of factors caused most of its members to fall away (e.g., Prussia and Spain in 1795), leaving Britain and Austria to prosecute a war against France. The Revolutionary Wars revealed a number of talented French generals, who quickly rose through the ranks, the most important of them being General Napoleon Bonaparte. It was Bonaparte's successful campaigns in Italy in 1796–97 that brought the War of the First Coalition to its conclusion in 1797. A year later, in response to France's aggressive foreign policy, the European powers formed the Second Coalition, which included Austria, Britain, Russia, Naples, Portugal, the Papal States, and the Ottoman Empire. The coalition had considerable success in Italy, where the Austro-Russian forces expelled the French armies from almost the entire peninsula. But it suffered defeats in Switzerland and later collapsed as a result of internal tensions between the coalition members. In the early nineteenth century, France, led by First Consul Bonaparte, who had seized power in France in the coup of 18 Brumaire (November 9–10, 1799), defeated Austria in Italy and Germany and forced her to accept the Treaty of Lunéville, which further reduced Austria's sphere of influence. By 1801, Great Britain was the sole state still actively resisting rising French power.

The United States and the Great Powers during the Revolutionary Wars

The Revolutionary Wars had an important impact on the United States of America. Occupied in fierce and deadly struggle in Europe, the great powers had no forces to spare for North America. Thus, Europe's suffering became America's advantage. It was amid the revolutionary turmoil that the principles of American neutrality were enunciated and enacted. More importantly, these wars ended the Franco-American alliance and enabled the United States to settle its critical frontier issues with Spain and Britain without resorting to war.

At the start of the War of the First Coalition in 1792, the Franco-American Treaty of Alliance and the Treaty of Amity and Commerce (1778) were still in effect and raised some awkward questions, such as whether the United States was obliged to help defend French possessions in the West Indies or to deny ports and supplies to the British. President George Washington consulted his cabinet before declaring American neutrality and seeking warring parties' acknowledgment of the United States as the neutral nation. The US declaration of neutrality on April 22, 1793, greatly disappointed the French government, which expected support from the United States out of republican solidarity, hatred of Britain, and gratitude for aid during the War of American Independence. But it was the Anglo-American rapprochement that marked the turning point in relations between the United States and France. Following the independence of the United States, there remained the nagging problems in its relationship with the former metropole. Despite pledges made in the Treaty of Paris in 1783, the British had retained a string of forts along the Canadian border, arguing that their presence was justified by America's failure to pay its prewar debts to British creditors. In 1790, Gouverneur Morris, a talented American political personality who was engaged in private business in France, was dispatched across the English Channel to sound out the British government on the subject of establishing formal diplomatic relations and negotiating a settlement of outstanding disputes. Morris had several meetings with Prime Minister William Pitt and Lord Grenville, the secretary for foreign affairs, but they remained noncommittal. Only when the Nootka Sound Crisis brought Britain close to a war with Spain did the British government become more cordial to Morris and consider diplomatic relations between the United States and Britain.

The prospects of Anglo-Spanish confrontation alarmed President Washington and his advisers, who feared that Britain might request permission to march troops through American territory to threaten Spanish-held regions. This permission, in turn, could be exploited by the British to tighten their hold on the trans-Appalachian territory. The American government was divided on which course of action to follow.[1] Some members, most notably Secretary of the Treasury Alexander Hamilton, favored granting the passage rights and exploiting the opportunity to secure American interests along the whole of the Mississippi River.[2] But others, including Vice President John Adams, Secretary of State Thomas Jefferson, and Chief Justice John Jay, wanted to refuse to such a passage, believing that the United States should exploit its power over commerce to compel the British government to settle the outstanding issues. These differences were at the core of the growing struggle between Hamilton-led Federalists, who controlled the Senate and called for a strong centralized government, national bank, and good relations with Britain, and their political opponents, Jefferson-led Democratic-Republicans, who denounced most of the Federalist policies. The latter's efforts to introduce a national navigation act to prohibit imports from countries that refused the import of American products in American vessels facilitated the British decision to dispatch twenty-eight-year-old George Hammond, who despite his youthful age was already a seasoned diplomat, to Philadelphia. Arriving in October 1791, Hammond did his best to prevent Congress from passing the navigation act, which would have been detrimental to British interests. The British government was willing to consider a treaty of commerce with the United States, but only if payment of prewar debts was secured and a neutral Indian barrier state, under British protection, was set up along the whole northern frontier. The American government, of course, rejected these conditions as infringing on American sovereignty, so Hammond's mission produced limited results.

News of the French declaration of war on Britain reached the United States in April and came as a complete surprise. The 1778 Treaty of Alliance had made the United States was a perpetual ally of France, and therefore it was obligated to assist that nation. Yet, despite considerable Francophile sentiment among the American public, few Americans wanted to dive into the morass of European wars, especially when the fledgling republic still lacked a navy. Even such bitter rivals as Hamilton and Jefferson agreed that neutrality was the only sensible policy. The former favored declaring the French alliance invalid because it had been made with the French monarchy, which no longer existed. Jefferson, on the other hand, urged avoiding entanglement in the war and using the alliance as a bargaining tool with Britain. President Washington rejected the advice of both. On April 22, 1793, he signed a neutrality proclamation that declared the United States "friendly and impartial toward the belligerent powers" and warned US citizens that they might be prosecuted for "aiding or abetting hostilities" or taking part in other non-neutral acts.[3] Washington did, however, accept Jefferson's advice that the United States should recognize the new French republic. In the spring of 1793 citizen Edmond-Charles-Edouard Genet, France's new ambassador to the United States, landed at Charleston, South Carolina, and he was enthusiastically welcomed throughout his journey to Philadelphia. Yet Genet's actions and the growing radicalism of the French government soon dissipated this goodwill; for many Americans, what was occurring in France resembled their worst nightmares of anarchy and ochlocracy. Discourse on the French and British causes galvanized and divided American public opinion. In July 1793, unable to maintain his political influence in Washington's administration and embittered by his own ideological struggles with Hamilton, Jefferson resigned as secretary of state.

At the beginning of the French Revolutionary Wars, Britain informed the United States that it would take enemy property wherever it could find it, including on neutral ships on the high seas. Thus, an order in council of June 8, 1793, instructed British naval commanders to detain all neutral ships bound for French ports with cargoes of corn, flour, or meal.[4] In early November, an even harsher order in council was issued, ordering the British fleet to "stop and detain all ships laden with goods the produce of any colony belonging to France, or carrying provisions or other supplies for the use of any such colony."[5] Arriving in the Caribbean, the British captains thus targeted the American merchant fleet trading with the French islands; by early 1794 several hundred American ships in the West Indies had been confiscated. The news of the British attacks on American shipping reached Philadelphia in March 1794, just as a report was received that British troops in the Ohio River valley were arming Indians, who, in turn, attacked American settlers. Thus, a war crisis flared up between Britain and the United States. In April 1794 Washington appointed Chief Justice John Jay as a special envoy to Britain with instructions to negotiate and settle all major disputes.[6]

Over the next six months Jay conducted wide-ranging negotiations with the British that resulted in the conclusion of the Treaty of Amity, Commerce, and Navigation, commonly known as the Jay Treaty, on November 19, 1794. The treaty secured some American goals, including limited rights of American merchants to trade with the British West Indies, withdrawal of the British military from northwestern forts (the area west of Pennsylvania and north of the Ohio River), and reparations for the seizure of American ships and cargo in 1793–94. The parties agreed to submit disputes over wartime debts and the American-Canadian boundary to arbitration. But the American side also made important concessions, including accepting the British definition of neutral rights and granting Britain most-favored-nation status in American commerce.[7] In the words of one eminent American historian, the treaty was "one-sided in Britain's favor," but it was also "a shrewd bargain for the United States. It bet, in effect, on England rather than France as the hegemonic European power of the future, which proved prophetic. It recognized the massive dependence of the American economy on trade with England. In a sense it was a precocious preview of the Monroe Doctrine (1823), for it linked American security and economic development to the British fleet, which provided a protective shield of incalculable value throughout the nineteenth century. Mostly, it postponed war with England until America was economically and politically more capable of fighting one."[8]

The terms of the Jay Treaty caused public outrage in the United States and engendered such intense debate that some Americans feared an outbreak of civil strife. The Democratic-Republicans, who favored France, denounced the treaty and called for "a direct system of commercial hostility with Great Britain,"[9] even at the risk of war. The Federalists were much more receptive to the treaty, but even they were disappointed by the limitations on their trading rights in the British West Indies. The Senate debated the treaty in secret and consented to it on June 24, 1795. The news of the Jay Treaty prompted the French government to suspend diplomatic relations with the United States. The French decision was further buttressed when, in October 1795, the American minister to Spain, Thomas Pinckney, negotiated the Treaty of San Lorenzo (Pinckney's Treaty), securing the American boundary at the 31st parallel, strengthening US commercial rights to use New Orleans in Spanish Louisiana, and opening access to the Caribbean from the Mississippi River.[10] In response, France began seizing American ships trading with Britain, reasoning that American cargo heading for British ports could be interpreted as contraband subject to seizure. By summer 1797, French privateers and naval vessels operating in the Caribbean and along the American coast had seized more than three hundred American ships.

Following his inauguration as the second president of the United States, John Adams quickly moved to restore relations with France. Yet an American attempt at diplomatic settlement with France led to the infamous XYZ Affair, in which the French diplomats requested a $6 million loan to France and a $250,000 bribe as prerequisites for serious discussions. The French demands aroused a public outcry in the United States, with Representative Robert Goodloe Harper of South Carolina famously proclaiming, "Millions for defense, but not a penny for tribute."[11] American outrage did not lead to an all-out war between the United States and France, however. Instead, Congress suspended commerce with France and authorized the capture of armed French ships, creating a separate Department of the Navy to pursue this mission. By summer 1798 the fledgling American navy and privateers were involved in an undeclared war, or "Quasi-War," with French ships, mainly off the American coast and in the Caribbean. The Franco-American conflict saw numerous privateer actions and only a few significant naval engagements, such as the capture of the *Croyable* (14 guns) by the *Delaware* (20) off New Jersey in July and the capture of the *L'Insurgente* (40) by the *Constellation* (38) in February 1799. The only notable American loss in these actions was the retaking of the *Croyable* (which had been renamed the *Retaliation*) in November 1798.[12] By 1799, French ships had been driven from the American coast and French privateering had been largely eliminated from the Caribbean. In part, this result was owing to France's recognition of its naval limitations following the defeat in the Battle of the Nile (August 1, 1798). In 1800, First Consul Napoleon Bonaparte initiated a change in French policy opening negotiations with the United States that resulted in an agreement ending the Quasi-War. The Convention of Mortefontaine (or Convention of 1800) ended hostilities between France and the United States, restored normal diplomatic and commercial relations, and deferred discussion of the alliance and American claims for the seizure of more than eight hundred ships.[13]

In March 1802 France and Britain signed the Peace of Amiens, but its provisions satisfied neither side: France refused to open its markets to British goods and rein in its foreign policy, while Britain refused to evacuate Malta. With neither country willing to compromise, hostilities resumed on May 18, 1803, when Britain declared war on France. Although France possessed one of the most formidable armies in Europe, Britain's dominance of the seas meant that the French government could not invade the British Isles and end the war in triumph. The short respite in European affairs in 1802–3 was of momentous importance to the United States, since it was during this break in what proved to be twenty-three-year-long hostilities that the United States was able to complete its greatest territorial acquisition. In 1763, at the end of the Seven Years' War (known as the French and Indian War in North America), France had lost its Louisiana Territory to Spain. Forty years later, Napoleon made clandestine deals with the Spanish to regain control of this territory. Reclaiming the Louisiana Territory was in line with Napoleon's grand design to restore the French colonial empire in the Atlantic. Yet, the powerful slave revolt in Saint Domingue (Haiti), which Napoleon tried to suppress in 1802–3, had dashed this vision. Furthermore, with a new war against Britain nearly unavoidable, Napoleon was concerned about the prospects of a British invasion of Louisiana and therefore was receptive to American inquiries about purchasing New Orleans and the surrounding territory. Surprising American negotiators, Napoleon's minister of the treasury, François de Barbé-Marbois, offered the entire Louisiana Territory, and the two sides ultimately agreed on the price of $15 million ($11.25 million in cash and $3.75 million in canceled debts owed by the French government) for the vast territory of more than eight hundred thousand square miles.[14] Curiously, the purchase money was transferred, after the outbreak of the war between Britain and France, through English bankers.

The Louisiana Purchase marked a watershed moment in the history of the United States. It serves as the best example of the argument that Europe's distresses during the Revolutionary and Napoleonic Wars were America's advantage. It created an excellent opportunity to limit the influence of foreign powers in the region and to secure vast tracts of lands for future settlement by the Americans. The purchase gave the United States the ability to control the whole of the Mississippi River and much of the Gulf Coast. Finally, the Louisiana Purchase set in motion a pattern of expansion that radically altered the demographics of North America and proved catastrophic for the Native Americans. With France largely removed from the scene, the Native American tribes faced an increasingly assertive American government and had only a disinterested Britain and a weakened Spain to act as counterbalances to a rising US hegemony.

The Start of the Napoleonic Wars, 1803–1807

In the two years following the collapse of Amiens in 1803 there was little in the way of traditional fighting. Napoleon, who was proclaimed emperor in 1804, assembled his army in northwestern France and threatened to cross the English Channel but was unable to actually do so. By 1805 the British government was able to organize a powerful anti-French coalition that included Austria, Russia, Sweden, Naples, and Portugal. In 1805 Napoleon launched a complex and ambitious plan to lure the Royal Navy from the English Channel and allow his army to cross it unmolested. The plan called for a French fleet to distract the British by threatening their possessions in the West Indies. However, by the time the plan was carried out, Napoleon faced a more immediate threat in the form of a new coalition shaping up in central Europe. Furthermore, a Franco-Spanish fleet under Admiral Pierre-Charles Villeneuve failed in its mission; defeated in a minor combat off Cape Finisterre on July 22, the fleet was then destroyed by the British admiral Horatio Nelson at Trafalgar on October 21. The Battle of Trafalgar had a profound impact on the course of the conflict as Britain now enjoyed unchallenged dominance of the seas for the duration of the Napoleonic Wars. Her Continental allies were less fortunate.

Austria and Russia agreed to coordinate their actions, but the Austrian decision to invade neighboring Bavaria before the Russians arrived proved to be consequential. The French army, which Napoleon forged into his famous Grande Armée between 1803 and 1805, left its camps in northwestern France in mid-September and, in a stunning feat of maneuvering and speed, transplanted itself into the heart of central Europe by the end of the month. Napoleon surrounded the Austrian army, commanded by Karl Mack von Leiberich, at Ulm and forced it to surrender on October 20. With the main Austrian army, north of the Alps, destroyed and another, led by Archduke Charles, pinned down in Italy, the French occupied Vienna and pursued the Russian army, under the command of Mikhail Kutuzov. In a brilliantly conceived and executed battle at Austerlitz (Slavkov) on December 2, 1805, Napoleon defeated the Austro-Russian army, inflicting some twenty-five thousand casualties and losing about seven thousand of his own men. The battle effectively ended the Third Coalition, as Austria sued for peace and surrendered its influence in Germany. Napoleon asserted hegemony in central Europe, where he reorganized the German states by amalgamating them into the French-dominated Confederation of the Rhine.

In 1806, the Fourth Coalition was formed, made up of Prussia, Russia, Saxony, Sweden, Sicily, and Britain. Yet it proved to be short-lived. In October, Napoleon invaded Prussia, inflicting a crushing defeat on the Prussians in the battles at Jena and Auerstädt. Over the next two weeks the French forces eliminated the Prussian army as an effective military force and captured almost all the major Prussian fortresses, occupying Berlin on October 23. Only one small corps under the command of General Anton Wilhelm von l'Estocq escaped the destruction and joined the Russian army in Poland. In the next stage of the campaign, the French marched into Poland, where they defeated the Russian army in the decisive battle at Friedland on June 14, 1807. Following this defeat, Emperor Alexander I of Russia chose to negotiate with Napoleon. The Treaties of Tilsit, signed on July 7–9, 1807, had a profound effect on the political situation in Europe. After a string of triumphs in 1805–7, Napoleon seemingly dominated Europe. He and Alexander I proclaimed an alliance of two great empires, dividing the European continent into two spheres of influence. Russia pledged to join France in her struggle against Britain, while France accepted Russian territorial expansion.

These rivalries and wars of European powers proved of great consequence to the United States. The central theme of this period was the American quest for international respectability and true independence from Europe. The Napoleonic Wars permitted the fledgling American republic to develop unmolested for almost a decade, becoming involved in this worldwide conflict only in its later stages.

The United States and the Continental System

Writing in 1820, following the death of King George III, the American minister to Britain, Richard Rush, mused that "Britain and the United States are destined to become . . . the predominating nations of Christendom. . . . Each an encumbrance to the other when together, their severance seems to have been the signal for unequalled progress, and boundless prospects to each; not more in material dominion than in the solid and durable glory of widening the empire of rational freedom throughout the world."[15] Yet, a decade earlier Anglo-American relations had been far from "widening the empire of rational freedom." In fact, the two nations had engaged in a long quarrel that climaxed in the American declaration of war upon Britain in June 1812.

This dispute sprang from a crucial fact: America chose to remain neutral while Britain struggled against Napoleonic France. In 1806, the conflict between France and Britain entered its thirteenth year, and no resolution could be expected in the near future. Napoleon's military prowess secured French dominance on the Continent, while Britain was protected behind the "wooden walls" of its navy. The British government chose to fully exploit its naval supremacy. In May 1806, it began to institute unprecedented systems of blockade by means of orders in council. These orders placed the entire European coast from Brest to the River Elbe under a British naval blockade. In response, Napoleon issued the Berlin Decrees (November 21, 1806), which declared the British Isles to be in a state of blockade, imprisoned British subjects on the Continent, and prohibited all commerce and correspondence with them. The Berlin Decrees served as the foundation for the so-called Continental System, or Continental Blockade, which pursued three main goals: undermining the British economy by depriving it of access to European markets, securing French economic dominance in Europe, and promoting industrial development on the Continent. The British government responded to Napoleon's actions with more stringent orders of January 7 and November 21, 1807. These prohibited coastal trade between ports controlled by France and its allies and compelled neutral vessels, including American ones, to enter British ports before proceeding to their destinations, under threat of seizure; neutral ships had to pay duties and secure licenses in order to trade with enemy ports. On November 23 and December 17 Napoleon further tightened his blockade system by issuing the Milan Decrees, which authorized the capture of neutral ships sailing from any British port or any vessels that submitted to search by the Royal Navy.

Thus, the two chief causes of the War of 1812 were the orders in council and the impressment of American seamen. Because the French navy could not actually implement a blockade of the British Isles, the principal effects of Napoleon's regulations prohibiting trade with Britain were felt by neutral nations, particularly the United States, which since 1803 had been the world's most important neutral carrier, especially of foodstuffs. American goods and ships were now liable to seizure by both the British navy and French privateers; thus, between 1807 and 1812 some nine hundred American merchant ships were seized by Britain and France. The British also instituted the notorious policy of impressment, which involved British warships' stopping American merchant vessels and forcibly removing American seamen whom they claimed were British subjects or deserters. Impressment was fueled by the vast scale of British operations against Napoleonic France. Between 1793 and 1812 the number of warships in the Royal Navy increased from 235 to 584, with a corresponding increase in the number of seamen from 36,000 to 114,000 men. Obtaining seamen was difficult, however, because of poor pay, stern discipline, and poor working conditions. But Britain needed them badly in order to defend its interests in the Indian Ocean, South Africa, and the Mediterranean Sea and to blockade the French-controlled European ports on the Atlantic coastline. The exact number of sailors impressed by the British is difficult to establish, but as many as sixty-five hundred American seamen were taken by the British between 1803 and 1812.[16]

The orders in council caused great friction between Britain and the United States. Unwilling to go to war, President Thomas Jefferson nevertheless responded to the deprivations of both France and Britain with the Embargo Act (December 28, 1807), which prohibited US exports via land or sea, though coastal trade was permitted provided that a bond was posted. The purpose of this embargo was to compel Britain and France to modify their decrees by denying them access to American commerce. The embargo hit Britain harder than it did France, and Napoleon should have been content with Jefferson's policy, but he chose to further exploit it. On April 17, 1808, he issued his Bayonne Decree, which sanctioned the seizure of all US ships in European ports under the assumption that they must be British vessels in disguise.

Engendered by Anglo-French rivalry, Jefferson's embargo proved to be quite detrimental to the United States. As Rear Admiral Alfred Thayer Mahan, the American exponent of sea power, observed, it had all the deficiencies of a blockade by an enemy and none of the advantages of actual war, such as the opportunity to capture British ships or threaten British territory. This self-imposed blockade had a major impact on American ports, undermining American economic prosperity and cutting into government revenues. The British traveler John Lambert, who visited New York in the spring of 1808, described "the melancholy dejection that was painted upon the countenances of the people, who seemed to have taken leave of all their former gaiety and cheerfulness"; the grass was growing on the New York wharfs in the month of April.[17] The embargo, which it was impossible to enforce fully, produced widespread smuggling that benefited British ports in Nova Scotia and generated considerable disgruntlement in New England. With opposition to the embargo increasing, in March 1809 the US Congress repealed the Embargo Act, substituting for it the Non-Intercourse Act, which prohibited all British and French vessels from entering American waters but allowed American vessels to operate freely. At the same time, George Canning, the British minister of foreign affairs, dispatched D. M. Erskine to negotiate with the United States. The resulting Erskine Agreement (April 18–19, 1809), which Erskine concluded in violation of his instructions, pledged to end the orders in council, to allow free trade between Britain and the United States to resume, and to settle the *Chesapeake-Leopard* affair. President Madison pledged to repeal the American Non-Intercourse Act as soon as the British orders in council were withdrawn. But the British government repudiated the agreement because Erskine had been unable to meet Canning's requests of American acquiescence to British enforcement and acceptance of the colonial trade law known as the Rule of 1756.

The Erskine Agreement thus embittered Anglo-American relations. Madison felt insulted and quickly reinstated the Non-Intercourse Act against Britain on August 9. Napoleon exploited these circumstances to sanction confiscations of more American vessels (through the decrees of Vienna, August 4, 1809, and Rambouillet, March 23, 1810). He argued that since all American ships were banned from trading with France, any vessel claiming to be American while visiting French ports must be engaged in smuggling. In May 1810 the United States adopted Macon's Bill No. 2 (May 1, 1810), which was better designed to deal with European belligerents. It repealed the Non-Intercourse Act of 1809 and announced that the United States would resume trade with the two belligerents with the provision that if France repealed its decrees, the United States would renew nonimportation against Britain, but if Britain repealed its orders in council, the United States would impose nonimportation on France. Macon's Bill had a direct and important impact on the war in Europe. Over the next year and a half (1810–11), vast quantities of American wheat and flour—more than a million barrels of flour alone—were shipped to the Iberian Peninsula, where they sustained British military operations against the French.[18] This was a crucial moment in the Peninsular War. In the summer of 1810 the French marshal André Masséna led some seventy thousand men across the Portuguese frontier, rapidly moving on toward Lisbon to expel the British forces. However, the British commander Arthur Wellesley, the future Duke of Wellington, implemented a comprehensive plan for the defense of Portugal. In addition to his impenetrable Lines of Torres Vedras, which stretched from one side of the peninsula to the other, Wellington rebuilt the Portuguese army and called for a systematic destruction of the countryside in the path of the French army. All residents were evacuated, livestock were slaughtered or moved, and crops and supplies were removed or destroyed, leaving the French in a barren desert. Unable to penetrate the fortified Lines of Torres Vedras, Masséna spent months seeking other alternatives before lack of supplies forced him to abandon his position and return to Spain. Meanwhile, the British forces continued to be sustained by American provisions.

Napoleon was alarmed by the prospects of revived commercial ties between Britain and the United States, which would have undermined his ongoing blockade of Britain. So he quickly moved to preempt the British and keep Americans in line with his Continental System. On August 5, 1810, Napoleon, through his foreign minister, informed the American minister to France, John Armstrong, that he was prepared to revoke the earlier decrees if Britain ended its orders in council or the United States resumed its policy of no intercourse with Britain. Curiously, Napoleon had no intention of repealing the Berlin and Milan decrees, nor could a simple note from the French foreign minister suspend these fundamental laws of the empire. Yet, "hoodwinked" Madison, as the historian Henry Adams aptly described him, took the French ploy.[19] With no proof that Napoleon had repealed his orders (which he had not), the US Congress confirmed the Non-Importation Act (March 1, 1811), which forbade the entry of ships and goods from the British Empire into the United States.

Wellington closely followed American economic policies since they could have direct impact on his troops. In March 1811 he expressed his concerns to the British commissioner in Spain: "You will observe that the ports of America will have been shut against us on the 1st of February. It is possible, nay, probable, that the grain for which you sent the £400,000 may not have quitted the ports of America at that time, and it is at all events desirable not to neglect any means which can be adopted to secure so desirable an object."[20] But Wellington's concerns were allayed once he learned that the Non-Importation Act still allowed Britain to continue purchasing American produce, which had become so crucial to the British war effort in Portugal and Spain. Shipments of American grain continued to increase, from 80,000 bushels in 1807 to more than 230,000 in 1810 and an incredible 900,000 in 1812. On the eve of the War of 1812, a British observer wrote that "if it was not for the supplies from America, the army here could not be maintained."[21]

In the wake of the Non-Importation Act, the British government was quite bitter toward the US government for having rushed to embrace Napoleon. Yet, its options were limited. American supplies were critical to its war effort. The British economy was experiencing a major crisis, and business interests, especially in manufacturing, appealed to the British government to take whatever steps were necessary to reopen trade with the United States. Finally, following demands in Parliament, on June 16, 1812, the British government repealed its orders in council restricting neutral trade. It would be weeks before this information became known in Washington, however, and by then it was too late. On June 18, 1812, the US Senate approved a declaration of war against Great Britain.

The War of 1812

The War of 1812 both shaped and was in turn influenced by military events in Europe. In April 1812, as it moved closer to declaring war, the US Congress passed a ninety-day embargo stopping all exports from the United States. Wellington was soon astonished to learn from "a paper from America" that "the Americans have laid a general embargo on all vessels. This is a measure of importance as all this part of the Peninsula has been living this year on American flour."[22] He immediately began to consider other potential sources for supplies, including faraway Brazil and Egypt, which could "keep the stores supplied with corn in the event then expected [in March 1812] of the stoppage of the intercourse with America."[23] The flow of American supplies did not stop immediately upon the proclamation of the embargo. In fact, it even continued for some time after the declaration of war. As the price of grain increased in Portugal and Spain, many American merchants became willing to circumvent restrictions to reap profits. However, British authorities in the Peninsula had soon established sufficient supplies of provisions to enable Wellington to easily rebuff an American offer of sixty thousand barrels of flour.[24]

The American invasion of Canada commenced almost simultaneously with Napoleon's invasion of Russia, an event that would largely overshadow the Anglo-American conflict. On June 24, 1812, Napoleon's massive army of more than 450,000 men invaded Russia. The Franco-Russian alliance, created at Tilsit in 1807, had quickly withered away. Russia was disgruntled by economic losses sustained under the Continental System and concerned about Napoleon's plans for the restoration of the Polish kingdom and his aggressive policies in central Europe. Napoleon's invasion of Russia lasted six months, and although the French had scored important victories at Smolensk and Borodino and had occupied Moscow, they were ultimately forced to leave empty-handed. The Russian government refused to negotiate "as long as a single foreign soldier remain[ed] on Russian soil," as Emperor Alexander told a French envoy.[25] But the Russian war effort had been significantly hampered by the Anglo-American hostilities. The War of 1812 diverted the resources of Russia's key ally, Britain, and prevented the much-desired American trade from reaching the Russian ports in the Baltic Sea. In September, as Napoleon was about to occupy Moscow, the Russian government asked John Quincy Adams, the American minister to St. Petersburg, if the United States would be open to an offer of Russian mediation with Britain. Adams quickly conveyed the news to President Madison, who accepted the offer in March 1813, but by then Napoleon had already been defeated and Russia was about to embark on what became the War of German Liberation. Madison appointed two commissioners (Albert Gallatin, secretary of the treasury, and James Bayard, a senator from Delaware) to negotiate peace with the help of Russian mediators. However, this mission produced no results, because the British government rejected Russian mediation on the grounds that its disputes with the United States involved internal issues that were not susceptible to foreign meddling. But the real cause for British apprehension lay in the Russian support for American conceptions of maritime law, which assumed a narrow view of belligerent rights and a broader interpretation of neutral rights. Britain expected American negotiators to bring up these issues in any discussion of peace terms, and Russian mediation could have provided them with much-needed support. Indeed, in his instructions to the American commissioners, Secretary of State James Monroe observed that "since 1780, Russia has been the pivot on which all questions of neutral right have essentially turned."[26]

His second offer of mediation in Anglo-American conflict rebuffed (September 1813), Emperor Alexander of Russia concentrated on his war effort against France. The Russian Campaign had disastrous consequences for Napoleon. His military might was shattered following the loss of up to half a million men in Russia. The French cavalry was virtually wiped out and never fully recovered during the subsequent campaigns in 1813–14. Furthermore, Napoleon's allies, Austria and Prussia, exploited the moment to break their alliance with France and joined their efforts against Napoleon. The Sixth Coalition, formed in 1813, involved Russia, Britain, Prussia, Sweden, Austria, and a number of German states. In October 1813 the allies finally caught up with Napoleon's main forces at Leipzig, where the Battle of the Nations, which proved to be the largest of the Napoleonic Wars, involving more than five hundred thousand combatants, decided the fate of Europe. In a three-day battle Napoleon suffered a defeat and was forced to retreat to France. The battle had a direct impact on the military operations in North America. Once the tide in the European war had turned against Napoleon, the British began to redeploy significant resources across the Atlantic. By the spring of 1814, when Napoleon was finally overthrown, two British armies of veteran troops had been dispatched to America, one to invade from Canada via Lake Champlain and the other to harass the coast and threaten American interests in New Orleans. Of the forty-four units dispatched to America, about half (21) came from Wellington's Peninsular Army. Their arrival in late 1814 dramatically increased the size of the British forces in North America and facilitated new military operations.

In the late summer of 1814 Britain commenced a joint land and naval campaign against American targets on the Gulf Coast. The campaign sought to deprive the United States of access to the crucial areas around the Gulf and ultimately influence peace negotiations to safeguard British interests in the region. The principal focus of the campaign was the city of New Orleans, a large commercial hub that served as the main outlet of American goods in the Gulf region and controlled access to the Mississippi River basin. The British also hoped to exploit the fact of the recent incorporation of these areas into the United States and solicit support from the Spanish and French residents, as well as Native American tribes, against the Americans. As early as the spring of 1814, the British North American Station commander, Vice Admiral Alexander Cochrane, sought to incite the Seminoles, in Spanish Florida, to fight against the Americans.

As the Napoleonic Wars winded down after Napoleon's abdication in April 1814, Britain was able to divert substantial troop reinforcements to North America. The British campaign began in earnest in mid-August, when a small British detachment led by Major Edward Nicolls, of the Royal Marines, captured the naval anchorage at Pensacola Bay, West Florida, and received support from some local Indians. A month later, Nicolls, supported by a Royal Navy squadron under the command of Captain William H. Percy, marched against Fort Bowyer at the mouth of Mobile Bay but was unable to overcome the American garrison commanded by Major William Lawrence, losing one ship and suffering dozens of casualties; the British were forced to withdraw in mid-September.

The British assault soon provoked an American counterattack. In November, Major General Andrew Jackson, the American commander on the Gulf Coast, attacked the town of Pensacola, easily overcoming local opposition. He then moved against the British-held forts, causing the British to evacuate Pensacola Bay. By December 1, Jackson was already at New Orleans, just in time to supervise defensive preparations for an impending British attack. The British fleet, comprising seven ships of the line and numerous frigates and smaller vessels, as well as an even larger number of transports carrying an expeditionary force of some 6,500 British regular soldiers, 1,000 marines, and some 1,000 West Indian blacks, had sailed from Jamaica under the command of Admiral Cochrane and anchored in the Gulf of Mexico to the east of Lake Pontchartrain. By mid-December the British expeditionary force had begun to march toward New Orleans, where a decisive battle took place on January 8, 1815. The British commander, General Edward Pakenham, launched a frontal attack on Jackson's strong positions. American gun and musket fire mowed down large numbers of the attackers, including Pakenham, who was killed. After several hours of fighting, the British were forced to withdraw, leaving behind some 40 percent of their men as casualties. Sometimes regarded as "the Needless Battle," the Battle of New Orleans had no direct influence on the terms of the ongoing peace negotiations, but its outcome did compel Britain to abide by the final peace treaty. This was particularly important because of British interest in acquiring New Orleans and securing control over the Mississippi estuary and regional trade.

The defeat at New Orleans did not end the British campaign in the Gulf. In late January and February the British forces targeted American forts, including Mobile, along the Gulf coastline, but their efforts were interrupted by the news of peace. In August 1814 Britain and the United States opened formal peace negotiations in Ghent (Belgium).[27] After four months of negotiations the two sides finally agreed on the peace terms and signed the Treaty of Ghent on December 24, 1814. Because the news of the peace signing had to cross the Atlantic Ocean by sailing ship, it did not reach the United States until February 1815; by then, unaware that the peace had been signed, American and British forces had fought a bloody battle at New Orleans. In the Treaty of Ghent, both sides agreed to restore the status quo ante bellum, which meant releasing all prisoners of war and restoring all territory held by the other. Britain promised to return captured slaves but ultimately did not and instead paid compensation a few years later. The final treaty also did not reflect Britain's proposal for the creation of an Indian buffer zone in Ohio and Michigan, which could have constrained American territorial aspirations. Interestingly, the treaty made no mention of the direct causes of the war, including impressment of American citizens and freedom of the seas. But with the end of the Napoleonic Wars, Britain stopped impressing seamen and never again pursued its disputes with the United States to the point of war.

The War of 1812 was the direct result of a complex political reality in

Europe. If not for the Napoleonic Wars, this conflict probably would not have been fought. As it was, the war against America hurt Britain's standing in Europe. It sapped much-needed human and material resources and allowed the other powers to encroach on Britain's commercial hegemony. The British government was also under intense domestic pressure to bring an end to the war. The British public grew increasingly weary of continued mobilization and taxation. After two decades of warfare, national sentiments had largely subsided in the wake of Napoleon's defeat, and few Britons insisted on continuing war to chastise Americans. Perhaps the most important result of the war was the remarkable surge of nationalism throughout the United States and Canada as many Americans and Canadians came to believe that they had won their own "wars of independence." In both places, popular mythology sprouted surrounding the war, citizen-soldiers, and heroic officers, which in turn reaffirmed fledgling national identities and helped to bring respective peoples together as one nation.

NOTES

1. For an interesting discussion of foreign-policy details, see John Lamberton Harper, *American Machiavelli: Alexander Hamilton and the Origins of the U.S. Foreign Policy* (Cambridge: Cambridge University Press, 2004) 65–102.

2. Ron Chernow, *Alexander Hamilton* (New York: Penguin, 2004), 389–408.

3. "Proclamation 4—Neutrality of the United States in the War Involving Austria, Prussia, Sardinia, Great Britain, and the United Netherlands Against France," 22 April 1793, The American Presidency Project, www.presidency.ucsb.edu/ws/index.php?pid=65475&st=&st1=. An old but still useful study is C. M. Thomas, *American Neutrality in 1793: A Study in Cabinet Government* (New York: Columbia University Press, 1931).

4. *American State Papers: Documents, Legislative and Executive, of the Congress of the United States*, ed. Walter Lowrie and Matthew St. Clair Clarke, vol. 1 (Washington, DC: Gales & Seaton, 1833), 240. Orders in council were orders issued by the British sovereign on the advice of his Privy Council. Unlike statutes, orders in council were issued by the sovereign by virtue of the royal prerogative and did not require parliamentary sanction.

5. Ibid., 430.

6. In June 1794 the US Congress once again stressed American neutrality in European conflicts by adopting the Neutrality Act, which made it illegal for an American to enlist in the service of a foreign power and prohibited the "providing or preparing the means for any mil-

itary expedition or enterprise . . . against the territory or dominions of any foreign prince or state with whom the United States was at peace." Neutrality Act, 5 June 1794, in *United States Statutes at Large,* 3rd Cong., 1st sess., 381–84.

7. "The Jay Treaty 1794 and Associate Documents," The Avalon Project, Yale Law School, avalon.law.yale.edu/subject_menus/jaymenu.asp.

8. Joseph Ellis, *Founding Brothers: The Revolutionary Generation* (New York: Knopf, 2000), 136–37.

9. Baron William Wyndham Grenville et al., "American Affairs," in *Report on the Manuscripts of J. B. Fortescue, Esq. preserved at Dropmore . . . ,* 10 vols. (London: Eyre & Spottiswoode for HMSO, 1892–1927), 3:526.

10. "Treaty of Friendship, Limits, and Navigation Between Spain and The United States," 27 October 1795, The Avalon Project, Yale Law School, avalon.law.yale.edu/18th_century/sp1795.

11. Eric Robert Papenfuse, *The Evils of Necessity: Robert Goodloe Harper and the Moral Dilemma of Slavery* (Philadelphia: American Philosophical Society, 1997), 27–28.

12. For details, see George C. Daughan, *If By Sea: The Forging of the American Navy from the Revolution to the War of 1812* (New York: Basic Books, 2008), 325–45.

13. "Convention between the French Republic, and the United States of America," 30 September 1800, The Avalon Project, Yale Law School, avalon.law.yale.edu/19th_century/fr1800.asp.

14. For details, see Charles A. Cerami, *Jefferson's Great Gamble: The Remarkable Story of Jefferson, Napoleon, and the Men behind the Louisiana Purchase* (Naperville, IL: Sourcebooks, 2003); Peter Kastor and Francois Weil, *Empires of the Imagination: Transatlantic Histories of the Louisiana Purchase* (Charlottesville: University of Virginia Press, 2008); and Patrick G. Williams, S. Charles Bolton, and Jeanne M. Whayne, *A Whole Country in Commotion: The Louisiana Purchase and the American Southwest* (Fayetteville: University of Arkansas Press, 2005).

15. Richard Rush, *A Residence at the Court of London: Comprising Incidents, Official and Personal, from 1819 to 1825; Amongst the Former, Negotiations on the Oregon Territory, and Other Unsettled Questions Between the United States and Great Britain,* 2 vols. (London: Richard Bentley, 1845), 1:247–48.

16. Brian DeToy, "The Impressment of American Seamen during the Napoleonic Wars," in *Consortium on Revolutionary Europe, 1750–1815: Selected Papers* (Tallahassee: Institute on Napoleon and the French Revolution, Florida State University, 1998), 492–501; Keith Mercer, "Northern Exposure: Resistance to Naval Impressment in British North America, 1775–1815," *Canadian Historical Review* 91, no. 2 (June 2010): 199–232.

17. John Lambert, *Travels through Lower Canada and the United States of North America in the Years of 1806, 1807 and 1808, to Which are Added, Biographical Notices and Anecdotes of Some of the Leading Characters in the United States,* 2 vols. (London: Richard Phillips, 1810), 2:157.

18. W. Freeman Galpin, "The American Grain Trade to the Spanish Peninsula, 1810–1814," *American Historical Review* 28, no. 1 (1923): 24–25.

19. Henry Adams, *The Life of Albert Gallatin* (Philadelphia: J. B. Lippincott, 1879), 445.

20. Duke of Wellington to Charles Stuart, 1 March 1811, in *The Dispatches of Field Marshal, the Duke of Wellington, K.G. During his Various Campaigns in India, Denmark, Portugal,*

Spain, the Low Countries, and France. From 1799 to 1818, ed. John Gurwood, 13 vols. (London: John Murray, 1834–39), 7:324.

21. David Milne Home, report of 9 April 1812, in Home, *Report on the Manuscripts of Colonel David Milne Home of Wedderburn Castle, N.B* (London: Mackie for HMSO, 1902), 155.

22. Wellington to Lt. Gen. Sir T. Graham, 8 May 1812, in *Dispatches of Field Marshal, the Duke of Wellington,* 9:129–30.

23. Wellington to Stuart, 3 May 1812, ibid., 10:342–45. Wellington explored several other possible sources of supplies, including the Barbary States, "British settlements in North America," "Western Islands," and Mexico, which "ought to be able to supply some." Writing to his brother Henry, he expressed his irritation at the Americans, noting that "it would be capital to turn the tables upon these cunning Americans, and not to allow them to have any intercourse with those ports [Cadiz and Lisbon]." Wellington to Sir Henry Wellesley, 10 May 1812, ibid., 9:132–33.

24. Wellington to Robert Jenkinson, 2nd Earl of Liverpool, 12 May 1812, ibid., 9:137–40.

25. Adjutant General Alexander Balashev, memo, in *Russian Eyewitness Accounts of the Campaign of 1812,* ed. Alexander Mikaberidze (London: Frontline Books, 2012), 12.

26. US Congress, *State Papers and Public Documents of the United States, from the accession of George Washington to the Presidency, exhibiting a complete view of our foreign relations since that time,* 10 vols. (Boston: T. B. Wait and Sons, 1817), 9:358.

27. In 1814 Belgium was not yet an independent state. Annexed by France during the Napoleonic Wars, it was transferred to the newly established Kingdom of the Netherlands at the Congress of Vienna in 1815 and gained independence in 1830.

4

Objects of Scorn

Remembering African Americans and the War of 1812

GENE ALLEN SMITH

The War of 1812, described by the American historian Donald Hickey as a "forgotten conflict," represented a major watershed in both the history of Anglo-American relations and the history of North American racial relations.[1] While historians have scrutinized virtually every official action that drove the two nations to war, the story of black participation in the conflict generally has not been remembered. Some five years before the war officially began, the British frigate *Leopard* fired on the American frigate *Chesapeake* on Monday, June 22, 1807. Then, British sailors boarded the American vessel, mustered the crew, and impressed four seamen—Jenkins Ratford, William Ware, Daniel Martin, and John Strachan—who they claimed were deserters. The damaged *Chesapeake* limped back to Norfolk with three dead and eighteen wounded.[2] The *Chesapeake-Leopard* affair, as it has subsequently been remembered, represented one of the most demeaning episodes in the early history of the United States. This affair involved the boarding of a neutral US warship and forcing sailors to serve aboard British warships, both of which were contentious diplomatic issues that would divide the two countries well into the nineteenth century. Equally significant, three of the four impressed sailors—Martin, Strachan, and Ware—were black men, all of whom claimed to be Americans. While race did not figure into the national dialogue during the debates and protests that followed, it nonetheless remained central to this episode and to the history of the War of 1812. Yet black participation would be downplayed in the aftermath of the war and forgotten as quickly as possible.[3]

As they had the American Revolution, black sailors and soldiers would see the second war with Great Britain as a means to advance their own agenda, and they served in all theaters of operations.[4] For example, Oliver Hazard Perry had a considerable number of African American sailors serving with him at the Battle of Lake Erie, an estimated 15–20 percent of his total crew.[5] The British incarcerated nearly a thousand African American sailors at Dartmoor Prison, in southwest England, many of whom were inadvertently massacred after the war ended. Throughout their incarceration these men embraced their status as free black seamen, struggling to uphold their belief in "Free Trade and Sailors' Rights."[6] Other slaves and free blacks joined the US Army and Navy, the Spanish military, and even British forces during the conflict in hopes of bettering their material conditions or to fight for causes in which they believed—causes that, if successful, would permit them to define their identity.

The British invasion of coastal North America created even greater opportunities for slaves who wanted to flee to freedom. Just as John Murray, 4th Lord Dunmore, had attempted to mobilize Virginia blacks in 1775, in April 1814 Admiral Alexander F. I. Cochrane issued a proclamation that freed enslaved people who would join the British cause. The active presence of British forces in the Chesapeake and along the South Atlantic coast in 1814 created opportunities for several thousand enslaved peoples to gain their freedom, while some six hundred former slaves donned uniforms as Colonial Marines and participated in British operations against Washington, Baltimore, and along the South Atlantic. Britain's campaign in the Mid-Atlantic states created a serious problem for American planters: it emboldened slaves to flee, while also making the countryside virtually indefensible. Should the American militia be called out to confront a British threat, then slaves had free reign to flee or rise against their masters. British forces exploited that fear, leaving Americans in the region doubly exposed, threatened by a potential British invasion if the militia remained in the neighborhoods or exposed to a potential slave revolt if the militia advanced to meet the British threat. This dichotomy provided slaves with unusual opportunities.[7] The British eagerly recruited slaves from the Chesapeake, the South Atlantic, and the Gulf of Mexico region, giving them a chance to fight as soldiers against their former masters and providing them with an opportunity to relocate as freemen to a British colony. Ultimately the British decision to mobilize slaves as combatants to liberate and relocate them instilled a racial component in the War of 1812 that scholars have not addressed. This chapter uses case studies of four black men—Peter Denison of Michigan, George Roberts of Maryland, Ned Simmons of South Carolina, and Jordan Noble of Louisiana—to show the roles that blacks played during the conflict and how their stories have not been remembered. Moreover, these episodes reveal exactly how black contributions threatened the white status quo in the United States.

After the Revolutionary War, the American government's decision to limit the size of its army inadvertently created new opportunities for free blacks and slaves. The traditional fears of a large standing army, as well as burdening fiscal concerns, prompted Americans to rely upon citizen-soldiers. The 1792 federal Militia Act further defined the role of American citizens in defending their country by placing responsibility for arming the militia on the individual and making states responsible for training and enforcement of the federal and state statutes. Each state did have the authority to clarify the federal mandate, even though most simply mimicked the wording of the 1792 act. New Jersey (1792), Vermont (1797), North Carolina (1806), and New Hampshire (1808) required free white male citizens to serve but took no position on African Americans. Some states, such as North Carolina and Virginia, permitted blacks to muster alongside whites. Others, such as Connecticut (1784), Massachusetts (1785), and South Carolina (1800), exempted blacks from the militia altogether; South Carolina even forbade "negroes" to be "armed with any offensive weapons unless in cases of alarm." The action of the states did not create any significant problems for the country, as there were no serious "alarms" or crises necessitating troops. But by the early nineteenth century America's difficulties with Britain and with various American Indian tribes on the northwestern frontier forced a reevaluation of the federal mandate and permitted opportunities for individual slaves and free blacks to contribute to their chosen cause.[8]

Prior to 1807, the Detroit, Michigan, slave Peter Denison had been indentured to Elijah Brush for a year, after which Brush had granted Denison his freedom. Apparently Brush had taken this action without the knowledge or approval of Denison's owner, Catherine Tucker, who protested the emancipation and demanded Denison's return. Harris Hickman, Brush's friend and a lawyer, applied for a writ of habeas corpus on behalf of Denison, forcing the Michigan territorial government to decide on the validity of slavery in the region. Although the Northwest Ordinance had abolished slavery in the American Northwest after 1787, it was not clear whether this prohibition applied in the land the British turned over to the United States in 1796. Judge Augustus Woodward ruled in the case that property rights would be upheld and that any bondsman living in the territory as of May 31, 1793, and belonging to a slaveholder as of July 11, 1796—the day Britain turned the territory over to the United States—would remain a slave. Denison fit within this latter category and technically remained a slave, the property of Catherine Tucker.[9]

This story may be similar to that of other early nineteenth-century slaves who tried through the courts to secure their freedom, but Denison's tale differed from that of many others in that while he remained technically a slave, he did not act like one nor was he treated as one in the years that followed. After the 1807 *Chesapeake-Leopard* affair, the territorial governor, William Hull, offered Denison "a written license" permitting him to form a militia company of free blacks and runaway Canadian slaves. Apparently Denison had gained the confidence of Detroit's black population, and according to Hull, under Denison's leadership segregated troops "frequently appeared under arms" and "made considerable progress in military discipline." Hull maintained that these men demonstrated an unquestioned "attachment to our government, and a determination to aid in the defense of the country." Yet as soon as the crisis that had prompted Hull to turn to Denison and the city's black population passed, the governor disbanded the militia.[10]

Although Denison's black company was disbanded after the 1807 crisis passed, the controversy over the creation of a black militia unit came before the territorial legislature time and again. During the summer of 1811 the legislature debated "the propriety of organizing a military company comprised of slaves that had run away from gentlemen residing" in Canada. Judge Woodward, who also served in the legislature, sponsored an unsuccessful resolution that would have forbidden Hull from mustering fugitive slaves into the militia at all. Nonetheless, during the summer of 1812 Governor Hull issued militia commissions to three black men, Captain Denison, Lieutenant Ezra Burgess, and Ensign Bossett. After hearing of this transaction, Judge Woodward, disregarding the growing tension between Britain and the United States, instantly demanded that Hull address "two inconveniences" regarding slaves and the militia. He wanted to know under what authority Hull had granted the commissions and supplied the black militia with weapons, and he criticized the governor for flagrantly encouraging slaves from Canada to flee to the Michigan Territory. Woodward believed that Hull had committed a "train of unwarranted transactions" and said that when confronted on the issue, the governor "was insolent in the extreme." Hull maintained that the runaways were free citizens of the Michigan Territory and that they, like white citizens, could bear arms in times of crisis. They would shortly be needed in mid-August 1812, when General Isaac Brock's small British, Canadian, and Indian army crossed the border and took Detroit. Hull, fearing that the Indians would begin a war of extermination, surrendered Detroit; by doing so, he gave up the entire northwestern territory.[11]

After General William Hull surrendered Detroit, the American regulars were transported as prisoners to Lower Canada, while the volunteers and militia, most likely including Peter Denison and his black compatriots, returned to their homes on parole until they were exchanged. Peter Denison then disappears from the historical record, but by 1816 a black Peter Den*n*isson reportedly lived as a freeman in the community of Sandwich, Upper Canada, and attended the St. John's Church of England there, just east across the river from Detroit. This Peter Dennisson was probably Peter Denison. Either he spelled his name differently or he did not correct the church secretary.[12] In either case, it is likely that Denison, his wife, and his children crossed over into Upper Canada, illustrating how within a few short years the path to freedom had shifted dramatically north. Peter Denison's story reveals the changing nature of the Michigan-Canada borderlands, as well as the changing definition of slavery in this region. Initially Canadian slaves fled south to the freedom of Michigan, but by the end of the War of 1812 the path to freedom had shifted dramatically, leading north to Canada. For a very narrow window of time, the fluidity of the borderlands greatly altered the slave's path to freedom and our understanding of the North American slave diaspora.[13]

During the late eighteenth and early nineteenth centuries the route to freedom most commonly led enslaved peoples south from British Canada to free American territories in the Northwest. Upper Canada legislated against slavery in 1793, but not all enslaved people gained immediate freedom. Because slavery was phased out over time, the Michigan Territory held out the prospect of immediate freedom to those brave enough to cross the treacherous waters of the Detroit River. Indeed, many of Denison's men had fled from bondage in Canada to the freedom of Michigan during the prewar period, a southern exodus that undermines the traditional image of the Underground Railroad leading north to Canada and freedom. Yet by the end of the War of 1812, few enslaved people lived in Canada, and Canadian law prohibited the further introduction of slavery. This reality prompted enslaved Americans such as Peter Denison, his wife, and their family to venture along an emerging path or nascent Underground Railroad to a new Canadian land of freedom. Yet historical memory of the conflict does not equate the northern path to freedom to the consequences of the War of 1812.[14]

George Roberts experienced the War of 1812 very differently. When the war began, the then forty-six-year-old African American Roberts, from the waterfront Canton neighborhood of Baltimore, Maryland, signed aboard Captain Richard Moon's privateer *Sarah Ann.* The ship departed Baltimore in late July, only a month after the beginning of the war. While cruising off the Bahamas in late August, the *Sarah Ann* encountered a British ship from Kingston bound for London, laden with coffee and sugar. Since the British ship outgunned the privateer and the Americans did not want to get too close, they engaged the vessel for hours in a long-range artillery duel. Then suddenly the American privateer descended on the British vessel, and Roberts and his fellow sailors swept aboard, taking the ship as a prize within minutes. After convoying the prize to Savannah, the *Sarah Ann* quickly left to seek other victims.[15]

On September 13, 1812, while cruising again off the coast of the Bahamas, the *Sarah Ann* encountered the British frigate *Statira,* which quickly subdued the privateer. Forcing the Americans to muster on deck, British officers singled out six sailors and accused them of being British. George Roberts was one of the six taken to Jamaica in irons. The privateer captain reported to the ship's owners in Charleston that he feared the men would be tried as deserters, which could mean execution. Moon insisted that Roberts, "a coloured man and seaman," had been born in the United States. While the American captain had not questioned Roberts personally, the sailor apparently "had every sufficient document together with his free papers"; nevertheless, the British had taken him. Furthermore, the American captain swore that Roberts had enlisted "on board the *Sarah Anna* [*sic*] at Baltimore where he is married." The Charleston owners responded to the British action by seizing twelve British sailors and holding them hostage in confinement. The threat worked: the British eventually released Roberts and his fellow prisoners.[16]

Securing his freedom, Roberts eventually signed aboard other vessels before finding his way back to the United States. In late July 1814 he signed on as a gunner aboard the Baltimore-built privateer *Chasseur*, later hailed by Hezekiah Niles as the "Pride of Baltimore." The privateer slipped by the British blockading squadron and then unexpectedly sailed east, directly toward the British Isles. There Captain Thomas Boyle preyed on merchant shipping, and in late August he boldly proclaimed the entire British Isles to be under the blockade of the *Chasseur*. Boyle demanded that his proclamation be posted on the door of the offices of the shipping underwriter Lloyd's of London, driving up insurance rates and forcing the Admiralty to transfer vessels to guard merchant ship convoys. *Chasseur* captured or sank seventeen vessels, and as Roberts recalled, they had "many hairbreath escapes."[17]

Roberts and the *Chasseur* returned to Baltimore on the evening of April 8, 1815, and as the privateer passed Fort McHenry she fired her guns in a salute. Granted, the privateer had not contributed to the American victory at Baltimore, but the city nonetheless embraced the *Chasseur* and her crew as true heroes of the battle. During the years that followed, Roberts was "allowed to parade with the military of the city on all occasions of importance . . . generally mounted as [a] servant to the major-general of the division." He marched each year in uniform in the annual commemoration of Defenders' Day, September 12, and "throughout his long life [he] was always highly thought of by the citizen soldiery." He always carried himself erect and "never appeared on parade except in uniform." Roberts's patriotism exuded from him. "Though laboring under the weight of so many years," he considered it "one of his highest aspirations to still be considered one of the defenders of his native city." Moreover, throughout his life he maintained that he would gladly volunteer again, if necessary, to defend Baltimore. Remaining a lifelong resident of Canton, Roberts died peacefully at his home on January 16, 1861, at ninety-five years old, and the *Baltimore Sun* offhandedly proclaimed "Another Old Defender Gone."[18]

George Roberts's maritime career had taken him to a multitude of foreign ports, brought him thrills and excitement, and made him an acknowledged contributor to the city of Baltimore's privateering heritage. Yet he never assumed a central role in the city's postwar celebrations. Later in life, Baltimore's racial composition changed, and this undoubtedly affected Roberts. Between 1850 and 1860 the city's free black population found their rights greatly circumscribed, revealing an increased racial prejudice toward black residents. Because George Roberts had gained recognition as a War of 1812 hero, he could transcend that racism and prejudice for at least one day a year—September 12, when he put on his uniform and marched with other veterans during the Defenders' Day celebrations. In helping their country maintain its independence, men like Roberts had disregarded the fear and danger of war, fighting for a greater cause, social and economic equality and freedom for slaves. During the conflict Roberts may have been equal and free, but afterward armed and proud black men simply threatened the white status quo and undermined the established racial hierarchy of American society. As time passed and black combatants like Roberts died, the stories of their contributions quickly faded and were forgotten.[19]

Unlike Roberts, Ned Simmons was born a slave and lived most of his life as a slave at Dungeness Plantation on the Cumberland Island estate of General Nathaniel Greene. Born sometime during 1763 probably in South Carolina, during the American Civil War he recalled a story of "carrying" General George Washington through the streets of Savannah at the time of Washington's celebrated visit in May 1791. This southern expression meant that Simmons helped transport the president during the journey; he did not physically carry him through the streets on the momentous occasion. Even so, the festivities, celebrations, and glorious Savannah fireworks display left a memorable impression on the then twenty-eight-year-old Simmons.[20] Shortly before the War of 1812, Nat Greene, his siblings, and their mother, Catherine, began quarreling over the distribution of the late general's estate. The question of lands, slaves, ribbons, and medals bitterly divided the family. In 1810 Simmons and thirty-two other slaves were given to son Nat. But Nat did not want to be a slave owner, and he conveyed the slaves back to his mother in 1813. With his mother's sudden demise during early September 1814, the slaves returned to Nat and then passed to his sister, Louisa Shaw. Although Simmons and his fellow Cumberland Island slaves' ownership ping-ponged among the Greene family, their monotonous existence on the island changed very little until the waning weeks of the War of 1812.[21]

When Admiral George Cockburn's ships and soldiers invaded the area in early 1815, Simmons and other slaves took the opportunity to decide their own futures. When British forces occupied Cumberland Island and encamped on Dungeness Plantation on January 15, Ned immediately volunteered for military service with the British, taking the surname Simmons. His full name appeared on the Cumberland Island garrison list five days later. In fact, he was one of the first Cumberland Island slaves to volunteer for British service. On January 28 his name, Ned Simmons, appeared on the muster list of the "Black Company," and a month later he enlisted in the Third Battalion of Colonial Marines. Simmons received an old, 1808 version of a British red uniform. He soon received a weapon and began training to be a marine. Then disaster struck.[22]

Although Ned Simmons had voluntarily agreed to join the British force, his training had not yet taken him off Cumberland Island. During early March 1815 two American commissioners arrived to inform the British of the ratification of the peace agreement. They also intended to negotiate for the return of American property, including slaves, taken during the war. After days of contentious bickering between the commissioners and Cockburn, the admiral agreed that any property, including slaves, on Cumberland Island at 11:00 p.m. on February 17, 1815, would be returned. Yet even this narrow interpretation of the Treaty of Ghent adversely affected

Ned Simmons. He had been one of the first to volunteer, but he had not yet departed the island. Thus he fell victim to the dispute concerning the return of property. On March 10, 1815, British officers stripped Simmons of his uniform, his insignia, and his weapon, and he and eighty other slaves involuntarily returned to bondage on Cumberland Island.[23]

During 1834 Nat Greene and his family sold the plantation to Robert Stafford, and along with it went the seventy-one-year-old Ned. Despite being transferred from the Greene family, Simmons remained on Cumberland Island, embraced his Baptist faith, and apparently accepted his fate. As the aging patriarch of the slave community on the plantation, he occupied a large cabin with a fireplace. When archaeologists excavated the site during the late twentieth century, they uncovered an 1808 British military button. Certainly Simmons had not forgotten the freedom he had briefly acquired as a black soldier during the War of 1812. When the American Civil War finally came to Cumberland Island, Simmons again took the opportunity to flee to freedom. In February 1863 he crossed the Union lines at Fernandina, Florida, and registered as contraband, giving his age as one hundred years old. Union naval forces provided him with rations because of his age, his lack of vision, and his feeble condition. During the days that followed, the centenarian began learning to read. Some months later, in 1864, a northern journalist who had spoken with Simmons reported that "Ned Simmons, an old negro, died here last week, at the home of the lady teachers, who have kindly cared for him since their arrival here." Ned Simmons had finally found what he had been denied at the end of the War of 1812, freedom "where no slave-driver will ever follow; where he can sing 'de praises ob de Lord' in freedom and safety."[24]

Jordan Bankston Noble followed a very different path to freedom. When the ninety-year-old Noble died peacefully at his children's New Orleans home, at 713 Dryades, during the early morning hours of Friday, June 20, 1890, the *New Orleans Daily Picayune* sadly reported the death of "the Drummer Boy of Chalmette," ran a woodcut picture of the "Colored Veteran of Four Wars," and encouraged family and friends to attend his Saturday-afternoon funeral and look on the white hair and familiar face of "Old Jordan" one last time. The announcement stressed his patriotic service and that "army veterans are also invited to attend." Finally, some seventy-five years later, the "famous drummer boy of New Orleans ha[d] gone to join his comrades of many campaigns." He was buried in the city's St. Louis Cemetery No. 2, Square 3.[25]

Born a mulatto slave in Augusta, Georgia, on October 14, 1800, to African and European parents, Noble apparently arrived in New Orleans sometime in 1812. By 1813 the then teenage Noble had joined the US Army as a drummer in the Seventh US Regiment. Whether he had secured his free-

ANSWERED THE LAST ROLL

Death of "the Drummer Boy of Chalmette."

JORDAN B. NOBLE, COLORED,
Veteran of Four Wars.

The familiar face of "Old Jordan" will no longer be seen upon the streets of New Orleans. After a life of nearly a century's duration, he died yesterday morning in the home of his three children, all of whom are far past the prime of life.

Jordan B. Noble was born in Georgia, of slave parentage, about 1798, and was brought to New Orleans when but a child. At the outbreak of the war of 1812 he enlisted as a drummer boy, serving under General Jackson on the memorable plains of Chalmette, where the rattle of his drum was heard amidst the din of battle.

He afterwards served in the Everglades of Florida, under General P. F. Smith, and went through the Mexican war with the Washington Artillery of this city.

In 1863, this veteran of three wars, nearly 70 years of age, organized a colored command, the Native Guards, under General Butler.

When "Old Jordan," as he was familiarly known, became too old to work he gave frequent "field music" entertainments with the historic drum that he had carried with him through all his service, and many will remember the white-headed old man and his well-worn drum, so often seen during the exposition of 1884 and 1885.

The famous drummer boy of New Orleans has gone to join his comrades of many campaigns. Peace to him and honor to the brave man who served his country so often and so well.

FIG. 4.1. Obituary of Jordan Noble, "Drummer Boy of Chalmette," *New Orleans Daily Picayune*, 20 June 1890.

dom or remained a slave is unclear. Though only a teenager, Noble nonetheless handled his drum like a veteran during the New Orleans campaign of December 1814–January 1815. He kept a steady beat and led Major Louis D'Aquin's company to meet the British for the fierce night of fighting on December 23, 1814. On January 8, 1815, at the Battle of New Orleans, "the rattle of his drum was heard [even] amidst the din of battle," "in the hottest hell of fire" during the chaotic main British attack at Chalmette. If, in fact, he had been a slave, perhaps his distinguished service to Jackson and the army won him his freedom.[26]

After the war, Noble reportedly remained in New Orleans, maintaining his military connections and marrying into the free black community. He participated in the 1836 Seminole War in Florida, serving with the Louisiana Volunteers in the Everglades under Colonel Persifor F. Smith. During the Mexican War, Noble enlisted as a musician with the New Orleans Washington Artillery of the First Regiment of Louisiana Volunteers, for which he earned a bounty. His name appears in the service record as "Noble, J.B. Company Field and Staff, First Louisiana Military Volunteers. Principal Musician. Enrolled May 9, 1846 at New Orleans, Louisiana, for six months. On roll dated August 1846. Book Mark 970 B 1884, Mexican War." In fact, Noble was one of the few African Americans to participate in the Mexican War. Returning to New Orleans after the conflict, Noble became a highly respected citizen with the unique distinction of having served as a drummer in three of his country's wars.[27]

Sometime before 1840 a supposed freeman of color, writing in French under the pseudonym Hippolyte Castra, composed a poem entitled "The Campaign of 1814–1815." Claiming to have served in Andrew Jackson's ranks at Chalmette, the author, in five of the eight stanzas of the poem, describes and praises the contributions of free black soldiers, while lamenting the demise of the colored militia corps, as well as the overall plight of the free people of color:

> I remember that, one day, during my childhood,
> A beautiful morning, my mother, while sighing,
> Said to me; "Child, emblem of innocence,
> "You do not know the future that awaits thee.

"You believe that you see your country under this beautiful sky
"Renounce thy error, my tender child,
"And believe above all your beloved mother. . . .
"Here, thou art but an object of scorn."

Ten years later, upon our vast frontiers,
One heard the English cannon,
And then these words: "Come, let us conquer, my brothers,
"We were all born of Louisiana blood."
At these sweet words, and embracing my mother,
I followed you, repeating the crises,
Not thinking, in my pursuit of battle,
That I was but an object of scorn.

Arriving upon the field of battle,
I fought like a brave warrior;
Neither the bullets nor the shrapnel,
Could ever fill me with fear.
I fought with great valor
With the hope of serving my country,
Not thinking that for recompense
I would be the object of scorn.

After having gained the victory,
In this terrible and glorious combat,
All of you shared a drink with me
And called me a valiant soldier.
And I, without regret, and with a sincere heart,
Helas! I drank, believing you to be my friends,
Not thinking, in my fleeting joy
That I was but an object of scorn.

But today I sigh sadly
Because I perceive a change in you:
I no longer see that gracious smile

> Which showed itself, in other times, so often
> Upon your honeyed lips.
> Have you become my enemies?
> Ah! I see it in your fierce looks,
> I am but an object of your scorn.[28]

The righteous indignation expressed in the poem was undoubtedly shared by many black veterans of the Battle of New Orleans. Not until January 8, 1851, thirty-six years after the glorious victory at Chalmette, were ninety free "veterans of color" finally invited to march for the first time in the Annual January 8th Parade, commemorating Jackson's victory. Previously black veterans had mustered in honor of the victory at Chalmette at the St. Louis Cathedral, but otherwise state pension legislation had been the only public recognition they had received. The 1851 parade finally recognized publicly in New Orleans their service to the city, the state, and the nation. During the procession, "Old Jordan" provided the same beat that he had provided as a fourteen-year-old on the Plains of Chalmette years earlier, and the black veterans marched in the center of the parade. The freemen of color had finally achieved community recognition. It was an honor long overdue. The *Daily Picayune* sheepishly acknowledged that "their good deeds have been consecrated only in their memories." The paper then asked rhetorically: Who had "endured the hardships of the camp, or faced with greater courage the perils of the fight?" Who had "rallied with more alacrity in response to the summons of danger?" "Who more than they deserve the thanks of the country and the gratitude of the succeeding generations?" Finally, it reported that "the respectability of their appearance, and the modesty of their demeanor, made an impression on every observer and elicited unqualified approbation," even as they passed in a feebly slow and steady cadence. Perhaps the graying of hair and the slow steadiness of movement finally made this group acceptable to the public rather than threatening or intimidating.[29]

Noble's drumbeat became the symbol for aging Battle of New Orleans veterans, black and white. He became a de facto leader of this aging group, his drumbeat reminding all of them of the sacrifices they had made and the victory they had assured the country. Three years later, on January 8,

1854, Noble received an invitation to play at the St. Charles Theatre in association with the battle celebration. In October 1855 Noble and his band led the Continental Guards' moonlight drill, and he later regaled all who would listen about his service under Generals Andrew Jackson and Zachary Taylor. During the years that followed, Noble instituted his own New Year's Day tradition, a public performance honoring the city's leaders, the military, and the press. These performances became well-attended events that demonstrated the public appetite for formal military marching music. They also cemented Jordan Noble's position within society as a freeman of color, a musician, and a three-time veteran.[30] The parade on January 8, 1860, according to the *Commercial Bulletin,* was the largest and most festive held during the pre–Civil War era, even though the number of aging veterans had greatly declined. The freemen of color still held a prominent place in the center of the parade, but they now rode in carriages rather than marched—their marching days were over. After imposing civic and military ceremonies at Jackson Square and a procession to the St. Louis Cathedral for the Te Deum, the St. Charles Hotel held a dinner for veterans of the battle. At Major General Winfield Scott's request, Jordan Noble was honored with a medal for his contributions at the Battle of New Orleans. The aging crowd became rowdy, cheering and applauding for their fellow soldier. When called upon to offer remarks, Noble had to wait for the cheering to stop before he boldly announced that he was ready to serve his country again as he had done at New Orleans, in Florida, and in Mexico.[31]

Within a few years Noble's wish would be fulfilled. In April 1861, as the United States descended into Civil War, Noble and approximately fifteen hundred Louisiana freemen of color offered their services to the Confederacy to defend the city of New Orleans. Within this force Noble raised a company of free blacks known as the Plauché Guards, named after Major Jean Baptiste Plauché, who had been his commander during the Battle of New Orleans. This force served only until Federal troops occupied the city during the spring of 1862. Then Noble volunteered for the Union army, organizing a company of free blacks for General Benjamin Butler. This unit became Company C, Seventh Louisiana Volunteers, also known as the "Native Guards." It remained active only from July to August 1863. Noble's immediate switch of sides reflected his long-standing service as a federal soldier and his desire to be an American. Despite his short federal service, Noble's participation with the Union forces won him a state pension of one hundred dollars for his service during the War of 1812. It also permitted Noble to claim service in support of the United States during four wars, giving him a unique distinction that he proudly proclaimed.[32]

Jordan Noble's life spanned the period from the early republic to near the end of the nineteenth century. He participated in four wars and gained distinction for doing so. After his fighting days had passed, he also contributed to the civic life of the community. His activities bridged the civic and military divide, winning respect from members of both communities. In fact, during the 1881 funeral ceremonies for President James Garfield in New Orleans, one writer commented that "Old Jordan, strong and portly, is still about and despite his eighty one years, walks the streets as a sedate looker-on, reads the paper, writes letters, chats with old acquaintances, watches the military parades with interest, and stoutly maintains his ability still to rub-a-dub-dub all its music out of a drum." Although too old to work, a few years later during the New Orleans Exposition of 1884–85 Noble and his "well-worn drum" entertained audiences with "field music." While the music lent him respectability, he held on tightly to his position within the New Orleans free black community and his military legacy as the drummer boy of the Battle of New Orleans. His distinction and talent, combined with an intense patriotism to Louisiana and the United States, permitted Noble to navigate the perils associated with pre– and post–Civil War American race relations. When discrimination and persecution came his way, Noble simply took out his drum and beat it away. Yet too many of Jordan Noble's contemporaries did not enjoy the same talent and advantages for orchestrating the perils of life.[33]

When Jordan Bankston Noble died on June 20, 1890, American race relations had evolved from the slave-based southern plantation system into which Noble had been born. In that two-tiered, segregated world he and his fellow black compatriots had made sacrifices in the hopes that they would gain freedom and equality. In other words, they had been searching and fighting for freedom, and many found it. Some free black Louisianans had hoped that the war with Great Britain would permit them to solidify and perhaps expand the rights they possessed. They had made conscious choices to side with the Americans because they had much to lose if the British succeeded. If the British made good on their promises of freeing the slaves, the free black community would expand greatly, which in the end would lessen their collective status in Louisiana's tricornered society. Those who sided with the Americans also represented a prominent social group of skilled artisans and small businessmen, and serving in the free black militia had been a way to express publicly their status. Likewise, joining with Jackson fulfilled their civic obligations to Louisiana and the United States—the promises of land and money served as but icing on the cake. Unfortunately, military service did not elevate the status of free blacks. Instead it created renewed suspicion and distrust. Nor did their service win for them the immediate state pensions, federal land warrants, and bounties promised by Jackson. In fact, a generation passed before black soldiers began receiving pensions, and many had to be renewed periodically by the state legislature. The promised land did not arrive until the 1850s, and even then most of the survivors or their descendants sold their holdings for cash. The promises Jackson made were eventually fulfilled but not in time for those who sacrificed to benefit from them and to realize the possibility of both freedom and opportunity. Those like Jordan Noble would suffer through the slavery controversy, the American Civil War, and emancipation and in the late nineteenth century would find themselves living in a segregated society. Whether they were slaves or freemen, they remained objects of scorn.[34]

The documentary record that chronicles black service during the War of 1812 is fragmentary at best. Peter Denison, George Roberts, Ned Simmons, and Jordan Noble were slaves and free blacks who chose sides during the War of 1812, and their choices ultimately defined their individual and collective identities. Denison fled to the freedom of British Canada, while Simmons tried to join the British army. Roberts and Noble sided with the Americans. As their stories testify, men of African descent did serve as soldiers and sailors aboard warships and on privateers during the war. Chesapeake Bay slaves joined the British Colonial Marines and marched with redcoats on Washington, DC, and Baltimore, while others chose to remain with their American masters and fight for the United States. The American army had not opened its enlistments to black troops, and most states did not permit blacks to muster. There were no all-black Regular Army units in

1812 and 1813, and the black presence, when noted, was poorly documented. Along the coast of Georgia and South Carolina, enslaved peoples faced the same choices as did those in the Chesapeake, while along the Gulf Coast they found additional choices—some joined with the Spanish or with Native American tribes, and others with Andrew Jackson or the British. Jackson ultimately secured the assistance of blacks in New Orleans with promises of freedom and equality that never were completely fulfilled.[35]

In some instances, the feats of men like Denison, Roberts, Simmons, and Noble were recorded for posterity, but often the stories of noncombatants are chronicled only in statistics. In the Chesapeake, as many as 4,500 to 5,000 enslaved people fled to British protection and were evacuated to Bermuda, Belize, Canada, or Trinidad. In New York, Philadelphia, and Baltimore, enslaved people and free blacks worked alongside whites to dig entrenchments for those cities, loudly proclaiming their civic and patriotic duty. Yet, black-white relations worsened after the war. Collectively, black unity had demonstrated a powerful threat, engendering fears in white America that were exacerbated by memories of the recent revolution in nearby Haiti (1791–1804).

In the aftermath of the conflict, Americans destroyed free mulatto Gulf communities in former Spanish Florida, which they viewed as a threat to peace and a challenge to the white status quo. Later, the removal of American Indians east of the Mississippi River bolstered the southern plantation system, creating the Cotton Kingdom of the mid-nineteenth century and further altering race relations. Meanwhile, in British dominions former American enslaved people clung tenaciously to the freedom they had obtained with evacuation, though the British government abandoned them in a segregated naval base in Bermuda or herded them into ill-provisioned camps in Canada and then into unsettled regions of Trinidad or Belize; they struggled economically, but they remained free.

In the end, the War of 1812 did not provide the greater opportunities or equality for free blacks that they had anticipated, nor did it initiate a wave of emancipation for enslaved Americans seeking freedom. They would find themselves wedged between slavery and freedom and between race discrimination and egalitarianism. Their patriotic efforts had not changed white minds regarding what role they should play in society, and public memories of the war largely ignored their contributions. New prejudicial racial distinctions replaced class differences among blacks and destroyed once and for all the optimism of the Revolutionary era. For African Americans, the "forgotten war" portrayed them as but "objects of scorn," delaying their quest for equality and freedom until the American Civil War.

NOTES

1. Donald R. Hickey, *The War of 1812: A Forgotten Conflict,* Bicentennial Edition (Urbana: University of Illinois Press, 2012).

2. Spencer C. Tucker and Frank T. Reuter, *Injured Honor: The Chesapeake-Leopard Affair, June 22, 1807* (Annapolis, MD: Naval Institute Press, 1996), 1–16.

3. Robert E. Cray Jr., "Remember the USS *Chesapeake:* The Politics of Maritime Death and Impressment," *Journal of the Early Republic* 25, no. 3 (Fall 2005): 464–66.

4. This essay builds upon Gene Allen Smith, *The Slaves' Gamble: Choosing Sides in the War of 1812* (New York: Palgrave Macmillan, 2013). See also Benjamin Quarles, *The Negro in the American Revolution* (Chapel Hill: University of North Carolina Press, 1961).

5. Gerard T. Altoff, *Amongst My Best Men: African Americans and the War of 1812* (Put-in-Bay, OH: Perry Group, 1996); Altoff, *Deep Water Sailors and Shallow Water Soldiers: Manning the United States Fleet on Lake Erie* (Put-in-Bay, OH: Perry Group, 1993).

6. Robin F. A. Fabel, "Self-Help in Dartmoor: Black and White Prisoners in the War of 1812," *Journal of the Early Republic* 9, no. 2 (Summer 1989): 165–90. Paul A. Gilje, *Free Trade and Sailors' Rights in the War of 1812* (New York: Cambridge University Press, 2013), details how the slogan "A free trade and sailors' rights" embodied the American decision to go to war with Great Britain during the summer of 1812.

7. Charles Ball, *Slavery in the United States: A Narrative of the Life and Adventures of Charles Ball, a Black Man, Who Lived Forty Years in Maryland, South Carolina and Georgia, as a Slave Under Various Masters, and was One Year in the Navy with Commodore Barney, During the Late War* (New York: John S. Taylor, 1837), 11–23.

8. C. Edward Skeen, *Citizen Soldiers in the War of 1812* (Lexington: University Press of Kentucky, 1999), 4–7; Robert J. Gough, "Black Men and the Early New Jersey Militia," *New Jersey Militia* 88 (Winter 1970): 231, 236; Act of the General Court of Connecticut, frame 296, Act of the General Assembly of North Carolina, frame 313, and Act of the General Assembly of South Carolina, frame 372, all in "The Negro in the Military Service of the United States, 1639–1886," M858, roll 1, vols. 1–2, 1639–1862, RG 94, National Archives.

9. Reginald R. Larrie, *Makin' Free: African-Americans in the Northwest Territory* (Detroit: Etheridge Books, 1981), 6–7; Clarence Edwin Carter, ed., *Michigan Territory, 1805–1820,* vol. 10 of *Territorial Papers of the United States* (Washington, DC: GPO, 1942), 252n.

10. Carter, *Michigan Territory, 1805–1820,* 252n; "Report of Legislative Committee," in William Hull to James Madison, 22 December 1808, Augustus B. Woodward Papers, Burton Historical Collection, Detroit Public Library; Daniel G. Hill, *The Freedom-Seekers: Blacks in Early Canada* (Agincourt, ON: Book Society of Canada, 1981), 114; Woodward to Secretary of War, 28 July 1812, in Carter, *Michigan Territory, 1805–1820,* 389–92.

11. Woodward to General Leib, 14 June 1811, Woodward Papers; Woodward to Secretary of War, 28 July 1812; Woodward to Hull, 23 July 1812, in Carter, *Michigan Territory, 1805–1820,* 389–92, 320–24; Smith, *Slaves' Gamble,* 39–40.

12. Shirley Wilcox, Mary Lou Little, and Wendy Barry, *Register of St. John's Church of England at Sandwich, 1802–1827* (Chatham, ON: Kent and Essex Branch, Ontario Genealogical Society, 1990), 43.

13. William C. H. Wood, ed., *Select British Documents of the Canadian War of 1812,* 3 vols. (New York: Champlain Society, 1968), 1:461; Robert S. Quimby, *The U.S. Army in the War of 1812: An Operational and Command Study* (East Lansing: Michigan State University Press, 1997), 43–46; Carter, *Michigan Territory, 1805–1820.*

14. Hull to Henry Dearborn, 22 June 1807, in *Michigan Historical Collections,* vol. 40, *Documents Relating to Detroit and Vicinity, 1805–1813* (Lansing: Michigan Historical Commission, 1929), 141; William Kenny to Alexander McKee, 30 September 1795, quoted in William Renwick Riddell, "A Negro Slave in Detroit when Detroit was Canadian," *Michigan History Magazine* 18 (1934): 49–50; Register of Blacks in Ohio Counties, 1804–1861, Ohio Historical Society Papers, Ohio Historical Society, Columbus; Hill, *Freedom-Seekers,* 113, 224n; Petition for Runaway Slave, 19 October 1807, Alexander David Fraser Papers, Burton Historical Collection, Detroit Public Library; Norman McRae, "Blacks in Detroit, 1736–1833: The Search for Freedom and Community and its Implications for Education" (PhD diss., University of Michigan, 1982), 105.

15. Christopher T. George, "Mirage of Freedom: African Americans in the War of 1812," *Maryland Historical Magazine* 91, no. 4 (Winter 1996): 446; George, *Terror on the Chesapeake: The War of 1812 on the Bay* (Shippenburg, PA: White Mane Books, 2000), 13.

16. *Niles' Weekly Register,* 14 November 1812; George, *Terror on the Chesapeake,* 13.

17. *Niles' Weekly Register,* 25 March 1815; "Another Old Defenders Gone," *Baltimore Sun,* 16 January 1861; George, "Mirage of Freedom," 446; Edgar Stanton Maclay, *A History of American Privateers* (New York: D. Appleton, 1899), ch. 5.

18. *Niles' Weekly Register,* 15 April 1815; Scott S. Sheads and Anna Von Lunz, "Defenders' Day, 1815–1898: A Brief History," *Maryland Historical Magazine* 93, no. 3 (Fall 1998): 301; *Baltimore Sun,* 16 January 1861.

19. Christopher Phillips, *Freedom's Port: The African American Community of Baltimore, 1790–1860* (Urbana: University of Illinois Press, 1997), 235–38.

20. Frank Moore, ed., *Anecdotes, Poetry and Incidents of the Civil War: North and South, 1860–1865* (New York: Publications Office, Bible House, 1867), 117–18; Mary R. Bullard, "Ned Simmons, American Slave: The Role of Imagination in Narrative History," *African Diaspora Archaeology Network Newsletter,* June 2007, 20–21, www.diaspora.uiuc.edu/news0607/news0607-7.pdf.

21. Mary R. Bullard, *Cumberland Island: A History* (Athens: University of Georgia Press, 2003), 139–40.

22. "Fleet Orders, January–April, 1815," George Cockburn Papers, 46:12, Library of Congress, Washington, DC.

23. George Cockburn to Thomas Spalding and Thomas Newall, 7 March 1815, Cockburn Papers, 26:97 and subsequent unnumbered pages; Mary R. Bullard, *Black Liberation on Cumberland Island in 1815* (DeLeon Springs, FL: E. O. Painter, 1983), 88–90; Bullard, *Cumberland Island,* 121–22.

24. Moore, *Anecdotes, Poetry and Incidents,* 117–18; Bullard, "Ned Simmons, American Slave," 18, 10, 44, 139–40.

25. *New Orleans Daily Picayune,* 21 June 1890.

26. Ibid.; Roland C. McConnell, *Negro Troops of Antebellum Louisiana: A History of the Battalion of Freemen of Color* (Baton Rouge: Louisiana State University Press, 1968), 74, 85; Marcus Christian, *Negro Soldiers at the Battle of New Orleans* (New Orleans: Battle of New Orleans 150th Anniversary Committee, 1965), 32.

27. *New Orleans Daily Picayune,* 21 June 1890; McConnell, *Negro Troops of Antebellum Louisiana,* 114–15; Military Pension File of Jordan B. Noble, RG 15, National Archives.

28. Hippolyte Castra, "La Campagne de 1814–1815," in Rodolphe L. Desdunnes, *Nos Hommes et Notre Histoire* (Montreal: Arbor et Dupont, 1911), 8–9; McConnell, *Negro Troops of Antebellum Louisiana,* 106–8; Kimberly S. Hanger, *Bounded Lives, Bounded Places: Free Black Society in Colonial New Orleans* (Durham, NC: Duke University Press, 1997), 167–68, 219–20.

29. McConnell, *Negro Troops of Antebellum Louisiana,* 112; *New Orleans Daily Picayune,* 9 January 1851; Donald E. Everett, "Émigrés and Militiamen: Free Persons of Color in New Orleans, 1803–1815," *Journal of Negro History* 38, no. 4 (October 1953): 398, 400–401.

30. Freddie Williams Evans, "Jordan B. Noble: The Drummer of Chalmette," *Preservation in Print* 27, no. 10 (24 February 2001): 24–25, www.prcno.org/programs/preservationinprint/piparchives/2001%20PIP/February%202001/25.html.

31. McConnell, *Negro Troops of Antebellum Louisiana,* 114–15; *Commercial Bulletin* (New Orleans), 9 January 1860.

32. *New Orleans Daily Picayune,* 21 June 1890; Evans, "Jordan B. Noble," 24–25.

33. City of New Orleans, *A History of the Proceedings in the City of New Orleans, on the Occasion of the Funeral Ceremonies in Honor of James Abram Garfield, Late President of the United States* (New Orleans, 1881), 87, 192–93; *New Orleans Daily Picayune,* 21 June 1890.

34. George A. Levesque, "Interpreting Early Black Ideology: A Reappraisal of Historical Consensus," *Journal of the Early Republic* 1, no. 3 (Fall 1981): 274–75.

35. Smith, *Slaves' Gamble,* documents free black and slave participation throughout the War of 1812, concluding with an account of their status during the postwar period.

5

In Defense of Liberty

The Battalion d'Orleans and Its Battle for New Orleans

PAUL GELPI

While minister to France, Thomas Jefferson wrote to James Madison that "the people . . . are the only sure reliance for the preservation of our liberty."[1] As president, Jefferson recognized the necessity of an army, distrusted a permanent military establishment,[2] and relied on the American people to defend their nation's liberty. His solution to the United States' national-security concerns: a disciplined citizenry armed and mobilized through the militia. Soon after he took office, Jefferson drastically reduced the end strength of the US Army and made universal service in trained militias the cornerstone of his military program.[3]

The acquisition of the Louisiana Territory in 1803 provided Jefferson with a unique opportunity to put his military ideas into practice. Overnight, the infant United States doubled its territory, secured the valuable port of New Orleans, and claimed dominion over lands to the Pacific shore. Jefferson may have found this national expansion a fiscal bargain, but ideologically he paid a high price.[4] The purchase of Louisiana presented Jefferson with a philosophical dilemma. Not only did the purchase go against his political beliefs about the role and power of the president but the territory's population led him to question the applicability of democratic institutions to non-Americans.[5] Jefferson doubted Louisianans' loyalty to democratic ideals, for he believed their political philosophy to be that of Bourbon France and Spain. Thus, Jefferson wondered whether Louisiana would be assimilated into the American political system or revert back to France or Spain when the foreign majority overpowered the American minority. That the latter did not occur was in part owing to the territory's first governor, William Charles Cole Claiborne, whose political pragmatism fostered the rapid assimilation of Louisiana's Creole population and created a stable if at first culturally divided government.[6] Nonetheless, Claiborne's efforts would have been for naught if Louisiana's Creoles had not been sympathetic to American democracy.

Yet Jefferson did not know how Louisianans would react to American sovereignty in 1803. Adding to his uncertainty was the threat that Spain would seek to reacquire its former colony. Bordered by Spanish Florida and Texas, Louisiana required a large defensive force. In Jeffersonian fashion, Governor Claiborne used the militia to protect Louisiana. An examination of one of the territory's longest-serving Creole militia units offers insight into not only the process of Americanization that Creole Louisiana underwent but also the degree to which the liberty Louisiana's Creoles bore arms to defend was American liberty.

Established shortly after the Louisiana Purchase, the Battalion d'Orleans was an all-volunteer unit of New Orleans Creoles.[7] Since Louisianans considered the battalion an elite unit at the time of the British invasion in 1814, writers in the two centuries since have emphasized myth in their creation of a historical memory that presumed social prestige and economic standing, rather than service record, conferred an elite status.

Powell A. Casey's *Louisiana in the War of 1812* (1963) and his foreword to Ronald Morazán's *Biographical Sketches of the Veterans of the Battalion of Orleans* (1979) typified this mythology about the Battalion d'Orleans. This is underscored by the reliance on Vincent Nolte's autobiography, written in the mid-nineteenth century and rife with errors, as exemplified by the description of Pierre Roche, born in 1791, as a veteran of Napoleon's 1798 Egyptian campaign.[8]

As the centennial of the Battle of New Orleans approached, interest in the battle and Louisianans' role in the war grew.[9] In August 1908 the *New Orleans Daily Picayune* published "Officers and Soldiers of the War of 1812." The article included a letter from a Mrs. Pellitier, transcribed and translated in full, that proclaimed the city's martial heritage and provided an account of who had served in the Battalion d'Orleans.[10] Although the *Daily Picayune* story presented a somewhat fanciful account of Louisianans' martial accomplishments and early New Orleans society, it included an accurate tally of the veterans, in name if not social standing.

An investigation of who served in the Battalion d'Orleans in the winter of 1814–15 suggests the cultural and social milieu of early nineteenth-century New Orleans. An accurate roster of the battalion at the time of the Battle of New Orleans may be gleaned from a comparison of the *Daily Picayune* article with Morazán's volume and the battalion's muster roll when it left active service on March 20, 1815.[11] On paper, the battalion numbered 222 officers and men organized into five companies, although only 200 were mustered into service. A representative sample of those men suggests some general socioeconomic characteristics. The average age of enlisted men was thirty-five, and 80 percent of them resided within the city. The majority of the men were artisans, although a merchant and a bank officer served in the battalion's ranks. As a whole the men of the battalion displayed a strikingly middle-class character. In contrast, the officers hailed from the upper echelon of New Orleans society. All but the commanding officer were émigrés from France and Saint Dominique whose families had escaped the French Revolution and subsequent upheavals. As such, the officers represented the wealthiest elite in the city, the foreign French.[12] The commander, Jean Baptiste Plauché, was a wealthy Louisiana Creole whose distinguished service furthered his political ambitions and his military career in Louisiana. Indeed, Plauché may be seen as a symbol for the political journey of Louisiana Creoles. He continued his military service after 1815 and eventually became a brigadier general and commander of the Louisiana Legion. After serving in local politics, Plauché entered state politics, and in 1850 he was elected lieutenant governor on the Whig Party ticket.[13] In officers and men, the battalion shared social, economic, and political characteristics with volunteer militia units elsewhere in America, especially in the southern United States.[14]

Consequently, the military record of the Battalion d'Orleans offers a window onto Louisiana Creoles' attitudes toward military service, as well as the depth of their acceptance of Jeffersonian military thought and their allegiance to the principles of republicanism, all of which reveal that their attitudes were typically American. Governor Claiborne's ad hoc adaptation and mixture of Franco-Spanish and American elements characterized not only the gradual development of the Louisiana militia but also the political and cultural maturation of Louisiana. Thus, the history of the Battalion d'Orleans suggests the process of Americanization that Creole Louisiana underwent. Incorporated into the territorial militia as a Creole unit with suspect loyalties, the battalion proved its patriotism in much the same way that the citizens of Louisiana did, in a series of crises that shaped the territorial and early statehood eras. During the periods of martial law following the Burr Conspiracy and the British invasion, the unit displayed characteristically American attitudes toward military service and despotic professional soldiers, sentiments shared by their fellow Louisianans.[15]

The period from the Purchase to the Battle of New Orleans represents an evolutionary era for the Louisiana militia. Once the United States acquired the Territory of Orleans, it devised a new militia system to replace the one established under Spain. Although Pierre Clement Laussat commented on July 18, 1803, that "thanks to the militia, there is not an inhabitant of any little note who is not considered a military officer,"[16] the degree to which the Franco-Spanish population enrolled in the province's militia prior to the Purchase remains debatable. Spanish officials were inclined to confer military titles upon economically and socially prosperous men, which created the illusion of a large military establishment. Although a conscripted militia had existed since the early 1770s, by the turn of the century it was a paper tiger. Nonetheless, the very size of such a force on paper with the facade of a substantial Spanish militia predisposed the infant Claiborne administration to distrust the Creoles.[17]

Shortly after the United States took control of Louisiana, Jefferson queried Claiborne about the state of affairs in the territory. Jefferson asked whether the territory had a militia, and if so, what its composition was. Claiborne reported that the Spanish militia was a well-disciplined force that numbered between eight thousand and nine thousand men on paper and included some free blacks, as well as Native Americans. Despite Claiborne's optimism about the state of the militia, the reality was less prosaic: an 1803 return of the militia placed the number of men under arms in the territory at 5,440, which included troops stationed in Mobile and Galveston. Significantly for New Orleans, the report incorporated the city militia of five companies that numbered one hundred men apiece and included it in its return of the territory's military establishment.[18]

Louisiana faced possible invasion from both Spanish Florida and Texas;

consequently, Claiborne required a sizable military establishment to secure the territory, and a militia offered the least expensive solution to this problem. Claiborne, who was Jefferson's cousin, a fellow Virginian, and staunch political ally, shared the president's distaste for standing armies. In this respect, Claiborne's appointment was not accidental: Louisiana presented Jefferson the first opportunity to apply his theories of republicanism. As sparsely settled borderlands, Louisiana required a large constabulary to enforce US law and protect the dispersed population. Again, Claiborne found a militia the economically and politically palatable choice.

Many Americans, both in the territory and in the United States writ large, viewed the large "foreign" population of Louisiana as a security risk. Daniel Clark, a longtime resident of New Orleans, observed that the Creole composition of the militia posed a dilemma for the American government since it could not rely on the troops nominally in its service.[19] Likewise, Thomas Paine warned Jefferson of the problems presented by the "foreign" population of Louisiana, with its questionable loyalties. Paine suggested that until the number of Americans equaled the number of Creoles, Louisiana should not enjoy a democratic government.[20] Along with other Americans, Paine feared that granting equal rights and a constitutional government to French and Spanish Louisianans would put American settlers at their mercy.

Paine's ideas resonated with Jefferson, who urged upon Congress a militia scheme for Louisiana. Jefferson proposed to raise a thirty-thousand-man volunteer militia force of native-born Americans. Soldiers in this citizens' army would receive a 160-acre land grant in the Louisiana Territory, which they would be obligated to settle and defend for seven years. This vast influx of new settlers would create an American majority in Louisiana, albeit it an armed one with potentially questionable loyalties. Although Jefferson's plan may have alleviated some of the problems Claiborne faced, support for it was far from universal, and by March 1808 the bill had died in Congress.[21]

Jefferson, Paine, and Clark proved poor prophets. As the territorial period progressed, Louisiana's Creoles rapidly absorbed American philosophical and political ideals. A striking example of this Americanization was the Creole hostility to standing armies, exemplified in Claiborne's use of the

Battalion d'Orleans. Unlike their Anglo-American brethren, Creole Louisianans did not share in the antimilitary heritage of the Radical Whig tradition.[22] The incorporation of the territory into the United States provided Louisianans with an opportunity, heretofore denied, to voice their opinions about military and political power. Many Americans presumed that Louisiana's Franco-Spanish past, with its acceptance of monarchies, had resulted in a population unsympathetic to *liberté, égalité,* and *fraternité;* however, Louisiana's Creoles reached the same conclusion about the tyranny of absolutist rulers and standing armies as their fellow Americans. In this regard, the Battalion d'Orleans characterizes the experience of Creole Louisianans.

Claiborne approached the problem of defense with the same pragmatism he displayed in other aspects of governing Louisiana.[23] He took the volunteer militia companies as he found them and welcomed new units into service. Thus, he gave the Battalion d'Orleans assignments even as he drafted a comprehensive militia act for the territorial legislature.[24] Beginning in July 1804 several volunteer militia companies began to parade in New Orleans.[25] The Battalion d'Orleans was one of these units, and that month it participated in the parade at which Claiborne presented the city militia with its standard. Claiborne feared a slave insurrection in the territory and informed Jefferson that he had taken steps to prevent such an incident. He reported to the president that he had ordered nightly patrols and had placed the battalion in a state of "readiness for action at a moment's warning." Later he commented to James Madison, then secretary of state, that the patrols had been strengthened.[26]

From late 1804 on, Claiborne increasingly relied on the battalion and appointed Eugene Dorcier to command it. Dorcier was a Revolutionary War veteran and Swiss émigré who had lived in Louisiana since the early 1780s. During the early days of Claiborne's administration, Dorcier served as a justice of the peace, in which office he "manifested a great share of zeal, integrity, prudence, and a sincere attachment to the United States."[27] In appointing Dorcier, Claiborne drew upon his experiences in Virginia, where justices were appointed to command militia contingents.

The following year, the legislature incorporated the battalion into the territorial militia, an act required because the battalion had been organized before the first territorial legislature met. Claiborne and the legislature addressed the issue in a Jeffersonian fashion with the 10 August 1805 passage of an act for regulating and governing the militia of the territory of Orleans, which drew heavily on an 1803 Virginia statute. Along with requiring universal service for all males aged sixteen to sixty, the 1805 legislation recognized the existing volunteer companies, such as the Battalion d'Orleans, and enrolled them in the territorial militia. Significantly, the 1805 act recognized militia service as a contract between an individual and the government, a traditionally American idea. In passing this act, the legislature acknowledged and protected the different contracts of the independent companies. For those units without set terms of service, the legislature specified those of the Battalion d'Orleans as the standard.[28]

Once incorporated into the new territorial militia, the battalion served as Claiborne's principal weapon in meeting the military crises he faced down to 1814: the expulsion of the Marqués de Casa Calvo, the Burr Conspiracy, and the British invasion of Louisiana. The last two episodes compelled him to declare martial law and to keep the battalion in arms for extended periods of time. For Louisiana's Creoles, these episodes of military rule gave substance to the threat to liberty that Americans associated with standing armies.

As the last Spanish governor of Louisiana, Casa Calvo had amassed a considerable power base among the Creoles. He had served as an adviser to Claiborne and the unofficial Spanish consul in New Orleans; however, his continued presence in the territory was a political problem for Claiborne. In an effort to remedy this, the governor let it be known that the marquess's residence in New Orleans was unwelcome, whereupon Casa Calvo decamped for Spanish territory across the Sabine River from Natchitoches. En route, he circulated a rumor of Louisiana's imminent return to Spain. Claiborne soon realized that the marquess's actions threatened both his political authority and national security. He then appealed to Secretary of State Madison for federal assistance and mobilized the Battalion d'Orleans; however, Claiborne chose to pursue a diplomatic solution to the growing security problem and elected not to apprehend the marquess. Yet Casa Calvo ignored repeated instructions to leave Louisiana and only left on 15 February 1806, when Claiborne's show of military force persuaded him to depart Louisiana.[29] The governor's handling of the affair exemplifies his attempts to assimilate rapidly the Creole population in the governance of the territory. As their role in the affair was brief, the men of the battalion came to see active duty as a short-term obligation, just as Americans had traditionally viewed it. In deploying the battalion, Claiborne tested and confirmed their allegiance to the United States and to the principles of republicanism. No sooner had Claiborne dealt with the Marqués de Casa Calvo than he confronted another, more serious crisis that required the Battalion d'Orleans.

In December 1806 General James Wilkinson revealed the existence of a plot to ignite revolutions in Louisiana and Mexico with the aim of creating a new republic in the Americas. Wilkinson related that Aaron Burr, Jefferson's first vice president, was the plan's architect. The Burr Conspiracy grew out of attempts to launch a filibuster against Mexico. When the scheme fell apart, those behind the intrigue—Wilkinson, Burr, and Edward Livingston, among others—conspired to create a republic out of the western territories of the United States and invade Mexico. In time, Wilkinson, who had been a double agent in the employ of Spain since the 1780s, betrayed Burr to curry favor with Jefferson. Meanwhile, Burr's agents in New Orleans made it known that their boss sought to secure the city as the port of embarkation for the troops he had assembled in Tennessee.[30]

Claiborne suspected Wilkinson of complicity in Burr's schemes.[31] He knew, as well, that many of his political rivals favored Burr; thus, he could scarcely distinguish friend from foe. Likewise, Claiborne was unsure of the militia's loyalty and did not know what units he could trust. He wrote to Madison that he hoped the Battalion d'Orleans would remain loyal to the United States and alluded to its past patriotism. Within a week of writing, he mobilized the battalion and placed it under Wilkinson's direct command at the latter's behest.[32]

When Wilkinson had yet to employ the battalion by early 1807, Claiborne moved to deactivate it to avoid further public expense. Despite his fiscal worries, Claiborne wrote to Wilkinson to reaffirm that the battalion remained under the general's command.[33] If Claiborne had sent his letter to test Wilkinson's loyalty, he failed in his effort to gauge in which camp the general stood. In placing the battalion under Wilkinson's command, Claiborne had displayed an atypical lack of political savvy. Louisiana's militia had not been federalized, and its men owed only territorial service. Thus, Claiborne could have forced Wilkinson to release the battalion but chose instead to allow the unit to remain in service.

When the Battalion d'Orleans's active service lasted more than a few weeks and required it to winter far from home along the territory's northwest frontier for no apparent reason, the men displayed a characteristically American attitude toward military service. Writing to Secretary for War Henry Dearborn, Claiborne complained that since it had entered service under Wilkinson the battalion had lost much of its military ardor and that the territory's militia in general was in a desultory state. He lamented that the Battalion d'Orleans, "once a highly respectable corps is now nearly dissolved." In a letter to Jefferson, Claiborne further commented on his bewilderment at the militia's general hesitancy to serve under martial law.[34] Yet the experience of the battalion under Wilkinson illustrates the Creole population's assimilation of American political philosophy, especially Jeffersonian republicanism.

Following the Burr affair, the territorial legislature reformed the militia. An act of 1807 charged units to perform routine patrols throughout Louisiana and required the Battalion d'Orleans to guard New Orleans. From 1807 to the Battle of New Orleans, the battalion continued to muster occasionally and execute its duties; however, during the 1811 slave uprising on Louisiana's "German Coast" the unit was not called out.[35] Spared the distasteful task of putting down a slave revolt, the Creoles continued to guard New Orleans and were at the forefront of the city's defenses when the British invaded Louisiana three years later.

After two years of war with Great Britain, the United States had not accomplished any of its military objectives. At the peace table the nation faired no better, and its ambassadors failed to achieve any of their diplomatic goals. Moreover, the defeat of Napoleon allowed the British to bring additional forces to bear against the United States. In the summer of 1814, British armies invaded the United States and burned its capitol. As the war grew increasingly unpopular on both sides of the Atlantic, diplomats moved toward closure. By the end of 1814, Britain and the United States had reached an accord, which marked a return to the status quo ante bellum. American and British diplomats signed the agreement in Ghent on

December 24, 1814, but news of the peace accord traveled slowly. It did not reach New Orleans until after Major General Andrew Jackson's forces defeated the British forces on January 8, 1815, and the two governments did not formally ratify the treaty until 18 February 1815.[36] Jackson's distrust of any news of a peace between the United States and Great Britain until it was officially confirmed in February and the delay in lifting martial law resurrected traditional fears of professional soldiers among Louisianans.

On December 15, 1814, one day before his declaration of martial law, Jackson issued a proclamation to the citizens and soldiers of New Orleans warning them of a rumor that Louisiana would be returned to Spain.[37] For the second time in a decade, Claiborne faced a military crisis that could divide the state if the rumor received any credence. In order to generate a patriotic fervor among the populace, Jackson warned of the atrocities that had occurred elsewhere in the United States in the wake of a British invasion. Jackson admonished Louisianans to guard their liberty, their property, and the "chastity" of their "wives and daughters."[38] Despite the sizable non-Creole population in Louisiana, Jackson addressed his communiqué to the Creoles, who were the target of the rumor.

In correspondence with Jackson, Claiborne reported on the condition of the state's militia. He specified that many of the state's units placed under Jackson's command enjoyed unique privileges because of his previous experience with a federal military commander and his dissatisfaction with martial law. He cited one of the volunteer rifle companies as an example and warned the general that it was "an independent corps; organized under a particular law, which accords to it peculiar privileges." Claiborne's rebuke served as a reminder that Louisianans viewed military service in the same contractual manner as their fellow Americans in New York and elsewhere.[39] His fears proved prophetic in the months following the Battle of New Orleans, as Jackson chose to ignore the terms of service for Louisiana's militia.

For two months after the battle, as the British gradually withdrew from Louisiana, Jackson kept New Orleans under martial law, which antagonized Claiborne and the city's population, Creole and American alike.[40] Their aversion to martial law and their distrust of federal authority intensified when Jackson kept the Louisiana militia on active duty in the quagmire of Chalmette while the Regular Army, along with the Tennessee and Kentucky militias, walked the streets of New Orleans on furlough. Fears of dictatorial professional soldiers found a voice in Judge François-Xavier Martin of the Supreme Court of Louisiana.

A native of Marseilles, France, Martin immigrated to the United States in 1783, shortly before the war for independence ended. He settled first in North Carolina, before moving west to Mississippi and Louisiana. Through his activities as a printer, lawyer, and jurist, Martin shaped much of early American jurisprudence. In North Carolina, he published legal treatises, statute compilations, and newspapers, along with other assorted works. His publishing and legal careers continued with increasing success until President James Madison appointed him to a federal judgeship in the Mississippi Territory in 1809. Martin sat on the Mississippi bench for only a brief period before he was transferred to the Territory of Orleans. In the chaotic early Louisiana judiciary his talents as a printer and lawyer enabled him to clarify complex civil codes, as well as untangle the morass of laws created by the juxtaposition of civil and common law.[41]

On January 1, 1815, Martin, then the state attorney general and the principal figure in Louisiana jurisprudence, was appointed to the state supreme court. As a jurist, lawyer, and commentator, Martin viewed Jackson as a backwoods harlequin who was woefully ignorant of the law. A Jeffersonian, Martin seized upon the first case before his court as an opportunity to lambaste Jackson. Although *Johnson v. Duncan et al.'s Syndics* had nothing to do with the war, it became the platform from which Martin launched his critique. Writing for the majority in the court's decision, Martin savaged Jackson for having proclaimed martial law.[42] When Jackson had issued his proclamation, he had suspended all legal proceedings in Louisiana. Martin argued that Jackson lacked the authority to declare martial law and could not suspend legal proceedings, which was his prerogative. In his opinion, Martin averred, "Martial law, what? An act suspending legal proceedings during an actual invasion, is not a law impairing the obligation of contracts." Although he recognized the supremacy of article 1, section 9, of the US Constitution over any state legislation, Martin asserted that the US Supreme Court had recognized limits to federal power. The judge based his conclusions on *Ex parte Bollman* and *Ex parte Swartout,* which affirmed that Congress alone could suspend the writ of habeas corpus. He also cited the Louisiana Constitution, which declared that no laws of the state could be suspended without the state legislature's consent.[43] In expressing his fears, as well as those of his fellow Louisianans, Martin, like the men of the Battalion d'Orleans in 1807, exhibited a characteristically American animus toward military authority and power.

Writing a decade after the Battle of New Orleans in *The History of Louisiana, From the Earliest Period,* Martin equated Jackson's declaration of martial law with the tyrannical power the British monarch had wielded in America until the Revolution, the same abusive power that he interpreted as the cause of the colonists' rebellion.[44] As a consequence of their experiences with federal military authorities, Louisiana's Creoles exhibited quintessentially American ideas and principles in their understanding of both standing armies and civil liberties. In this light, the Battalion d'Orleans stands as a striking example of the Creole experience of Americanization and testimony that the liberty that Louisiana's Creoles bore arms to defend in their battle for New Orleans was American liberty.

NOTES

The substance of the present essay is contained in Paul Gelpi, "Mr. Jefferson's Creoles: The Battalion d 'Orleans and the Americanization of Creole Louisiana, 1803–1815," *Louisiana History: The Journal of the Louisiana Historical Association* 48, no. 3 (Summer 2007): 295–316.

1. Thomas Jefferson to James Madison, as extracted, revised, and enclosed by Jefferson in a letter to Uriah Forest, 31 December 1787, in *The Papers of Thomas Jefferson,* vol. 12, *7 August 1787 to 31 March 1788,* ed. Julian P. Boyd (Princeton, NJ: Princeton University Press, 1955), 475–79.

2. For Jefferson's military philosophy, see Lawrence Delbert Cress, "A Well-Regulated Militia: The Origins and Meaning of the Second Amendment," in *The Bill of Rights: A Lively Heritage,* ed. Jon Kukla (Richmond: Virginia State Library and Archives, 1987): 55–65, which provides an excellent introduction to the debate surrounding the militia and a standing army; and J. C. A. Stagg, "Enlisted Men in the United States Army, 1812–1815: A Preliminary Survey," *William and Mary Quarterly* 43, no. 4 (October 1986): 616. Cress's "Republican Liberty and National Security: American Military Policy as an Ideological Problem, 1783–1789," *William and Mary Quarterly* 38, no. 1 (January 1981): 73–96, and his "An Armed Community:

The Origins and Meaning of the Right to Bear Arms," *Journal of American History* 71, no. 1 (June 1984): 22–42, also examine the debate. Although Jefferson bore chief responsibility for the US Military Academy, established at West Point, New York, in 1802, the emphasis in its curriculum on engineering and the use of the army in civil construction projects, as well as its role in the settlement of the western frontier, throughout the first half of the nineteenth century illustrate Jefferson's conception of the proper military establishment. Indeed, in his first inaugural address Jefferson emphatically stated that "a well-disciplined militia" is "our best reliance in peace." Thus, the presence of a professional military need not be understood as an endorsement of a European-style standing army. The small professional military was less a war-making force than an agent of American expansionism and civilization. It is within this paradigm that Jefferson's view of the proper role of a military establishment should be understood. For the text of Jefferson's address, see *Thomas Jefferson: Writings,* ed. Merrill D. Peterson (New York: Library of America, 1984), quotation on 495.

3. By summer 1802 the army numbered only 4,051 officers and men divided unequally among artillery, cavalry, and infantry. Shortly thereafter the War Department reorganized the army, restructured the artillery and infantry, and eliminated the cavalry altogether. See Russell F. Weigley, *History of the United States Army* (London: B. T. Batsford, 1967), 105–9; and Weigley, *The American Way of War: A History of United States Military Strategy and Policy* (Bloomington: Indiana University Press, 1973), 40–55.

4. On Jefferson and expansionism, see Joyce O. Appleby and Arthur M. Schlessinger, *Thomas Jefferson* (New York: Time Books, 2003); Howard Jones, *Crucible of Power: A History of American Foreign Relations to 1913* (Wilmington, DE: SR Books, 2002); Lawrence S. Kaplan, *Thomas Jefferson: Westward the Course of Empire* (Wilmington, DE: SR Books, 1999); James E. Lewis, *The Louisiana Purchase: Jefferson's Noble Bargain?* (Chapel Hill: University of North Carolina Press, 2003); and Frank Lawrence Owsley Jr. and Gene A. Smith, *Filibusters and Expansionists: Jeffersonian Manifest Destiny* (Tuscaloosa: University of Alabama Press, 1997).

5. On Jefferson's attitudes toward the nation's newest citizens, see George Dargo, *Jefferson's Louisiana: Politics and the Clash of Traditions* (Cambridge, MA: Harvard University Press, 1975).

6. For an erudite study of Claiborne and Louisiana, see Joseph T. Hatfield, *William Claiborne: Jeffersonian Centurion in the American Southwest* (Lafayette: University of Southwestern Louisiana, 1976). See also Joseph F. Stoltz III, "'An Ardent Military Spirit': William C. C. Claiborne and the Creation of the Orleans Territorial Militia, 1803–1805" (MA thesis, University of New Orleans, 2009).

7. The term *Creole* is used in this essay to describe anyone of European or African descent born in the Americas. This is the most traditional definition of *Creole,* as well as one that reflects how early nineteenth-century Louisianans understood and used the term. For an analysis of the term *Creole* and its use in Louisiana, see Joseph G. Tregle Jr., "Early New Orleans Society: A Reappraisal," *Journal of Southern History* 18, no. 1 (February 1952): 20–36, as well as Tregle, "Creole and Americans," in *Creole New Orleans: Race and Americanization,* ed. Arnold R. Hirsch and Joseph Logsdon (Baton Rouge: Louisiana State University Press, 1992), 131–85.

8. See Powell A. Casey, *Louisiana in the War of 1812* (Baton Rouge: n.p., 1963), 30–32; and Casey, foreword to *Biographical Sketches of the Veterans of the Battalion of Orleans,* by Ronald

Morazán (Baton Rouge: Legacy, 1979), i–iv. Although Morazán's work is primarily genealogical, it provides a useful database from which the socioeconomic state of the battalion can be fashioned. See also Ella Rightor, "Military," in *Standard History of New Orleans, Louisiana*, ed. Henry Rightor (Chicago: Lewis, 1900), 129–70.

9. See Grace King, *New Orleans: The Place and the People* (New York: Macmillan, 1895); King, *Stories from Louisiana History* (New Orleans: L. Graham, 1905); Alcée Fortier, *A History of Louisiana* (Paris: Manzi, Joyant, 1905); and Rightor, *Standard History of New Orleans, Louisiana*.

10. "Officers and Soldiers of the War of 1812," *New Orleans Daily Picayune*, 23 August 1908.

11. The men were selected by comparing the muster rolls of the battalion when it was deactivated on March 20, 1815, with a 1908 *Daily Picayune* article, which served as the basis for both Casey's and Morazán's studies. See Morazán, *Biographical Sketches;* "Muster rolls of companies and battalions of troops and officers under General Jackson at the Battle of New Orleans, 1814–1815," RG 68, Louisiana State Museum, New Orleans; and "Officers and Soldiers of the War of 1812."

12. For an overview of the socioeconomic distinctions within New Orleans society, see Tregle, "Early New Orleans Society."

13. Morazán, *Biographical Sketches*, 188–89.

14. For analyses of antebellum militia units in the southern United States, see G. Ward Hubbs, *Guarding Greensboro: A Confederate Company in the Making of a Southern Community* (Athens: University of Georgia Press, 2003); and W. Eric Emerson, *Sons of Privilege: The Charleston Light Dragoons in the Civil War* (Columbia: University of South Carolina Press, 2005).

15. Despite their antipathy toward martial law, the men of the battalion held Andrew Jackson in high regard for defeating the British. He felt likewise and praised the battalion for its loyalty, as well as bravery, in an address to the unit shortly before it was deactivated in March 1815. Nonetheless, the men chafed under martial law and criticized Jackson accordingly.

16. James Álexander Robertson, *Louisiana under the rule of Spain, France, and the United States, 1785–1807; social, economic, and political conditions of the territory represented in the Louisiana Purchase, as portrayed in hitherto unpublished contemporary account by Dr. Paul Alliot and various Spanish, French, English, and American officials*, 2 vols. (1911; reprint, Freeport, NY: Books for Libraries Press, 1969), 2:44. Laussat was the French prefect in New Orleans during the transfer of Louisiana from Spain to France and thence to the United States. See also José Montero de Pedro, Marqués de Casa Mena, *The Spanish in New Orleans and Louisiana*, trans. Richard E. Chandler (Gretna, LA: Pelican, 2000).

17. Clarence Edwin Carter, ed., *The Territorial Papers of the United States*, vol. 9, *The Territory of Orleans, 1803–1812* (Washington, DC: GPO, 1940), 18, 33, 117. See also John Preston Moore, *Revolt in Louisiana: The Spanish Occupation, 1766–1770* (Baton Rouge: Louisiana State University Press, 1976), 222.

18. Moore, *Revolt in Louisiana*, 222; Carter, *Territorial Papers*, 9:33.

19. Dargo, *Jefferson's Louisiana*, 143–46.

20. Thomas Paine to Jefferson, 25 January 1805, The Thomas Jefferson Papers at the Library of Congress: Series 1: General Correspondence, 1651–1827, Manuscript Division, Microfilm reel 032.

21. Dargo, *Jefferson's Louisiana.* For an overview of American attitudes toward military service and a military establishment in the early republic, see Lawrence Delbert Cress, *Citizens in Arms: The Army and Militia in American Society to the War of 1812* (Chapel Hill: University of North Carolina Press, 1982), 150–71.

22. For the influence of Radical Whiggery on Anglo-American attitudes toward the military, see Lawrence Delbert Cress, "Radical Whiggery on the Role of the Military: The Ideological Roots of the American Revolutionary Militia," *Journal of the History of Ideas* 40, no. 1 (January–March 1979): 43–60. His "Republican Liberty and National Security" and "Armed Community" explore the Radical Whig influence as well.

23. For Claiborne's governing style, see Thomas P. Abernethy, *The Burr Conspiracy* (1911; reprint, Gloucester, MA: P. Smith, 1968); Dargo, *Jefferson's Louisiana;* and Hatfield, *William Claiborne.*

24. The unit is variously referred to as the Battalion d'Orleans, the Uniformed Battalion of Orleans Volunteers, and the Orleans Volunteers in the contemporary literature. To avoid confusion, the unit is styled the Battalion d'Orleans throughout this essay.

25. Carter, *Territorial Papers,* 9:266; W. C. C. Claiborne, *Official Letter Books of W. C. C. Claiborne, 1801–1816,* ed. Dunbar Rowland, 6 vols. (Jackson, MS: State Department of Archives and History, 1917), 2:236–37; An act recognizing the Battalion of Orleans Volunteers, and providing for a troop of horse, in *Acts Passed at the First Session of the Legislative Council of the Territory of Orleans . . .* (New Orleans: James M. Bradford, 1805), 26–28.

26. Claiborne, *Official Letter Books,* 2:339; Carter, *Territorial Papers,* 9:298 (quotation).

27. Claiborne, *Official Letter Books,* 3:241; Gerard Toups, "The Provincial, Territorial, and State Administrations of William C. C. Claiborne, Governor of Louisiana, 1803–1816" (PhD diss., University of Southwestern Louisiana, 1979), 63–87.

28. An act for regulating and governing the militia of the territory of Orleans, in *Acts Passed at the First Session of the Legislative Council of the Territory of Orleans,* 263–304; An act to reduce into one, all acts and parts for regulating the Militia of this Commonwealth, in *The Revised Code of the Laws of Virginia* (Richmond: Thomas Ritchie 1819), 93–130.

29. Carter, *Territorial Papers,* 9:596–97.

30. Abernathy, *Burr Conspiracy,* 3–100; Carter, *Territorial Papers,* 9:713; Claiborne, *Official Letter Books,* 4:42, 50, 58. Abernathy provides a concise account of the affair.

31. In private correspondence, Claiborne expressed his doubts about Wilkinson's loyalty. In his public correspondence with Jefferson and Madison, which Wilkinson might see, Claiborne praised the general's performance. As a result, he placed the territory's militia under Wilkinson's command in the hopes that the general would act as he did. Carter, *Territorial Papers,* 9:713–18, 729–31, 739–40; Claiborne, *Official Letter Books,* 4:42, 50, 58.

32. Carter, *Territorial Papers,* 9:596–97.

33. Claiborne, *Official Letter Books,* 4:75, 103, 105.

34. Ibid., 4:288–89, quotation on 288; Carter, *Territorial Papers,* 9:740.

35. An act to establish patrols for the internal police of the territory, in *Acts Passed at the Second Session of the First Legislature of the Territory of Orleans* (New Orleans: Bradford & Anderson, 1807), 98–102; An act supplementary to an act, entitled an act to establish patrols

for the internal police of the territory, *Acts Passed at the Second Session of the Second Legislature of the Territory of Orleans* (New Orleans: Bradford & Anderson, 1808), 82–86. The 1808 law was an amplification of the earlier statute. For a concise overview of the slave rebellion, see Paul Gelpi, "Slave Rebellion, Territory of Orleans," in *The Encyclopedia of the Wars of the Early Republic: A Political, Social, and Military History*, ed. Spencer C. Tucker (Santa Barbara, CA: ABC-CLIO, 2014).

36. Reginald Horsman's *The War of 1812* (New York: Knopf, 1969) provides a concise account of the war, as does Donald R. Hickey's *War of 1812: The Forgotten Conflict* (Urbana: University of Illinois Press, 1989). Robin Reilly's *The British at the Gates: The New Orleans Campaign in the War of 1812* (New York, 1974) examines the battles for New Orleans within the wider contexts of British operations in 1814 and the war itself. For concise overviews of the battles, see the following entries by Paul Gelpi in *The Encyclopedia of Warfare*, ed. Sarah Uttridge and Charles Catton (London: Amber Books, 2013): "Fort Bowyer, First Battle of," "Fort Bowyer, Second Battle of," "Fort Peter, Battle of," "Fort St. Phillip, Siege of," "Lake Borgne, Naval Battle of," "New Orleans, Battle of," and "23 December 1814, Battle of."

37. Andrew Jackson, *The Papers of Andrew Jackson*, vol. 3, *1814–1815*, ed. Harold D. Moser, David R. Hoth, Sharon Macpherson, and John H. Reinbold (Knoxville: University of Tennessee Press, 1991), 204–5.

38. Ibid., 204.

39. Ibid., 211–12.

40. Ibid., 303.

41. Michael Chiorazzi, "Francois-Xavier Martin: Printer, Lawyer, Jurist," *Law Library Journal* 80 (1988): 63–97, esp. 63–76 and 76–78. Although an influential printer and jurist, Martin (1762–1846) has been the subject of few biographies; indeed, he has no modern biographer. Chiorazzi's essay provides an overview of Martin's life and comes the closest to being his biography. The inclusion of an annotated bibliography of works by and on Martin provides a detailed summary of his biographers.

42. François-Xavier Martin, *Louisiana Term Reports, or Cases Argued and Determined in the Supreme Court of that State*, vol. 3 (New Orleans, 1815), 530–58; Joseph G. Tregle Jr., "Andrew Jackson and the Continuing Battle of New Orleans," *Journal of the Early Republic* 1, no. 4 (Winter 1981): 373–93.

43. Martin, *Louisiana Term Reports*, 530; Charles L. Thompson, *United States Supreme Court Reports, Lawyers' Edition* (Rochester, NY: Lawyers Co-operative, 1917), 554.

44. François-Xavier Martin, *The History of Louisiana, From the Earliest Period* (1827–29; reprint, 2 vols. in 1, Gretna, LA: Pelican, 1975), 405–12.

6

Lessons Learned from the War of 1812 for the US Military in the Twenty-First Century

BLAKE DUNNAVENT

Freshmen students every semester ask why we study history. It is pointless, they say, anxious to get right into their major fields of studies and cease focusing on ancient battles, politics, and economics. And by *ancient* students mean everything before the late 1990s. In a twenty-first-century global environment, preoccupied with technological innovation, what nuggets or gems can be gleaned by examining the past to demonstrate their applicability in a modern, high-tech world? Practically speaking, history is very relevant to the present. Whether or not they are aware of it, college freshmen, corporations, and financial institutions, as well as the US government, draw upon historical concepts in daily life. Among the most salient of those concepts is leadership. Though often overlooked, America's second conflict with Great Britain gave rise to some of the nation's most iconic leaders, such as Oliver Hazard Perry and Andrew Jackson, who continue to represent leadership in the minds of many Americans today.

Quality leadership, from the enlisted ranks to senior officers, has been of critical importance to America's military, both past and present. The importance of quality leadership is underscored by the absence of it, as evidenced in the memoirs of General Winfield Scott, who noted that officers appointed during the War of 1812 were often political appointments, describing them as "swaggerers, dependents, decayed gentlemen and others—'fit for nothing else.'" Consequently, the first two years of the conflict were marked by administrative anarchy and military defeat, which the historian William B. Skelton observed were reversed only in the final stages of the war as younger officers who had learned their trade by experience pushed gradually into the higher command levels. Skelton noted that military service was an extension of leadership roles in local, state, and national affairs for a large number of the high commanders. Only three of the high commanders were alumni of the US Military Academy.[1] Today, courses in leadership prevail at the war colleges for officers and at noncommissioned-officer academies in all branches of the armed forces. However, Samuel J. Watson, in his study of the army officer corps on the American frontier in 1810–20, argued that nineteenth-century military professionalism was not simply a matter of growing expertise in the art of warfare. According to Watson, nineteenth-century American military history and professionalism revolved around two fundamental issues: civil-military relations, evaluated by the degree of military accountability to civilian control, and the military's ability to accomplish the missions assigned to it.[2]

Prominent in the War of 1812, as in the present, were three types of leadership: operational, strategic, and tactical. In *Nineteen Gun Salute*, published by the Naval War College Press, John Hattendorf and Bruce Elleman define operational leadership as "activities within a single theater of war. It is the act of leading a large and complex naval or joint forces command in accomplishing political and military strategic objectives assigned by the national or coalition leadership through the direct application of armed force." "The essence of operational leadership," they write, "is to make decisions on how to act effectively with feasibility." Elleman and Hattendorf describe strategic leadership as "activities with broad national scope. It is the act of interrelating and harmonizing, at the national level, a nation's ends and means through a comprehensive direction of its armed forces." This can include "other elements of national power—such as diplomacy, intelligence, and economics—to control broad situations in order to obtain broad national or coalition objectives." Hence, "the essence of strategic leadership is to make broad decisions, often on a national or even a global level, as to where and when to act." Tactical leadership is a bit more basic. According to Jay Stratton, director of Air Warfare/SPEAR, Office of Naval Intelligence, it involves "motivating your men to act and accomplish the mission with flexibility and latitude in decisions and actions to achieve commander's intent."[3]

In the War of 1812, Oliver Hazard Perry demonstrated leadership in all three areas. Perry was among those young officers who had learned his trade through experience. The son of a naval captain with his own ship, Perry had entered the navy at the age of thirteen as a midshipman. In 1809 he had received his first command, the schooner USS *Revenge*, in the Atlantic. When President James Madison signed the declaration of war with Britain on June 12, 1812, twenty-six-year-old Oliver Hazard Perry was ordered to take command of the vessels in Newport, Rhode Island.[4] In 1813 the US military sought to reverse some of the many setbacks that occurred in the land campaign along the Canadian border in the first year of the war. To that end, in February 1813 Commodore Isaac Chauncey, the US naval commander of the Great Lakes, ordered Master Commandant Oliver Hazard Perry "to travel westward with some of his Rhode Island men to Presque Isle on the south shore of Lake Erie, and there to build a naval squadron with which to wrest control of the lake from the British, who, at the time, dominated it." Despite the frigid temperatures, Perry and his one hundred or so men sloshed to their destination on Lake Erie. They immediately set to the task of felling trees and constructing suitable vessels to engage the British. Chauncey had given Perry a daunting logistical task. Not only did his men have to cut down the forests of the American wilderness for the hulls and decks but Perry had to requisition critical supplies for construction and arming the fleet from locations more than one hundred miles away. In addition to these obstacles, Perry's command remained desperately short of manpower. In an effort to alleviate this problem, Perry wrote to his commander requesting more able-bodied sailors. His missives produced a mere trickle of seamen to add to Perry's inadequate numbers. Months later, the continued severe manpower shortages forced Perry to "publish handbills . . . to raise volunteers from the local militia; and frontiersmen." When this action proved inadequate, Perry contacted the army for assistance. The regional army commander responded by dispatching more than one hundred volunteers and sharpshooters to fill out Perry's crews, to the chagrin of the secretary of the navy.[5]

Once his command had prepared the small American armada for action, Perry directed his men to deploy the squadron beyond the Presque Isle bar. Geographically, Perry's location provided shelter from the British vessels, but the shallowness of the water made it difficult to maneuver the larger vessels from their anchorage over the bar. With painstaking effort, Perry's command, assisted by the nearby militia, successfully floated the American vessels onto the lake. Perry could now give battle to the British. Next, Perry contacted the regional army commander who had provided him manpower, Major General William Henry Harrison, and the two gentlemen "reconnoitered the upper lake and selected South Bass Island as the staging point for action against the British." The island's harbor, Put-in-Bay, provided a good anchorage, "and it was a logical place to move the army from the American mainland if and when it could invade." Following this joint decision, the American squadron sailed for its new destination in mid-August and dropped anchor off South Bass Island, just under forty miles away from the British fleet, which was located on the Detroit River at Amherstburg.[6]

In the British sector, upriver in Canada, Commander Robert H. Barclay—faced with food shortages and a whole host of other logistical deficiencies owing in part to the American flotilla's location, which interdicted any possibility of British supplies arriving—believed he had no choice but to commit to battle. On September 9, 1813, Commander Barclay's forces "slipped their moorings and floated down the Detroit River onto Lake Erie." While the small British fleet had awaited supplies and reinforcements, Perry's squadron had been training and readying for combat. The contest began on September 10, 1813.[7]

At dawn, Perry's lookouts spotted British masts about nine miles from their position. The American sailors feverishly scrambled to make their vessels ready in the early morning light. By 6:00 a.m. Perry's nine vessels had set out to intercept the oncoming seven British craft. Initially, Perry directed his fleet to maneuver about to gain a favorable position with respect to the wind. Four hours later, the lake's meteorological situation changed in favor of the American squadron. With the wind now on his side, Perry steered directly toward the British fleet. At 11:45 a.m., both sides fired their opening salvos. For the next two and a half hours, as the broadsides belched their merciless iron, creating wooden splinters capable of shredding human flesh, from the deck of his flagship Perry continually ordered his crew to load the powder and shot and engage the enemy. Keenly aware that more than 90 percent of his crew were dead or wounded and that his ship had sustained crippling damage, Perry chose to transfer to another vessel to continue the fight. After the precarious transit to his new command, Perry pressed hard against the British squadron, inflicting severe damage to the already punished vessels. By 3:00 p.m., the British had suffered enough; one by one the vessels of Barclay's force struck their colors. The hard-fought battle was over. America had attained victory and control of Lake Erie.[8]

In 2013 the United States commemorated the two-hundredth anniversary of the Battle of Lake Erie. To acknowledge Perry's signal victory, Vice Admiral Michelle Howard gave a presentation at the National Museum of the US Navy in Washington, DC. "There are multiple lessons to be learned from Commodore Oliver Hazard Perry and the campaign of the Great Lakes," she stated. One of these lessons was operational leadership. "The battles on the Great Lakes took place at the very edge of our nation. For Commodore Perry, who had to build his ships first, resourcing at the end of a long and vulnerable logistic trail was an immediate problem." Despite supply difficulties, Perry acted "effectively [and] with feasibility" in order to build and outfit a respectable flotilla to engage the British force. "But of greater concern to him was the lack of Sailors and Marines," Howard noted. However, "there was a joint solution." Unlike the nineteenth-century military, in which "jointness" was anathema, today's armed forces actively embrace this concept, which is why the Battle of Lake Erie provides such an important lesson in operational leadership. Despite the ire he drew from his superiors, Perry, who failed "to achieve sufficient numbers through volunteers" and from the Navy Department, appealed to his army counterpart, whose much-needed assistance enabled Perry to sail to victory. The acquisition of logistics and manpower and working jointly with the army all fit the definition of operational leadership. Moreover, all of Perry's actions took place within a single theater of war, and he seized a key strategic objective by engaging the enemy in combat. Thus, Perry's actions in 1813 provide sound operational-leadership lessons for today's military.[9]

The lessons learned from Perry are not limited to operational leadership; strategic-leadership examples also emerge. Perry successfully used his small portion of America's military arsenal in 1813 "to control broad situations in order to obtain broad national or coalition objectives" on Lake

Erie. Admiral Howard succinctly posited, "The British captured the Northwest bringing strategic importance for both American and British governments to gain control of the Great Lakes." Perry and his amalgamated band of brothers wrested control of Lake Erie, thereby giving the United States a strategic edge, which was recognized by both belligerents.[10]

The Battle of Lake Erie also provides tactical-leadership lessons, albeit less encompassing than the operational- and strategic-leadership lessons. Regardless of the hardships suffered by his men during the march to Lake Erie, Perry continually motivated them to fulfill the assigned missions. His direction and inspiration invigorated his men as they constructed the American flotilla and persisted during the arduous task of deploying the vessels beyond the Presque Isle Bar. Perry's encouragement continued throughout the voyage to Put-in-Bay and the training that ensued at anchorage. Just before the battle began, Perry ordered the flag carrying the words "Don't Give Up the Ship" to be hoisted high for his command as a rallying cry. In the hours and days following the sanguinary duel between the two small navies, Perry ceaselessly looked after the well-being of his crews. Officers in America's twenty-first-century military would do well to follow Perry's leadership style as they prepare for and engage in combat.[11]

Admiral Howard also made some general comments about the Battle of Lake Erie and the War of 1812 as a whole. The "Battle of Lake Erie," she observed, "has much to say as we move into the next few decades and create our own defense strategies. . . . We are closer now to the Red Coats in the strategic implications of the War of 1812. We have the Navy that dominates the seas. Our Navy can project power across the oceans." In addition, she said, the United States relies upon its allies or coalition partners to conduct missions globally in the twenty-first century just as the British used partners during their campaigns against the United States in the War of 1812. Our fighting partners worldwide sometimes "live in the area, and conflict will impact their families and lives." For our allies, "winning the conflict is tied to survival." Hence, "timing becomes a strategic issue." The leadership of the United States and our partners typically apply "pressure to defeat the adversary quickly [as] long campaigns can run against the partnership as the will to fight together is tested." The partnership status of the United States today mirrors that of Britain in 1813. England had many Native American allies, which the British military used in both its army and its navy. Eager for assistance, the British made far too many logistic pledges to their Native American allies. Later, when the British failed to meet their promises, the partnership dissolved. Distance from adequate supply lines severely hampered the British commanders' ability to provide their Native American cohorts with the vital stores agreed upon.[12]

Another iconic leader was Major General Andrew Jackson, who proved adept at making the most of unlikely partnerships in the Battle of New Orleans.[13] On December 23, 1814, in a downpour, British Major General John Keane dispatched sixteen hundred British troops to Bayou Bienvenue from Pea Island, thirty miles east of New Orleans. At 6:00 a.m. they reached the mouth of the bayou, at 9:00 they proceeded inland through the soggy terrain, and by noon they had reached the Mississippi River. Throughout the day reinforcements continued to arrive at Keane's position on General Jacques Villiere's plantation, nine miles from the Crescent City. The British, although they posted pickets around their perimeter, did not prepare camp defenses adequate to repulse an attack. Confident of their abilities—especially following their victory at Washington—and of certain American ineptitude, at about 5:00 p.m. the redcoats built large campfires to cook dinner, and shortly thereafter the unsuspecting British troops readied for bed. At the same time, General Jackson, who had received word that the British had taken a position on the Mississippi, planned a three-pronged night attack using both military and naval forces. While the ground elements would hit the British from two different flanks, naval forces would provide fire support from the river. Shortly after nightfall Lieutenant John D. Henley maneuvered the schooner *Carolina* down the river from New Orleans and anchored across the river from the British camp. Armed with a variety of weapons, the US Navy fired the opening shots of the night engagement. At 7:30 p.m. the *Carolina* fired into the heart of the British camp, causing widespread confusion among the redcoats. Meanwhile, Jackson's ground forces attacked the confused and startled British army, but by 9:30 p.m. he had withdrawn from the action because of a thick fog that engulfed the battlefield, making military targets difficult to distinguish.[14]

On Christmas Eve, as the *Carolina* maintained a continual bombardment of the British position, the sloop *Louisiana,* commanded by Commodore Patterson, slipped into a position a mile north to support the *Carolina,* which was then on the western bank of the river, and harassed the British with cannon. For two more days the American naval forces continued to fire salvos from their long-range cannon into the British camp. In the hours before dawn on December 27, the British, using howitzers and a mortar, fired red-hot shot at the *Carolina.* On the second round the British shot "lodged in the schooner's main hold under her cables." With fire sweeping through the ship, the crew abandoned her, and at dawn the flames reached the magazine, detonating the ship.[15]

After the December 23 engagement, the British forces grew with reinforcements that plodded in soaked to the skin from the incessant southern winter rains. On Christmas Day, Major General Sir Edward Pakenham arrived and took command of the fifty-three hundred dispirited and drenched British soldiers, who were expected to eliminate Jackson's force and seize New Orleans. As the crisp morning of December 28 became illuminated by the sun's rays, Pakenham decided that it was time to attempt a reconnaissance in force against the American forward positions. After the redcoats had marched about five miles, they spotted American forces dug in ahead of them. When the British began to attack, Jackson's five field pieces and the sloop *Louisiana,* which provided fire support for Jackson's right flank, discharged a devastating amount of iron into the two British columns. The *Louisiana*'s accurate naval gunfire forced the British infantry to dive into muddy ditches for protection. For seven hours the *Louisiana* and Jackson's artillery bombarded the British with more than eight hundred shots. The effective American artillery and naval gunfire forced the shattered British lines to pull back in the evening to avoid further losses. Some authors note that while the two adversaries engaged in furious combat, Jackson also had to contend with the Louisiana legislature. He had received word that the legislature intended to surrender to the British, an idea he quickly rejected.[16]

The final two clashes took place on January 1 and January 8, 1815. As the morning dawned on the New Year, fog obscured both the American and British positions. Between 8:00 and 9:00 a.m. the mist cleared, and an artillery duel erupted between Jackson's batteries and those of Packenham. After three hours of sustained bombardment, both sides suffered casualties and the exchange concluded. In the days following the cannon fight, both sides prepared for the final contest. Jackson had chosen his defensive ground well. He had anchored his right flank to the Mississippi and his left to an almost impenetrable muddy morass known as the Cypress Swamp. Jackson had connected his flanks with a mud rampart more than ten feet thick and tall enough that enemy forces assaulting the American position would require ladders to overcome it. Jackson, through his telescope, observed the activity of the British forces for the next six days and deployed his men accordingly. The bulk of his forty-three hundred fighters would defend the muddy rampart from the Cypress Swamp to the Mississippi, while about seven hundred men would defend the west bank of the Mississippi. Behind the earthen defenses, Jackson's command manned nearly twenty artillery pieces aimed at the open landscape that the redcoats would traverse. Around sundown on January 7, Jackson received intelligence that the British assault would commence shortly after dawn on January 8. That evening he walked the entire length of his defenses, talking to the men and commanders of the batteries. As the sun broke through the winter morning of January 8 and slowly climbed in the chilly air, the Americans peered over their soggy walled entrenchments to see the British begin their march to the muzzles of the American cannon, muskets, and rifles. Moments later, as more than five thousand British infantry came in range of the American guns, Jackson yelled "Fire!" The British forces walked straight into a slaughter. Throughout the duration of the battle, Jackson continually moved up and down the line shouting orders and words of encouragement to his odd-looking crew of defenders. In less than an hour it was over. The Chalmette battlefield was littered with British dead and dying. An American army had defeated a numerically superior and experienced foe.[17]

As from Perry's leadership at the Battle of Lake Erie, there are lessons to be learned from General Jackson's leadership at the Battle of New Orleans. In terms of operational leadership, Jackson did command in a single theater of war, the Gulf Coast. Militarily he was directed to defend New Orleans from the British, and like Perry, he achieved his objective with a joint coalition of forces. Maurice Matloff's *American Military History* colorfully describes the nature of Jackson's command as follows: "It was a varied group, composed of the 7th and 44th Infantry Regiments, Major Beale's

New Orleans Sharpshooters, LaCoste and Daquin's battalions of free Negroes, the Louisiana militia under General David Morgan, a band of Choctaw Indians, the Baratarian pirates, and a motley battalion of fashionably dressed sons and brothers of the New Orleans aristocracy." Jackson's willingness to work jointly with the navy's two small vessels on the Mississippi also paved the way for victory at New Orleans. Like Perry, Jackson had supply problems. Despite waiting for months to hear from Washington to augment his stores, Jackson relied upon existing stockpiles and what he could acquire locally. Hence, Jackson acted "effectively and with feasibility" to achieve the government's directives. Regardless of the logistical situation, simply stated, as America's twenty-first-century armed forces must do on repeated deployments, Jackson made the best of what he had. In the 2004 book *Generation Kill,* made into an HBO miniseries that aired in 2008, a Marine preparing for the invasion of Iraq in 2003 commented about logistics, "The Marines make do"—as General Jackson demonstrated at the Battle of New Orleans.[18]

Jackson's performance in the Battle of New Orleans also exemplifies strategic and tactical leadership. Strategically, Jackson used his hastily formed coalition "to control broad situations in order to obtain broad national or coalition objectives." Jackson's success can be attributed in part to his strategic leadership in that he chose at a local level, with national implications, "where and when to act." Lastly, Jackson demonstrated tactical-leadership traits that can be applied to today's battlefields. By continually conversing with his men before and during the battle, he discovered the logistical needs of his men and provided the necessary motivation "to act and accomplish the mission . . . in decisions and actions to achieve commander's intent."[19]

The War of 1812 altered how the US government viewed America's armed forces—to a point. For the first time in the young country's brief history, the US Army wanted combat leaders of the officer corps to remain in the military to prepare for future war. Although it was by no means a panacea, as William Skelton states, it laid the "foundation for the American profession of arms." The US Navy also had a renaissance of sorts in the postwar years. According to the historians Harold and Margaret Sprout, the

Navy Department recognized that its prewar deployment of a few vessels in crisis situations was no longer sufficient. Therefore, the navy "gradually established permanent squadrons on a number of stations. Each station was simply a more or less well defined area within which several naval vessels cruised all the time. And the vessels assigned to each station at any given time comprised a squadron." All of this, whether it be the Army or the Navy, would have been meaningless without appropriate leadership.[20]

Two centuries later, the present US military can draw upon the lessons learned about leadership in the cases of Commodore Perry and General Jackson in the War of 1812. Perhaps it is not going too far to suggest that the War of 1812 provided the building blocks for the creation or the adoption of formalized institutions to study the past for future war scenarios and leadership. In 2002 a team of Harvard researchers studying what makes a great leader posed the timeless question why certain people seem to naturally inspire confidence, loyalty, and hard work, while others (who may be just as smart and visionary) stumble again and again. Their research led them to conclude that one of the most reliable predictors of true leadership is an individual's ability to find meaning in negative events and to learn from even the most trying circumstances. It is a timeless lesson, as pertinent to modern college freshmen eager to launch successful careers in diverse fields as it is to the modern military. Purposely or by accident, historians and society in general tend to mythologize military leaders of the past, such as Perry and Jackson, for their exploits on inland waters, the seas, or muddy battlefields where they fought with little knowledge or understanding of their context. Great commanders and popular men at arms they were, but they were also mere mortals, in tumultuous times, during crucible events in American military history. They demonstrated what two Harvard researchers concluded nearly two hundred years later: the skills required to conquer adversity and emerge stronger and more committed are the same ones that make for extraordinary leaders.[21]

NOTES

1. William B. Skelton, "High Army Leadership in the Era of the War of 1812: The Making and Remaking of the Officer Corps," *William and Mary Quarterly* 51, no. 2 (April 1994): 253–54 (quotation), 260.

2. Samuel J. Watson, *Jackson's Sword: The Army Officer Corps on the American Frontier, 1810–1821* (Lawrence: University Press of Kansas, 2012), 5.

3. John B. Hattendorf and Bruce E. Elleman, eds., *Nineteen Gun Salute: Case Studies of Operational, Strategic, and Diplomatic Naval Leadership during the 20th and Early 21st Centuries* (Newport, RI: Naval War College Press, 2010), 245; Jay Stratton, phone interview by author, 25 October 2014.

4. Oliver Hazard Perry Rhode Island, "Commodore Oliver Hazard Perry," accessed 30 October 2015, www.ohpri.org/history-details/commodore-oliver-hazard-perry.

5. Vice Admiral Michelle Howard, "Battle of Lake Erie 200 Years Later: Lessons Learned" (paper presented at Naval History and Heritage Command's National Museum of the U.S. Navy, Washington, DC, September 2013), navylive.dodlive.mil/2013/09/10/battle-of-lake-erie-200-years-later-lessons-learned/; John K. Mahon, "Oliver Hazard Perry," in *Command under Sail: Makers of the American Naval Tradition, 1775–1850*, ed. James C. Bradford (Annapolis, MD: Naval Institute Press, 1985), 126–41.

6. Mahon, "Oliver Hazard Perry."

7. Gerard T. Altoff, *Oliver Hazard Perry and the Battle of Lake Erie* (Put-in-Bay, OH: Perry Group, 1999), 30.

8. Ibid., 30–59; Mahon, "Oliver Hazard Perry."

9. Howard, "Battle of Lake Erie"; Hattendorf and Elleman, *Nineteen Gun Salute*, 245.

10. Hattendorf and Elleman, *Nineteen Gun Salute*, 245.

11. Howard, "Battle of Lake Erie"; Mahon, "Oliver Hazard Perry"; Richard Dillon, *We Have Met the Enemy: Oliver Hazard Perry; Wilderness Commodore* (New York: McGraw-Hill, 1978), 154–72.

12. Howard, "Battle of Lake Erie."

13. See Robert C. Vogel, "Jean Laffitte, the Baratarians, and the Battle of New Orleans, A Reappraisal," *Louisiana History* 41, no. 3 (Summer 2000): 261–76.

14. R. Blake Dunnavent, *Brown Water Warfare: The U.S. Navy in Riverine Warfare and the Emergence of a Tactical Doctrine, 1775–1970* (Gainesville: University Press of Florida, 2003), 25–26.

15. Ibid.

16. Ibid.; Robin Reilly, *The British at the Gates: The New Orleans Campaign in the War of 1812* (New York: G. P. Putnam's Sons, 1974), 194–300.

17. Reilly, *British at the Gates*, 194–300; John K. Mahon, *The War of 1812* (New York: Da Capo, 1972), 354–72.

18. Mahon, *War of 1812*, 354–72; Maurice Matloff, ed., *American Military History* (Washington, DC: Center of Military History, 1988), 144–45; Evan Wright, *Generation Kill: Devil*

Dogs, Iceman, Captain America, and the New Face of American War (New York: G. P. Putnam's Sons, 2004).

19. Hattendorf and Elleman, *Nineteen Gun Salute,* 245; Stratton, phone interview.

20. Harold Sprout and Margaret Sprout, *The Rise of American Naval Power, 1776–1918* (Princeton, NJ: Princeton University Press, 1944), 94–95.

21. Warren Bennis and Robert J. Thomas, "Crucibles of Leadership," *Harvard Business Review* 80, no. 9 (September 2002): para. 1, hbr.org/2002/09/crucibles-of-leadership.

7

One Hundred Years of Old Hickory and Cotton Bales

The Battle of New Orleans Centennial Celebration

JOSEPH F. STOLTZ III

The monument made for an impressive sight: a one-hundred-foot tower of marble that shone brightly in the crisp winter air. Only a decade earlier, the Chalmette Monument had sat half-finished and nearly forgotten in a cow pasture. Now, in January 1915, it stood overlooking the fifteen thousand spectators gathered around its base. These admirers had come from around the United States to be on the spot where, exactly one hundred years earlier, Andrew Jackson and his army had defeated the invading forces of Great Britain.

Five "true daughters" of the engagement's participants sat in the shadow of the monument as the United States Daughters of 1812 organization dedicated the obelisk, in the words on the plaque affixed on the monument's observation deck, "to the memory of the American soldiers who fell in the Battle of New Orleans." With that, American and British flags rose up the shaft of the monument celebrating a century of peace between the United States and Great Britain since the battle.[1]

Once a national holiday celebrated across the United States, Jackson Day (January 8) commemorations declined greatly over the course of the nineteenth century. First as a result of Jackson's divisive presidency and then because of the sectional politics of the American Civil War and Reconstruction, celebrations of the Battle of New Orleans's anniversary were at an all-time low in the 1880s. Even in New Orleans, forever a stalwart supporter of Jackson, many people found it hard to commemorate a victory by the same United States that had recently subdued the South. The re-emergence of Battle of New Orleans commemorations and the form those celebrations would take during the centennial celebrations make a strong argument that festivities rarely had anything to do with Andrew Jackson and his soldiers' victory over the British. Instead, commemoration centered on the types of issues that early Jazz Age Americans needed the Battle of New Orleans to represent in the heydays of Jim Crow, the Lost Cause, and the eve of American participation in the Great War.

Considering the apathy toward the battle's commemoration at the turn of the twentieth century, the 1915 event had been a remarkable success. From the 1890s to the second decade of the twentieth century, the public memory of the Battle of New Orleans received bursts of attention and enthusiasm, thanks to women's patriotic organizations around the country. These groups played an important role in the preservation of battlefields and other historic sites across the United States. In the South, groups like the Daughters of 1812 were especially important because they provided opportunities for white southerners still upset over the Civil War to reengage in American patriotic events.

In the early 1890s, numerous ladies' patriotic organizations formed across the country, such as the Colonial Dames, the Daughters of the American Revolution (DAR), and the United Daughters of the Confederacy (UDC). The UDC in particular played a prominent role in shaping American historical memory, especially in the South. The UDC formed in 1894 through the national consolidation of numerous state organizations. These hereditary patriotic organizations originally organized with the intention of caring for Confederate veterans, widows, and orphans. Yet they quickly became vehicles for airing southern grievances and coordinating resistance to interference by the federal government in southern society. The US government paid little attention to the meetings of these organized women's groups, which it considered less threatening than gatherings of men, who might take up arms. Groups like the UDC played a critical role in shaping the memory of the Civil War and in developing the Lost Cause in the South.[2]

The United Daughters of 1812 also wrote its official charter in Washington, DC, around the time the UDC formed. Slightly predating the UDC, the Daughters of 1812 formed with the purpose of promoting US rather than Confederate patriotism. The 1812 organization even chose blue and gray for its official colors, ostensibly for the blue worn by the navy and the gray worn by the army during the war. This color scheme also represented a less than subtle suggestion of the group's true intentions. The organization strove to emphasize an era before the Civil War, when, as they saw it, regional division did not threaten to tear the country apart. By the early 1900s the popular memory of the War of 1812 was of a second American Revolution in which the various states of the Union fought as one in a common cause. That memory appealed to some southerners who had grown tired of the Lost Cause and the constant emphasis on a lost war. The successes of the War of 1812 in the West appealed to people during the 1890s and 1900s for the same reasons that historians have identified for the Daughters of the Republic of Texas's advances in the same period. In New Orleans especially, home to the South's greatest non–Civil War military success, the membership of the Daughters of 1812 grew dramatically.[3]

The New Orleans–area Daughters of 1812 had assistance in their chapter's formation because they possessed a tangible goal with which to rally support: the completion of the Chalmette Monument. Only one year after the chapter's formation in 1893, the Daughters successfully petitioned the state of Louisiana to hand over administration of the land surrounding the monument to the organization. The state also granted the Daughters a paltry two thousand dollars, which the basic care and maintenance of the grounds quickly exhausted. Undeterred, the Daughters commissioned an engineering report, focusing on the necessary steps to finish the memorial to Jackson and his army. Armed with this report, the Daughters traveled to Washington, DC, to meet with President Theodore Roosevelt and a House of Representatives committee. They persuaded the federal government to contribute twenty-five thousand dollars toward the completion of the monument. However, the appropriation made it clear that the Daughters would fund all future care and maintenance. The state of Louisiana transferred ownership of the land to the US War Department in 1907.[4]

Upon completion of the monument in 1908, the New Orleans–area Daughters of 1812 assumed official stewardship of the battlefield and monument. Unlike the Ladies Hermitage Association in Nashville and the Mount Vernon Ladies Association in Virginia, the Daughters had limited opportunities for fund-raising at the Chalmette battlefield. While the historic homes of Nashville and Mount Vernon required constant renovation and upkeep, they also were showpieces that could help generate funds. Tourists could make a day trip from Washington or Nashville to visit the homes of Jackson and Washington and escape the rigors of the urban scene, but Chalmette offered few comforts. The rural pastureland surrounding the battlefield began to change even as the Daughters took over the battlefield's stewardship.[5]

The Chalmette battlefield sits on valuable waterfront property along the Mississippi River. In 1905 the New Orleans Terminal Company announced plans to build a docking slip a few hundred yards from the monument. Construction crews completed the slip two years later, and by the time they finished, the location of Jackson's headquarters lay underwater. The development of the shipping slip also cut motor access to the battlefield, which had traditionally been from a road along the Mississippi River. In addition, the river itself, long the primary method of travel, became increasingly less frequented as the twentieth century progressed.

The Terminal Company also purchased land between the Chalmette Monument and the US military cemetery built during the Civil War, land over which British and American forces had fought throughout the New Orleans campaign. Yet, the company could not develop the property, because the residents of Fazendville, an African American neighborhood that sat in the center of the parcel, refused to sell. Industrial development continued further downriver, a location where the British had headquartered and the December 23 night battle had occurred. The Daughters, who relied on the sale of pecans from the battlefield's trees, raised funds through membership dues and by renting the land north of the monument for pasture. They still had trouble competing with the industrialization transformation surrounding their site. Luckily for the Daughters and the community of Fazendville, the slip's construction affected access to the military cemetery. The War Department persuaded the Terminal Company to provide land for a right-of-way over nearby train tracks and persuaded the Parish of St. Bernard to extend a nearby highway so that visitors could have access to the cemetery. By extension, this right-of-way also preserved road access for the battlefield and the community of Fazendville.[6]

The New Orleans Daughters constantly battled industrialization, lack of funds, and even Mother Nature. After lightning struck the monument, the Daughters asked the War Department to help defray the cost of the repairs. Legally, though, the federal government could do little unless Congress amended the law preventing the US government from providing money for the site's maintenance. Further, powerful commercial interests worked against the Daughters. Unlike Mount Vernon and the Hermitage, which were located in rural areas, the battlefield rested on property that a 1921 report found to be worth five hundred thousand dollars on the open market.[7]

Despite what must have been a frustrating decade of lobbying and petitioning, the Daughters of 1812 had a great deal to celebrate. Through their efforts, they raised awareness concerning the plight of the Chalmette Monument, organized a campaign to complete the structure, and renewed efforts to memorialize the Battle of New Orleans. They did so in the face of pervasive industrialization in Chalmette and a resilient Lost Cause sentiment in the City of New Orleans itself, buoyed by vast amounts of private money for Confederate memorialization. Also, despite the construction around the battlefield, as well as the difficulty of getting to it, the most important sixteen acres of the battlefield remained intact. With the centennial of the battle just a few years away, the group could feel optimistic.[8]

Although the Daughters of 1812 made many positive gains in New Orleans and played a major role in advocating for a restored Chalmette battlefield, they made no such headway in Tennessee. This lack of enthusiasm may seem surprising in light of the Volunteer State's prominent role in the War of 1812 and at the Battle of New Orleans. Even so, the Tennessee Daughters of 1812 counted only twenty members statewide in the second decade of the twentieth century. Instead, the Ladies Hermitage Association took the lead in Tennessee's War of 1812 memorialization.[9]

After the Civil War, the state used Andrew Jackson's home, the Hermitage, as a respite for aging southern veterans. In 1856 the state of Tennessee paid forty-eight thousand dollars to needy descendants of Old Hickory who could no longer take care of the five-hundred-acre property. By 1889 the newly chartered Ladies Hermitage Association (LHA) had taken possession of the twenty-five acres that included Jackson's mansion and tomb, holding the state land in trust for the specific purpose of promoting patriotism and tourism in the Nashville area.[10]

The LHA soon decided that the best way to promote interest in the site, and by extension in Jackson and patriotism, would be to restore the house to its former glory. Restoration took money, but the founding ladies of the LHA moved in Nashville's most elite social circles. The women quickly recruited new members and planned an event that would make their organization the talk of the Cumberland Valley. The first Jackson Day Ball was held in 1892, and the ball remains one of Nashville's more prestigious social events.[11]

Other events also offered creative opportunities to raise money for the Hermitage's restoration and for the promotion of knowledge about the general and the Battle of New Orleans. The LHA persuaded local businesses across Nashville to hold a Jackson Day Sale and donate 5 percent of their profits to the organization. In addition, the Hermitage's distance from the hustle and bustle of Nashville provided the LHA opportunities to rent the site for barbeques. During the early 1900s, a day traveler from Nashville could travel by riverboat up the Cumberland to tour the general's former property for only a nominal fee.[12]

The LHA was not the only high-profile commemorative group in the Nashville area at the turn of the century. With an eye toward the centennial, area businessmen formed the Andrew Jackson Memorial Association in 1914. The group decried what its members viewed as a lack of enthusiasm toward the upcoming Battle of New Orleans centennial. They also were unhappy that the replica of Clark Mills's equestrian statue was the only memorial to Jackson in the Tennessee state capital. Unaware of the statue's historical or technical significance, the organization blustered that the monument was "not of very great artistic merit."[13]

The businessmen of the Memorial Association felt that the general's memory deserved a grand "Jackson Boulevard" to serve as "a second Champs-Elysses." As envisioned, the road would proceed from the steps of the capitol to the doors of the Hermitage, a distance of some twelve miles. To pay for the estimated $1 million cost of construction, the group proposed to solicit funds from local, state, and federal governments. By 1915 the monetary plan for the boulevard called for $250,000 each from the city, the county, and the state, in addition to $500,000 from Congress and $50,000 to $100,000 that the association would obtain from private donors. As spectacular as the finished result might be, the organization never garnered serious momentum toward the project's completion because of the cost.[14]

Unlike the short-lived Andrew Jackson Memorial Association, the Ladies Hermitage Association had no such qualms about Clark Mills's statue. In fact, it greatly distressed the organization to learn in 1914 that Congress questioned the placement of the Jackson statue in Lafayette Square, near the White House. In 1824 the federal government named the square after the famed French noble turned American patriot Gilbert de Lafayette during the former general's visit. In the corners of the square stood monuments to Lafayette, Friedrich von Steuben, Thaddeus Kosciuszko, and Jean de Rochambeau, all prominent foreign-born generals of the American cause during the Revolutionary War. Then, conspicuously out of place in the center of the square rose a bronze image of Jackson on his horse. For the sake of theme, Congress wanted to move Jackson's statue to another location. The Ladies protested and quickly sprang into action. They solicited the assistance of Tennessee congressman Joseph W. Byrnes, and Congress's plan soon faltered.[15]

The Ladies also used gendered social norms to their advantage whenever doing so helped promote Jackson and the Battle of New Orleans. The areas of education reform and criticism were among the few areas in which women could affect public policy in early twentieth-century America. To that end, the LHA regularly monitored the publication of schoolbooks to make sure that children learned the "real" history of the Battle of New Orleans. The association even published in 1935 the *Battle of New Orleans: Its Real Meaning; Exposure of Untruth Being Taught Young America Concerning the Second Most Important Military Event in the Life of the Republic.* The book is an impassioned response to those who would argue that the battle lacked significance because of the Treaty of Ghent. It also places the success of Jackson's army squarely in the hands of the southern frontiersman and his trusty squirrel rifle.[16]

The members of the LHA did not limit their attention to schools merely to textbooks. The children of Tennessee had to prove that they had learned the story of the battle and its accompanying mythology by participating in essay contests held around Jackson Day. The third grader Christine Tarwater informed all of Nashville that "Gen. Andrew Jackson made breastworks of mud and cotton bales" after he "formed a small army of Tennessee riflemen." A classmate of Tarwater's further elaborated: "When the British came up the bank at New Orleans they laughed" because "Andrew Jackson's men were just squirrel shooters." The Tennesseans soon halted the British laughter, even though Jackson only "had one cannon." The backwoodsmen put the field piece to effective use, firing "scraps of iron and spikes." Despite the dramatics, Everett Carlton summed up the moral of the story nicely, proclaiming, "From that day on the British never fought with the Americans."[17]

Everett Carlton probably never realized it, but in third grade he succinctly explained the driving theme of Battle of New Orleans commemorations around the United States in 1915, namely, one hundred years of peace between Great Britain and the United States. Rather than focus on a war marked by domestic unpopularity and fought between nations whose international relations had greatly improved, the United States, Great Britain, and Canada chose to highlight the Treaty of Ghent. In the United States, the development of the Perry's Victory and International Peace Memorial on Lake Erie exemplified these efforts. In Great Britain, the government sponsored the promotion of a grand Anglo-American exposition. The exposition, as planned, would last six months and celebrate peace, prosperity, and the advancement of the arts and sciences that became possible when nations did not go to war.[18]

In a tragic twist of fate, Anglo-American plans to celebrate peace experienced a dramatic change as Great Britain entered World War I. Logistically, the United Kingdom could no longer honor its commitment to hold the planned grand exposition. Further, it became increasingly dangerous for Americans and Britons to traverse the Atlantic Ocean because of German naval activities. As a result, the American Peace Centennial Committee, along with its sister agencies in Great Britain and Canada, decided to modify the events planned for 1915. The American group called for the "postponement of all public rejoicing until the war in Europe is ended." The only exceptions would be "churches, schools and colleges in the program of peace celebrations already arranged." Negotiation between Canada and the United States resulted in a limited future schedule of official events. President Woodrow Wilson still spoke at the unveiling of a monument to the Treaty of Ghent in Washington, DC, and made a national address on December 24 to mark the day the peace commissioners had signed the treaty. Finally, New Orleans would host a three-day event for the centennial of the war's last major battle. The century "of peace between English-speaking peoples which followed that battle" was to be the focus of the occasion.[19]

As politic as an emphasis on peace would be, it did not always sit well with some Americans. Until war actually began in Europe, some women involved in memorialization efforts such as those of the Daughters of 1812 and the Ladies Hermitage Association rejected the idea of emphasizing the peace rather than the battle that had brought it. Writing to the *Nashville Tennessean,* one woman expressed concern that she had only heard plans to commemorate the Treaty of Ghent and peace. She remarked that the *New York Times* had recently published drawings of "a costly bridge across the Niagara River and huge memorial monuments at Detroit." She was at a loss to explain how any commemoration of the peace treaty could occur without "some very large hint of Gen. Andrew Jackson and his victory over the British forces at the world-famous Battle of New Orleans." Without Jackson and his men, the "unparalleled prodigious success, which demolished British forces, driving them from [American] shores by land and sea" would have left the Treaty of Ghent a "rope of sand."[20]

Mary C. Dorris shared similar sentiments. She penned a historical treatment summarizing the War of 1812 and the Treaty of Ghent for the *Nashville Tennessean,* which ran her story under the large bold headline "Treaty of Ghent—Last Stand Against American Liberty."[21] The editors assured their readers that the long piece contained "an absorbing narrative of how Americans, forced to fight the British a second time on account of injustices and outrages on the high sea, carried the War of 1812 to a victorious climax with the signing of the Treaty of Ghent." They also explained that "the figure of Andrew Jackson looms high above any other American in this war, and the writer has vividly visualized the stalwart American General." Despite the efforts of peace centennial committees in Great Britain, the United States, and Canada to temper the celebratory aspect of the 1915 commemoration, Tennesseans had their own plans.

Mary Dorris took her case directly to the Ladies Hermitage Association later that year. She suggested that a commemoration of the battle, and not the Treaty of Ghent, "ought now to bend our energies and attention." And not surprisingly, the LHA leant a sympathetic ear. After all, whatever was good for the memory of the Battle of New Orleans bolstered the memory of Andrew Jackson, which in turn benefited the preservation efforts of the LHA. Just like the Mount Vernon Ladies Association in Virginia and the Daughters of the Republic of Texas, the Ladies Hermitage Association faced the political and ethical realities of their commemoration efforts. These groups had a vested interest in defending the historical understanding that most profited the promotion of their respective topics regardless of current politics or even the most recent scholarship. The US government's preference for a change in the commemorative efforts to focus on peace rather than martial success threatened the LHA's carefully constructed narrative of the battle. For the Ladies, the greatest son of the Volunteer State had led an army of backwoods frontier Tennessee rifleman in a desperate gamble that saved the Louisiana Purchase for the United States. If that event had not occurred, then why would anyone donate money to preserve Jackson's mansion and promote the history? The centennial festival arranged by the LHA in Nashville existed to promote the Ladies' interpretation of the battle, not to preserve the diplomatic relations of the United States.[22]

The LHA mustered all of its available clout in the Nashville-area business and political communities. The group successfully petitioned local railroad operators to offer tickets to and from the city at a reduced rate on the day of the centennial. They also encouraged local businesses to give their employees a day off work on the holiday. The festivities opened with a two-mile-long parade that included numerous area organizations. Marching bands saluted the crowd with airs of both "The Star-Spangled Banner" and "Dixie" as the column moved toward the state capitol building. Behind the bands, units of local police, Confederate veterans, and Tennessee National Guard soldiers formed, adding a martial element to the proceedings.[23]

Once the procession arrived at the capitol building, the grand event of the Nashville Battle of New Orleans centennial celebrations commenced. For weeks, newspapers had teased their readers with promises of a sham battle meant to re-create Jackson's famous victory. Event organizers built a replica of the "fort" the Tennesseans had hid behind one hundred years earlier. The structure consisted of cotton bales placed near the steps of the state capitol building. The rather elaborate structure stretched the length of a number of city blocks and stood shoulder high to the men placed behind it.[24]

Confederate veterans had the honor of portraying the Tennessee soldiers who served under Andrew Jackson. Dressed in Confederate uniforms and wielding Civil War–era muskets and campaign equipment, the men valiantly fired blank rounds at the troops of the Tennessee National Guard. Smoke filled downtown Nashville as the khaki-uniformed National Guardsmen fell before the withering fire of the Confederate veterans. Eventually, with the "British" assault decimated, the attackers slowly retreated, leaving the cheering Confederates in command of the state capitol. One Confederate veteran interviewed after the event pridefully noted, "The boys in grey are the victors." Another newspaper remarked that "the old guard were there" and that "it was an inspiring site to watch these veterans in battle lines again and to hear the 'crack, crack' of their rifles in the battle on the boulevard."[25]

Other events only obfuscated further which war the events sought to commemorate. At the Hermitage, Mary Dorris—the same woman who wanted to make sure that the battle's memory took precedence over the peace treaty's—laid a wreath on Jackson's tomb. A gift of the Thomas Hart Benton Chapter of the Daughters of 1812, the wreath was made from tree branches from the Civil War–era Battle of Franklin site. Presumably, the USD chapter chose Franklin because of its nearby location and its association as the site of a famous Tennessee military event. Yet the selection of Franklin was ironic because Confederate forces had fought the battle in a useless attempt to take a heavily entrenched Union position. In fact, the Battle of Franklin stands as one of the Civil War's most needless engagements and as a testament to the foolishness of charging a heavily fortified enemy. Dorris had fought tirelessly both to highlight the importance of the New Orleans battle despite its late date during the War of 1812 and to promote the idea of American (and southern) superiority by emphasizing British arrogance in charging Jackson's line in 1815. Lost Cause ideals dominated white southern culture in the twentieth century though. It is not clear that anyone in attendance saw the paradox of placing a wreath gathered from the location of a Confederate military disaster on the tomb of a man who had once uttered the words, "Our federal union; it must be preserved."[26]

Untroubled by these inconsistencies, the Nashville celebrations proceeded as planned. The LHA arranged for the culminating events of the festivities to be a grand banquet at the Maxwell House and the annual Jackson Day Ball at the Hermitage Hotel. At the banquet, the city elite sat among local politicians, judges, the governor of Tennessee, and the chancellor of Vanderbilt University. The banquet speeches centered on the need for a new, grander memorial to Jackson reflecting the importance of the Battle of New Orleans. If the state did not provide for the monument, then "Tennessee has degenerated," said one speaker. Apparently still unaware of the commemoration's many ironies, another informed the crowd of wealthy supporters that "Jackson was a student of the common people" and a man "who restored this government to the plain people."[27]

After the banquet, the three hundred attendees left for the ball. To commemorate the one hundredth anniversary, the Ladies Hermitage Association had planned a special event. At the beginning of the ball, "eighteen of Nashville's most popular girls," wearing "gowns of white, sashes of red, and badges of blue," entered the ballroom. Each girl wore a badge bearing the name of one of the eighteen states in the Union at the time of the battle. Around the room, the LHA hung banners proclaiming the names of Jackson's military victories during the conflict, along with laurels of Spanish moss and cotton bolls, cotton reportedly having played an important part in Jackson's victory.[28]

The Ladies Hermitage Association's plans for centennial celebrations in Nashville occurred just as advertisements for the events said they would. By all accounts, the festivities were a resounding success, if not quite what the peace centennial committees in Washington and London had in mind. The ceremonies in Nashville were nothing if not triumphant, and in the recorded speeches there was little about the importance of peace and understanding between English-speaking peoples.[29]

Though a celebration of the War of 1812 and the Battle of New Orleans, the Nashville centennial ceremonies could not escape the shadow of the Civil War and Reconstruction. The events became an opportunity to highlight southern military prowess in the wake of the South's greatest defeat. The commemoration efforts in Nashville typified a South still struggling with the memory of its past and trying to find a way to rewrite the history of the Civil War. At the same time, the ceremonies in Nashville marked a distinct success for the idea behind groups like the Daughters of 1812. Promotion of the battle once again encouraged patriotism in southerners. It might be a patriotism that skewed the historical facts when convenient, but the centennial ceremonies in Nashville had managed to persuade Confederate veterans literally to march again to the beat of the "Star-Spangled Banner."

The centennial celebrations in New Orleans shared many similarities with the Nashville ceremonies. Because events in the Crescent City carried the official sanction of the American Peace Centennial Committee, organizers were more concerned about British sensitivities. According to the official program, at 8:20 a.m. on Friday, January 8, 1915, the Louisiana National Guard began a twenty-one-gun artillery salute timed so "that the last shot will be fired exactly one hundred years after the last cannon was discharged from the American lines." The careful timing continued until 10:15 a.m., as public-school children from around the city departed a train station en route to the battlefield. Less than an hour later, the adults boarded a fleet of small watercraft in a "river parade" descending the Mississippi.[30]

At the battlefield, the celebrants cheered as a Congreve rocket arced above the crowd and the drum of Jordan Noble sounded "The Long Role," marking noon and the opening of the ceremonies. A series of speeches were followed by a wreath-laying on the Chalmette Monument by the Ladies Hermitage Association. Made from evergreens growing on General Jackson's old property, the LHA's choice appeared more apropos than the one selected for Jackson's tomb by the Tennesseans. After the wreath-laying, the festivities continued with the flag-raising detailed earlier. The ceremonies in Chalmette concluded with a close-order-drill demonstration by the Seventh US Infantry Regiment, the unit that had guarded the extreme right of Jackson's line one hundred years earlier.[31]

Elsewhere in New Orleans, other events celebrated various aspects of the New Orleans campaign. The YMCA sponsored a six-and-a-half-mile race from Lake Pontchartrain to the French Quarter. The run commemorated the Orleans Battalion of Volunteers's forced march from Fort St. John to join Jackson's column descending the river on the night of the British landing. The Ursuline nuns hosted a benediction, Te Deum, and hymn to Our Lady of Prompt Succor, to whom the nuns had prayed the night before the final battle. Mrs. W. C. C. Claiborne, president of the Ursuline Academy Alumni Association and a direct descendant of the governor of Louisiana at the time of the battle, gave the opening address.[32]

The festivities lasted well into the first night. Military bands played in Lafayette and Jackson Squares, and the Louisiana National Guard and the Louisiana Naval Battalion hosted a military ball for visiting US Army and US Navy units. At the Athenaeum, the Women's Section of the American Peace Centennial Committee oversaw an event featuring historic tableaux by students. The scenes depicted women sewing clothes for soldiers, a campfire scene of American troops guarding the Rodriguez Canal, and a street scene of the troops' triumphant return. Period dances conducted in period costumes closed out the opening day.[33]

While the second day of festivities largely centered on the activities of the Louisiana Historical Society and the unveiling of what eventually became the Louisiana State Museum, the third day opened in spectacular fashion. The event organizers arranged for a reenactment of the elaborate ceremony the city had conducted upon Jackson's return after the battle. Twenty women adorned in white "Greek robes" stood in Jackson Square. Eighteen of them wore sashes with the names of the eighteen states of the Union in 1815, and two wore sashes bearing the words *justice* and *liberty.* The girls paraded in two lines from the gated entrance of Jackson Square to the doors of the St. Louis Cathedral, forming a corridor. A Mr. Charles C. Hard, playing the role of Andrew Jackson, entered the line of girls and received the "palm of victory" from the woman representing Louisiana. The "general" and his staff made their way to the steps of the cathedral, where the Right Reverend J. M. Laval greeted them. Laval played the part of Abbe Dubourg, the highest-ranking priest in New Orleans at the time of the battle. Laval gave the exact speech Dubourg had given a century earlier and then placed a laurel-wreath crown upon Hard's head. Hard then turned to the crowd and, addressing "Abbe Dubourg," gave Jackson's speech as onlookers had recorded it one hundred years earlier. With that, the assembly proceeded inside the cathedral.[34]

After a High Mass, a parade marched from Jackson Square to Jackson Avenue, three miles away. The procession included mounted police, state officials, and schoolchildren, followed by members of fraternal organizations such as the Knights of Columbus, the Woodsmen of the World, the Elks, and the Druids. Unlike in Nashville, the name of no Civil War patriotic organization appeared in the official program of the centennial ceremonies. Granted, members of the Daughters of 1812 could also be members of the Daughters of the Confederacy, but the UDC apparently had no official role in the centennial ceremonies.[35]

Unlike in Nashville, the specter of the Civil War did not hang over the centennial ceremonies in New Orleans. Rather, World War I affected the mood of the centennial ceremonies in New Orleans. When organizers originally planned the events, they envisioned a reenactment of the battle occurring on the location of the original event. To add to the novelty, descendants of the battle's original participants would defend what remained of the ramparts. By the time of the final preparations, though, the reality of World War I trench warfare had begun to unfold. Suddenly, the idea of showing "British soldiers" charging an entrenched position seemed extremely insensitive and politically incorrect.[36]

Instead, events and commentators focused on the marked contrast between the centennial events and the horrors of Europe. They emphasized the century of peace between Great Britain and the United States, suggesting that if other nations got along as well as the two Anglophone countries did, there would be less violence in the world. Many of the speakers made overt efforts to avoid any sense of triumphalism.[37] The description of Samuel Wilson's speech is representative. He "dwelt at length on the Battle of New Orleans and the events that led up to it. He was lavish in his praise for everyone connected with the victory; but brought out the fact that the greatest result was not the victory itself but in the century of peace that followed it."[38]

One of the few exceptions to this trend occurred during the International Peace Banquet on the second night. After a round of toasts at the Hotel Grunwald, Major General Franklin Bell, of the US Army, rose to speak. He assured the crowd that "the army of the United States stood for peace" and had "always stood for peace." A nation that prepared to defend itself did not automatically deserve the accusation of militarism. Clearly responding to the antiwar movement in the United States and the pacifism expressed numerous times at the centennial's events, Bell suggested that "the soldier does not protest that you teach your children it is disgraceful to fight for his rights." He added, "The soldier has the right to protest, and does protest, against turning the other cheek whether right or wrong. Every human right that has been won . . . has been won at the point of the sword." At that point a disgusted spectator shouted "No!," but those shouting "Yes!" drowned out the attempted rabble-rouser.[39]

The American Peace Centennial Committee's efforts to avoid offending Great Britain and Canada during the Battle of New Orleans commemorations went well, probably better than most had hoped. Not only had the forum provided an opportunity to focus on the friendship between the Anglophone nations, but it also offered an opportunity for encouraging the United States to side with Britain should America enter the war.

For the Daughters of 1812 in New Orleans, the event had also been a great success. Despite the meager and sometimes superficial commemoration of the battle that had occurred at the beginning of the century, by 1915 the Daughters had helped to reinvigorate interest in Jackson's victory. The attention again paid to the event dramatically reduced the likelihood that the monument and what remained of the ramparts would succumb to Chalmette's growing industrialization. Could the Daughters translate the new public interest into the financial or political clout necessary to expand the battlefield?

Prior to the centennial, the Daughters paid for the construction of a five-room on-site caretaker's cottage. In June 1915 Marcel Serpas became the caretaker and moved into the cottage with his family; the Serpases remained the caretakers of the Chalmette battlefield for seventeen years and even named one of their children Andrew Jackson Serpas, at the urging of the Daughters of 1812. The Serpas children gave tours of the site and also gathered the pecans the Daughters sold, eventually receiving a portion of the proceeds as their salary. Marcel also kept the money from the ten-cent deposit charged to visitors for borrowing the key to the monument in order to climb to the observation deck at the top. Despite the hopes of the Daughters, visitation remained low following the centennial commemoration, averaging only one group per day. Despite the advances in transportation, Chalmette was simply too far off the path of most tourists, and the site had little to offer beside the monument. In 1929 the Daughters informed the War Department that their organization could no longer serve as the financial stewards. If the US government wanted to preserve the site of Jackson's famous victory, it needed to take over the management of the site.[40]

The federal government doubted it could do a better job. While to maintain the current property cost only twelve hundred dollars annually, expanding it would cost significantly more. Because of the rampant industrialization surrounding the site, the War Department felt that failing to expand the park's footprint would only result in to even lower attendance, as businesses were constructing factories only a hundred yards from the monument. Congress balked at spending the necessary money, as the War Department contended against influential industrial interests desirous of the same land. Despite the monetary concerns, the government realized that if it could barely plan on winning the battle to preserve the site, it certainly could not ask the Daughters of 1812 to do so. The Daughters had done as much work as they could, and Secretary of War Patrick Hurley informed Congress that if it wished to preserve the site "in a manner commensurate with the importance of a great national victory," the federal government had to help.[41]

Though the New Orleans Daughters of 1812 had not been as successful as the Ladies Hermitage Association in fund-raising for their historic site, they played an important role in preserving and shaping the memory of the Battle of New Orleans. By the closing years of the nineteenth century, the commemoration of the battle had faded considerably. The nation still struggled with the events of the Civil War, and the efforts of groups like the United Daughters of the Confederacy only further intensified the mythologies and the romanticism of the Lost Cause. The western South had always been the epicenter of Battle of New Orleans celebration, but by the 1880s fewer and fewer southerners commemorated Jackson's victory. Women's organizations like the LHA and the Daughters of 1812 used the UDC's methods to reinvigorate public attention about the War of 1812 and the Battle of New Orleans. White southerners in Nashville and New

Orleans quickly bought into the renewed interest. It gave them an opportunity to focus on a portion of their past that highlighted the success of their ancestors rather than the failure of the Confederacy.

These successes did not occur without controversy. In Nashville, the UDC held enough power to insert itself into the Battle of New Orleans commemorations, and the reenactment of the battle embodied a Lost Cause sentiment. Further, the Nashville commemorations highlighted the power of the Civil War's memory. Southerners linked the Battle of Franklin, an overwhelming Confederate defeat, with a ceremony meant to commemorate the state of Tennessee's greatest military victories. The pain of the Civil War's loss altered Tennessee's historical memory.

The Louisiana ceremonies, while a dramatic celebration of Anglophone peoples' friendship, paid almost no attention to the role of nonwhite English speakers. The use of Jordan Noble's drum at the Chalmette ceremonies represented one of the only references to any African American participation in the battle. In a showcase of white pride meant to symbolize Anglo-American unity, many New Orleanians also conveniently forgot that many of their ancestors who had fought in the New Orleans campaign had spoken French. The proud Creoles of New Orleans had often used every trick at their disposal to preserve the Gallic nature of the city in the face of what they perceived as a torrent of Anglo-American immigration. The political needs of the present, though, dictated a focus on Anglo-American unity.

Great Britain and the United States needed that unity as the two nations prepared for possible joint military action. Accordingly, the federal government exerted its influence to halt Anglophobia or triumphalism from entering into the official commemoration. One cannot help but wonder how an ardent Anglophobe like Jackson felt about such sentiments. Then again, what Jackson would have wanted the commemoration to consist in mattered little; more important was what various segments of early twentieth-century America needed the commemoration to consist in and the Battle of New Orleans's legacy to mean.

NOTES

1. *New Orleans Times-Picayune,* 9 January 1915.

2. For more on the formation of the Daughters of the Confederacy and their impact on southern culture and the Lost Cause, see Karen L. Cox, *Dixie's Daughters: The United Daughters of the Confederacy and the Preservation of Confederate Culture* (Gainesville: University Press of Florida, 2003); and John A. Simpson, *Edith D. Pope and Her Nashville Friends: Guardians of the Lost Cause in the Confederate Veteran* (Knoxville: University of Tennessee Press, 2003).

3. For an excellent work on the history of women's patriotic organizations in general see Wallace Evan Davies, *Patriotism on Parade: The Story of Veterans' and Hereditary Organizations in America, 1783–1900* (Cambridge, MA: Harvard University Press, 1955). On the Daughters of 1812 specifically, see Frank J. Douglas, Robert Bachman, George Lynn Woodruff, and LeRoy Habenight, *National Society of United States Daughters of 1812, 1892–1989: History* (Metairie, LA: National Society of United States Daughters of 1812, 1989). On the role of groups like the Daughters of the Republic of Texas in the South, see Gregg Cantrell, "The Bones of Stephen F. Austin: History and Memory in Progressive-Era Texas," *Southwestern Historical Quarterly* 108, no. 2 (October 2004): 145–78.

4. Louisiana Act No. 8 (17 January 1894); An Act Providing for the Completion by the Secretary of War of a Monument to the Memory of the American Soldiers who fell in the Battle of New Orleans at Chalmette, Louisiana, and Making the Necessary Appropriation Thereof, 59th Cong., 2nd sess. (4 March 1907).

5. For more on the difficulties of administering historic homes, see Sherry Butcher-Younghans, *Historic House Museums: A Practical Handbook for Their Care, Preservation, and Management* (New York: Oxford University Press, 1993); and Patricia West, *Domesticating History: The Political Origins of America's House Museums* (Washington, DC: Smithsonian Institution Press, 1999).

6. Charles H. Browning, *American Historical Register and Monthly Gazette of the Patriotic-Hereditary Societies of the United States of America,* vol. 3 (Philadelphia: Historical Register, September 1895–February 1896), 400, 507.

7. F. Arnemann to United States Daughters, 1776 to 1812, 6 December 1909, in United States Daughters of 1812, Chalmette Chapter, Papers, Tulane University Special Collections, New Orleans; House Report No. 81 to accompany House Resolution 2232, An Act in Reference to a National Military Park on the Plains of Chalmette (19 November 1921).

8. From 1880 to 1915, prominent statues to memorialize the Confederacy appeared all over New Orleans, at considerable expense. The famed American sculptor Alexander Doyle produced five of the most famous statues: Washington Artillery Cenotaph (1880), Robert E. Lee Monument (1884), "Calling the Roll" (1886), General Albert Sydney Johnston Equestrian Statue (1887), and General P. G. T. Beauregard Equestrian Statue (1915). Considering the time it took to get Andrew Jackson's statue placed in Jackson Square and to get the Chalmette Monument completed, the Civil War clearly dominated southern minds and philanthropic donations in this period. For more on the role of statuary in memory and memorialization,

see Kirk Savage, *Standing Soldiers, Kneeling Slaves: Race, War, and Monument in Nineteenth-Century America* (Princeton, NJ: Princeton University Press, 1997).

9. Aline Gray Roberts, ed., *Celebrating One Hundred Years of the TN State Society United States Daughters of 1812* (n.p., 2009).

10. Mary C. Dorris, *Preservation of the Hermitage, 1889–1915: Annals, History, and Stories; The Acquisition, Restoration, and Care of the Home of General Andrew Jackson by the Ladies Hermitage Association for Over a Quarter of a Century* (Nashville, 1915).

11. Ibid.

12. Tom Kanon, "Forging the 'Hero of New Orleans': Tennessee Looks at the Centennial of the War of 1812," *Tennessee Historical Quarterly* 71, no. 2 (Summer 2012): 139–40. Kanon's article is an indispensable examination of Tennessee's attitudes toward both the Creek War and the War of 1812, one hundred years later.

13. Quoted in ibid., 137.

14. *Nashville Tennessean,* 21 June 1914; *Nashville Banner,* 9 January 1915; *Nashville Tennessean,* 22 July 1914.

15. Ladies Hermitage Association Board of Directors, Meeting Minutes, January 1906–September 1914, 129, Collections at the Hermitage, Nashville.

16. Reau E. Folk, *Battle of New Orleans: Its Real Meaning; Exposure of Untruth Being Taught Young America Concerning the Second Most Important Military Event in the Life of the Republic* (Nashville: Ladies Hermitage Association, 1935).

17. *Nashville Tennessean,* 21 January 1917.

18. Ibid., 12 April 1914. For more on the Ohio monument to the Battle of Lake Eerie, see *Interstate Board of the Perry's Victory Centennial Commissioners: Watterson, Henry, 1840–1921; The Perry memorial and centennial celebration under the auspices of the national government and the states of Ohio, Pennsylvania, Michigan, Illinois, Wisconsin, New York, Rhode Island, Kentucky, Minnesota and Indiana* (Cleveland, OH: The Board, 1912).

19. *Nashville Tennessean,* 29 November 1914.

20. Ibid. 28 March 1912.

21. Ibid., 22 March 1914.

22. Ladies Hermitage Association Board of Directors, Meeting Minutes, 141.

23. *Nashville Banner,* 8 January 1915.

24. Ibid., 9 January 1915.

25. Ibid.; *Nashville Tennessean,* 12 January 1915.

26. "The Celebration of Jackson Day, January 8, 1915," *Tennessee Historical Magazine* 1 (March 1915). For more on the Battle of Franklin, see James L. McDonough and Thomas Lawrence Connelly, *Five Tragic Hours: The Battle of Franklin* (Knoxville: University of Tennessee Press, 1983). There is also the irony that during the Battle of New Orleans Thomas Hart Benton was vehemently anti-Jackson; he had shot the general just a year before the British attacked the Gulf Coast. Jackson still carried Benton's bullet in him throughout the New Orleans campaign; and he did return it to Benton after they became friends again twenty years later.

27. Quoted in Kanon, "Forging the 'Hero of New Orleans,'" 149.

28. *Nashville American,* 3 January 1915.

29. *Nashville Tennessean,* 21, 27 December 1914.

30. *The Battle of New Orleans, Official Programme* (New Orleans: Louisiana Historical Society, 1915), 8.

31. Ibid., 8–9.

32. Ibid., 10.

33. Ibid., 10–11.

34. Ibid., 11–13; *New Orleans Times-Picayune,* 11 January 1913.

35. *Battle of New Orleans, Official Program,* 13–16.

36. *New Orleans Times-Picayune,* 12, 22 October 1914; Battle of New Orleans Scrapbook, 1815–1940, Louisiana Historical Center, Louisiana State Museum, New Orleans.

37. *New Orleans Times-Picayune,* 8–11 January 1915.

38. Ibid., 9 January 1915.

39. Ibid., 10 January 1915.

40. Robert W. Blythe, *Administrative History of Jean Laffite National Historical Park and Preserve* (Atlanta: Cultural Resources Division, Southeast Regional Office, National Park Service, 2013), 28–29.

41. House Report No. 194 to accompany House Resolution 6151, An Act to authorize the Secretary of War to assume the care, custody and control of the monument to the memory of the soldiers who fell in the Battle of New Orleans, at Chalmette Louisiana, and to maintain the monument and grounds surrounding it (2 June 1930); Secretary Hurley, quoted in Blythe, *Administrative History,* 30.

8

Continually Heroic
Portraying Andrew Jackson through Classical and Contemporary Heroic Devices

LESLIE GREGORY GRUESBECK

Prior to the Battle of New Orleans in 1815, Andrew Jackson was not a man whose image was widely recognized. He was noted as a military figure, having made his reputation as an Indian fighter and backwoods lawyer. The public was aware through talk that General Jackson was a man of great will who was sometimes given to great temper, but accounts of those who had met Jackson after hearing such rumors were filled with pleasant surprise at his impeccable manners and gentlemanly gestures. After the Battle of New Orleans was won, the public clamored for images of the country's newest hero. George Washington had been such a figure for the American public and had also played a heroic part in the founding of the nation and the defeat of the British. Now, sixteen years after Washington's death in 1799, the American public was ready to lavish adoration upon its new hero. Artists from American and Europe began creating a wealth of images portraying both Jackson and the Battle of New Orleans. This image-making would continue throughout Jackson's political career, including his presidency and beyond. In fact, much of this imagery would help shape the public's opinion of Andrew Jackson and help make his reputation one befitting a man who played increasingly more public and powerful roles, including that of our nation's hero.

Jackson remains one of the most widely painted presidents. He grew in status among the American citizenry first as the war hero, and he continued to excite and entice the public as he served as a statesman and then pursued the office of president. First attempts to portray the forty-eight-year-old Jackson often missed the mark. Jean François de Vallée, a French artist, painted an ivory miniature of the general that portrayed him as younger and in better health than he really was.[1] After all, one's heroes must be youthful, for in youth one has stamina and vigor and virility. From the ancient Greeks forward, artists have clung to this ideal. Vallée's miniature is painted in the Empire manner so popular in Napoleonic France, so that Jackson appears current in his styling and, perhaps at least in Vallée's mind, like Napoleon in magnitude. Although Vallée's depiction of Jackson may not have been immediately recognizable to the general American public, it was at least flattering. The portrait is a three-quarter-length view, the general's left shoulder turned slightly toward the background. Jackson looks full forward at the viewer. His abundant hair, not gray or white but instead of an almost reddish hue, is combed forward.[2] Although Jackson is dressed in military garb, he bears a slight resemblance to a courtier observing Napoleon's crowning in Jacque-Louis David's great work *Coronation of Napoleon in Notre-Dame,* completed between 1805 and 1807, with which Vallée may well have been familiar, as David's status as court painter to Napoleon was widely known.

Jackson must not have been displeased by the image, which he accepted and then presented to Edward Livingston, the American statesman appointed as US minister to France by Jackson in the 1830s, along with a note of thanks and friendship. Both the image and the note were made into engravings by Alexander Hay Ritchie in 1864 for publication in Charles Hunt's *Life of Edward Livingston* (see www.questia.com/read/9010537/b200766pn09/view), but not before the Vallée image was copied with less skill by Major Arsène Lacarrière Latour, Jackson's chief engineer during the Battle of New Orleans, for use as the frontispiece to his 1816 *Historical Memoir of the War in West Florida and Louisiana* (see www.ufdc.ufl.edu/UF00103020/00001/54j), which he dedicated to the general. Latour was a mapmaker, not a portrait artist; his copy of the Vallée miniature is crude at best and quite unflattering, which probably was not Latour's intention.[3]

The Latour engraving is not the only unflattering portrait of General Jackson. There were many, partially because of the popular practice of enlisting a limner, an itinerant, often untrained artist, to create portraits. This

FIG. 8.1. Jean François de Vallée, *Andrew Jackson.* Miniature, watercolor on ivory, 1815. Historic Hudson Valley, Pocantico Hills, New York, Gift of J. Dennis Delafield (MP.91.11 a-b).

custom began in America as portraiture became a popular status symbol—something it had long been in Europe. These artists, who often began as sign painters, traveled from town to town, supplying signs and portraits to the populace. And that populace wanted portraits of General Jackson, much as it had wanted images of Washington. Fortunately, many professional, highly trained artists also made portraits of General Jackson, including Nathan Wheeler, John Wesley Jarvis, Ralph E. W. Earl, Thomas

Sully, George Peter Alexander, Samuel Waldo Lovett, Rembrandt Peale, Anna Claypool Peale, and Jacques Amans.

Over time, artists portraying the Battle of New Orleans and Jackson came to rely upon sometimes ancient devices to illustrate power and importance. For instance, one is hard pressed to find a popular image of the battle that does not feature Jackson as the largest figure in the composition. Granted, Jackson was thin and tall, but in such images he is markedly larger than his fellow fighters. This device, which art historians refer to as hieratic scale, dates from the time of the Sumerians, about 4000 BCE, and the concept behind it is quite simple. The largest person in the composition is the most important and has the greatest power. Often in ancient art, that size and power placed the ruler in closer contact with the heavens and therefore closer to the ultimate power, the god or gods worshipped by the culture.

One popular example of hieratic scale is a series of lithographs illustrating the Battle of New Orleans issued by the lithographers Nathaniel Currier and James Merritt Ives in 1842. Currier and Ives were among the most important lithographers in the United States. Lithography was still in its infancy, having been invented by the German printer Aloys Senefelder in 1796.[4] Currier and Ives produced what they referred to as "Cheap and Popular Prints" on subjects ranging from melancholy events of the day to kitschy vignettes. They produced four prints dedicated to the Battle of New Orleans, as well as several prints illustrating the life of General Jackson, from one depicting his legendary childhood encounter with the English officer whose boots young Jackson refused to shine to a very dramatic interpretation of the president on his deathbed.[5]

In Nathaniel Currier's print *The Battle of New Orleans Fought Jany. 8, 1815*, General Jackson is depicted prominently in the right foreground, mounted on a white steed and impeccably garbed in full military regalia. His figure is the largest in the composition. He sits erect in the saddle, his face turned toward the viewer rather than toward the action surrounding him. Directly behind him and slightly smaller are his officers, also mounted. And all around the mounted Jackson are the firing troops—British and American—weapons, and a levee of cotton bales "protecting" the Americans from the British army, yet another bit of legend, which makes the entire battle more exciting and remarkable to the nostalgic audience at whom this print was aimed. One might view this as a example of atmospheric perspective, in which the artist makes objects closer to the viewer larger and objects further away smaller. However, the outsized Jackson cannot be denied status as the predominant character in these images.

There are many similar illustrations. In some compositions, Jackson stands upon the cotton bales, his coat tails waving dramatically behind him. Often he holds in one hand a spyglass, sometimes retracted, sometimes extended. A spyglass might not be necessary at all, as Jackson, whether on horseback or standing, is so close to the action of the front line, and so far above the front line. Sometimes a halo of gun and cannon smoke frames the general's placid visage. This sense of serenity and calm in the midst of mayhem is yet another characteristic of imagery of the heroic and royal—going back as far as the smooth, serene faces of the pharaohs and early Egyptian and Greek statuary. Washington too is often portrayed with this immense sense of calm—even in crossing the icy waters of the Dela-

FIG. 8.2. Nathaniel Currier, *The Battle of New Orleans Fought Jany. 8, 1815*, 1842. Prints and Photographs Division, Library of Congress, LC-3b49845u.

ware River in the famous, albeit slightly inaccurate painting *Washington Crossing the Delaware,* by the German artist Emmanuel Leutze. The hero's calm amid chaos shows that he is in command.

Often in these scenes, such as in the Currier and Ives print mentioned above, the only thing larger than Jackson is the resplendent, enormous American flag waving triumphantly in the distance. This flag may be symbolically larger than life, overwhelming in size, like the enormous flags that wave above car lots today. The flag reminds the viewer of the importance of America's liberty, which the Battle of New Orleans certainly represented, as well as the greatness of the United States. The flag may also represent a merging together on the part of the artists of images of the Battle of New Orleans with images the action that took place at Fort McKinley, where the flag made famous by Frances Scott Key in "The Star-Spangled Banner" waved. This hand-sewn wonder, measuring 30 feet by 42 feet, had been raised over Fort McKinley to signal American victory over the British at the Battle of Baltimore on September 14, 1814.[6] This overlapping imagery allowed the artist to further instill a sense of patriotism in the viewer and to indicate Jackson's importance. The imposing Jackson, whether on horseback or tall astride a cotton bale, reigning above the battle as an enormous American flag waves triumphant behind him, certainly convinces the viewer of Jackson's heroic nature.

Andrew Jackson's hair is another unavoidable topic. Historically, and even prehistorically, power has been illustrated by an abundance of hair. Early statues often had a healthy head of hair ornately arranged—like those on the Woman of Willendorf and the Lady of Brassempouy. Healthy hair in these cases may have been associated with fertility and general good health, both of which are considered attractive and reflect the power and ability to successfully reproduce and prosper. Assyrian cult figures (3000 BCE) often exhibit thick, abundant hair, as do Sumerian figures. In Egyptian art and culture (3000 BCE to 100 CE), as in eighteenth-century European cultures, massive wigs were styled to fit the roles of leaders. The stories of poor Sampson's plight once his hair was cut illustrate the importance of hair not only as representative of health and power but as the source of actual power. Because of this association of hair with power, many religions have very specific rules about how hair should be cut (or not cut), styled, or covered, not to mention whether it should be touched or seen.

Alexander the Great (356–323 BCE), another leader whose conquests and triumphs might be thought of as on the same scale as Jackson's, wanted images of him to be visually consistent.[7] He hired the sculptor Lysippos (390–300 BCE) to create a standardized portraiture. These portrait sculptures embody the visual standards that became representative of Alexander, especially his unruly hair and his renowned cowlick. Alexander's cowlick, like Jackson's, is emblematic of the wild, unbridled nature that allows heroes to conquer. Additionally, this unruly hair, like youthfulness, is a sign of virility and health. Into this history of health, power, sexuality, and strength comes Andrew Jackson. Jackson's hair has been described in texts as unruly and unkempt during his young days as a lawyer and Indian fighter. It ranges in portrayals from an extremely straight, high pompadour of solid white to a loose, tousled graying mane with a pronounced cowlick at the part. Jackson's hair, like Alexander's, befits a great conqueror. Portraits of Jackson vary as to the style and color of his hair, perhaps to emphasize certain personality traits. Thomas Sully's portraits of the cowlicked Jackson are probably the most familiar. It is Sully's portraits that are referenced on the US twenty-dollar bill and were re-created on a US postage stamp in 1903. In one of these paintings, a bust-length portrait completed in 1845, shortly before Jackson's death—the study for which Jackson sat in 1824—Sully portrays Jackson thoughtfully looking leftward; a dark cloak encases his shoulders. A small hint of white collar adds emphasis to the turn of Jackson's head and, above all, the uncontrolled curling mane. The engraver Thomas B. Welch, in 1852, blended the stylizing of the 1845 Sully with some exaggerations of style found in a portrait once attributed to Sully that hangs in the collection of the US Senate. These include the hair, the eyebrows, and facial furrows.[8]

Robert Eleaser Whiteside Earl, an artist whose career was intertwined with Jackson's, created many portraits of the general during his years as Jackson's "court painter." Earl first met and painted Jackson in 1817 at the Hermitage. Jackson and his wife, Rachel Donelson Jackson, embraced the young painter. Through Rachel Jackson, Earl met and married Jane Caffrey, a favorite niece of Mrs. Jackson's. But less than a year after the couple wed,

FIG. 8.3. Thomas Sully (attributed), *Andrew Jackson.* Oil on canvas, mounted on board, c. 1857. Collection of the United States Senate, Washington, DC.

Caffrey and her unborn child died during childbirth.[9] Earl remained active in the Jacksons' lives from this point on, even serving as a liaison between Jackson and other artists. Historians debate Earl's talent and intent. James G. Barber, in his 1991 book devoted to the imagery of Jackson, *Andrew Jackson: A Portrait Study,* refers to Earl thus:

At best, Ralph E. W. Earl's prospects as an artist were limited. His style was more primitive than refined, his portrait more wooden than lifelike. Earl probably would have had a difficult time sustaining himself in the cities along the eastern seaboard. His chances of success were not much better in the back country, where demand was less and, next to the axe and plow, portraits were deemed a luxury. Seemingly, the most he had in his favor were a few complimentary letters of introduction written on his behalf shortly after his arrival in Georgia.[10]

Although she praises Barber's attention to Earl's work, Rachel Elizabeth Stephens, in her 2010 dissertation, "America's Portraitist: Ralph E. W. Earl and the Imaging of the Jacksonian Era," speaks more to the impact Earl's portrait work had on Jackson's public image:

Based on his artistic lineage and European training, Earl assisted Jackson in using portraiture as political propaganda in the service of identity formation. As the first president elected by the people, not the Electoral College, Jackson was truly a democratic President, and he displayed his commitment to the people by becoming the first president to invite the public to his inauguration. Orphaned during the American Revolution as a teenager in the western Carolinas, Jackson trained to be a lawyer and moved to Tennessee in 1788. His 1791 marriage to Rachel Donelson connected him to one of Nashville's oldest families, yet his roots were humble. Jackson's conflicting identity as a rising star on the western frontier and a rough neck country gambler would become something Jackson would publicly grapple with for the rest of his life. Jackson became the first Tennessean on the national stage and the state's first Senator. The image Jackson projected and his actual background were fraught with tensions, and he employed Earl to remind the public of his heroics and respectability.[11]

Jackson, like Alexander the Great, clearly understood the importance of consistent visual imagery. Because of his singular relationship to Jackson and his family, we see in the series of Earl portraits—more than thirty-six of Jackson over a period of more than twenty years[12]—an interesting transition in hairstyles and styling in general. Earl's portraits of Jackson, as well as those of Rachel and her entire extended family, have a remarkable impact on the public perception of the Jacksons. In Earl's first portraits of Jackson, about 1817–18, Jackson's hair is brushed forward but with great lift and action; it is not highly coiffed. In these early portraits, whether full- or half-length portraits, Earl portrays Jackson as the military hero of the Battle of New Orleans. Dressed in military uniform, including a dark blue uniform coat very similar to the actual coat worn by Jackson in 1818, Jackson looks slightly to the viewer's left. In the full-length portrait, Jackson extends his right hand in the same direction as his head, to gesture to the left side of the canvas with his spyglass. In his left hand he holds his hat, which rests just above his left knee. Because of the accuracy of the details of the coat in these portraits, Barber believes that they may "indeed have been reasonably faithful."[13] As Jackson moves from the role of war hero to that of prominent citizen and finally president, Earl's depictions vary in pose and costume, but Jackson's visage and distinctively abundant hair become more standardized. "The variety of sizes, settings, and poses in Earl's canvases," writes Barber, "was seemingly endless and the demand was seemingly insatiable. Jackson, however, always looked the same, as if the artist had reproduced his facial features with a large rubber stamp!"[14]

Stephens notes the same effective use of costume to advance the pictorial message: "Earl would go on to meticulously depict, among other sitters, Andrew Jackson dressed variously as a civilian and a statesman later in his career. Earl Jr. seemed to realize from a young age that one's attire in a portrait played a large role in the painting's message."[15] But Stephens builds a more reasonable case for this standardization of Jackson's features in these portraits, which includes Jackson's hair combed gently back from his forehead, a more controlled yet substantial head of brilliant white. "Earl's repeated imagery of Jackson pictured him in ways similar to what . . . texts describe and reinforced a new widespread viewpoint for Jackson. His portraits cemented these positive ideas about his sitter in the popular imagination."[16] Stephens's point is salient, and the artistic merit of Earl's ability to render is really a non-issue. Earl did standardize the image of Jackson, creating a sort of brand that presented to the public a believable hero, a conscientious statesman, and a gentleman farmer. Earl's portraits have transcended time; even present-day audiences recognize Earl's portraits as being of Jackson.

The number of equestrian paintings and statues of Andrew Jackson are evidence that audiences love and admire the hero on a mount. Equestrian statuary can be traced back to the ancients. Triumphant rulers on horseback date from the time of the Mesopotamians (third century CE), who created scenes like that of the victorious Shapur I on horseback granting mercy to the defeated Roman emperors, Philip the Arab and Valerian. Possibly the most famous equestrian statue is that of Marcus Aurelius, which dates from 161–80 CE. The larger-than-life-size bronze survived being melted for scrap in the medieval period because Christians mistook the Roman emperor for Constantine the Great, the great champion of Christianity.[17] This work inspired the Renaissance artists Donatello and Verrocchio, who created large, imposing equestrian statues of the mercenary generals Gattamelta and Colleoni, respectively.[18] Although the equestrian statue has long been a device to elevate the ruler to even greater heights—often the rider is portrayed with a supplicant beneath the foot of the horse—until Clark Mills cast the enormous bronze equestrian statue of General Jackson, no sculptor had been able to portray a rider on a rearing steed without a visible counterweight. Mills's piece was praised in its day for accomplishing this engineering feat. There are four castings of this work. The first was cast for installation at Lafayette Park in Washington, DC, in 1853. A second was made and installed in 1856 in the Place D'Armes, in New Orleans, to commemorate the Battle of New Orleans. A third casting was commissioned for the east plaza of the Tennessee State Capitol in the 1880s. The fourth was commissioned in 1987 and placed in Jacksonville, Florida, in commemoration of Jackson's contributions to the settlement of Florida by Americans (see www.dcmemorials.com/index_indiv0000800.htm).[19]

In the 1920s, according to Andrew S. Keck, art historians and critics began to question the aesthetic contributions of the piece. In their view, it lacked the grandeur and emotion of seventeenth- and eighteenth-century equestrian statues. This might be attributed to the debate over craft versus fine art that was emerging as the American art scene struggled to define itself. Keck recalls two critics in particular who lambasted Mills's work: Lorado Taft and Charles Rufus Morey. Taft, a historian and sculptor, wrote in *The History of American Sculpture:*

Who begrudges to-day this brave pioneer his little meed of success? Let us hope that he never became conscious of his defects. No one of that first generation is more completely the machinist. His grasp of his subject is a purely mechanical one; his motif in the statue a problem of equilibrium. Having no notion, nor even suspicion, of dignified sculptural treatment of theme, the clever carpenter felt nevertheless the need of a "feature." Perhaps he had heard of "action"! Possibly he had seen an engraving of Palconet's Peter the Great. At any rate, he built a colossal horse, adroitly balanced in the hind legs; and America gazed with baited breath. Nobody cares whether the rider looks like Jackson or not; the extraordinary pose of the horse absorbs all attention, all admiration. There may be some subconscious feeling of respect for the rider who holds on so well, but in spite of his frank efforts to call attention to himself, the appeal is as meager as his personal charm, as precarious as his seat.

Morey, in the 1927 book *The Spirit of American Art,* sums up his dislike of the Mills bronze thus:

He has at least the distinction of creating both our first and worst equestrian monument. The tour de force of balancing the defender of New Orleans so gallantly upon his rearing steed absorbed the craftman's small creative ability; Mills was a caster rather than a modeler, giving the same metallic texture to Jackson's head, the horse's hide, and the holster, hat, and stirrup.[20]

These critics may have their points, and while Keck does agree that Mills's bronze lacks the naturalism and intricate modeling that previously created equestrian statues may have shown, he says that that was not the intent of the statue. Rather, the intent of this work was to present Jackson, both the hero and the president, as a man of the people, and to do so by focusing on a commanding silhouette.

His task was to present to an uncritical public a military hero who was a man of the people and a champion against aristocracy and privilege. Democracy and Equality were to be celebrated in this country in 1850 and not Aristocracy and Hierarchy. It is to the great credit of Clark Mills that he was sensitive to the spirit of his country and found the means to express its ideals as well as he did. His statue must be judged not in terms of the Seventeenth Century but in those of his own day, the Nineteenth Century.[21]

Certainly the use of this same silhouette as the backdrop to thousands of images of visitors to New Orleans each year, who line up diligently in Jackson Square to snap their own photos in front of General Jackson and his mount, as well as its appropriation for the Battle of New Orleans Bi-Centennial Commemoration on the state of Louisiana's auto plates, reinforces the power of Mills's image.

Jackson is portrayed on horseback not just in sculpture but in two-dimensional work as well. Again, a war hero and the nation's leader riding a fine steed is an image that one finds over and over throughout art history, including images of Jackson's contemporaries. And in most of the Jackson equestrian portraits created during Jackson's lifetime, the general is dressed in military garb. Sometimes he is alone on his horse, but more often he is presented, as in the Currier and Ives work mentioned above, in the midst of conflict. Regardless, Jackson's visage reflects a knowing placidness and a sense of control, as if he is sure of a positive outcome to the action going on around him. Interestingly, Jackson is portrayed on a variety of horses, even in depictions of the same scene. In one of Jackson's favorite portraits by Earl, he is shown on a white steed named Sam Patch, presented to Jackson by the citizens of Philadelphia in 1833.[22] Other artists depict Jackson, almost randomly, on a brown horse, a black horse, and, in an endearing primitive watercolor in the holdings of the Museum of Fine Arts Houston, a dappled horse. Again, the overriding impression is that these repetitious, very standardized images are working to solidify Jackson's status as a hero and a statesman.

Not everyone was an admirer of Andrew Jackson. His detractors were also eager to render Jackson, and their less flattering propaganda used ancient devices to show the extent of his evil. He is portrayed in *Office Hunters for the Year 1834*, a negative cartoon attributed to James Akin, as the devil, looming large in the sky above a sea of men seeking office and jobs within the "spoils system." Akin relies on hieratic scale to illustrate Jackson's overwhelming evil.[23]

Edward Williams Clay satirizes Jackson often through the use of the enthronement pose. This pose is associated with the early Greeks, who built monumental statues of gods and goddesses seated upon thrones. The figures face full forward and stare downward at the supplicants below. The popularity of this pose may be attributed to the influences of neoclassicism on the artists of the day. Neoclassicism in America was driven in part by

Thomas Jefferson's promotion of the movement as the "official architecture of the new American republic." The movement spread across America at the time of the American Revolution because ancient Greece and Rome served as models of enlightened political organizations. So by Andrew Jackson's era, enthroning a leader in a classically inspired seat or creating his toga-draped likeness in marble already had a short yet established precedent in American art.[24]

In Clay's 1831 cartoon *The Rats,* Jackson is depicted in the enthronement pose, but in a broken chair. This widely popular cartoon lampoons the president by illustrating him as enthroned but perplexed, the house crumbling around him and four rats with human heads scuttling about his feet in an attempt to reach safety. Clay reworked *The Rats,* using the same devices and diversifying the cast, in another lithograph from 1831 entitled *00001—The value of a unit with four cyphers going before it.*[25]

In 1834, Clay produced his famous broadside *King Andrew the First,* which does not rely on an enthronement pose of hieratic scale but instead portrays Jackson in a formal, full-length royal portrait with the throne visible behind him. Not dissimilar from those of English royalty and certainly meant to refer visually to David's portrayals of the emperor Napoleon, both at his coronation and on his throne, this engraving shows the president in full regalia, include ermine-lined cloak, crown, and scepter. But this regal portrayal is far from admiring. Clay shows "King Andrew" trampling the Constitution and alludes to other misuses of his power as president.[26]

And it was not just cartoonists who cast Jackson and his ideals in a less than friendly light. The founder of the Hudson Valley school of American landscape painting, Thomas Cole, was not a fan of Jackson or populism. And he painted about the evils of populism in his five-part series of allegorical paintings entitled *The Course of the Empire,* in which Jackson is cast as Caesar.

In *American Visions,* the art historian Robert Hughes writes about Cole's disenchantment with Jacksonian politics and his fears that populism might undermine not only the landscape, which he viewed as America's natural asset, but also the landed gentry for whom Cole painted, thus having an impact on his career. Hughes writes that "*The Course of the Empire*

FIG. 8.4. Edward Williams Clay, *King Andrew the First.* Lithograph, 1834. Tennessee Historical Society Collection, Tennessee State Museum, Nashville.

offers a cynical view of history. If America was a new Rome, as the Federalists have hoped, then Cole's series was meant to be a visual analogue to Edward Gibbon's *Decline and Fall of the Roman Empire.*"[27]

Cole painted these works for the New York millionaire Luman Reed, who owned a semipublic collection of art. The first work, *The Savage State* (1834), is a primitive scene. The second, *The Arcadian or Pastoral State* (c. 1836), features circular, Stonehenge-like architecture, circles of young girls dancing, and pastures filled with flocks being tended. The painting represents the ideal pastoral state of the early republic.[28] Of the third work, *Consumption* (1836), Hughes writes:

> The lesson of what can go wrong with the State unfolds in the third painting. . . . No more agrarian simplicity of the early Republic. Populism has led to mob rule, the fickle mob begets dictatorship, a culture of spectacle and patronage reigns. Here comes Caesar across the bridge, in triumph, holding the palm of victory and the trumpet of fame, with his slaves, lictors, and presumable corrupt senators. Cole didn't go so far as to give him Andrew Jackson's face, but he didn't need to, since both he and Luman Reed felt the moral would be plain enough.[29]

The fourth work, *Destruction,* and the fifth, *Desolation* (both 1836), complete the cycle. *Destruction* illustrates the fall of the imperial city as it is being overrun and sacked. The bridge that bore the triumphant Caesar is collapsing under the weight of embattled armies. *Desolation* emphasizes the landscape's return to the natural. Mere ruins of the former grandeur remain as the wilderness returns.[30]

Regardless of the artist's views on Jackson as a man and on Jackson's politics, Jackson remains heroic in present-day representations. Though heroic ideals have shifted slightly, some remain tied clearly to antiquity. The cover art for the soundtrack to the 2010 musical *Bloody, Bloody Andrew Jackson* features Jackson as a rock-and-roll star. Showing a man's lower waist and backside in tight blue jeans, an American flag tucked into his left back pocket, it is clearly an homage to the cover of the American rock star Bruce Springsteen's album *Born in the USA.* Jackson, like Springsteen, cocks his right hip out, but Jackson's hip holds a holstered gun, and his right hand appears ready to draw it. Springsteen's rock-star image—that of purely American and purely working class—is a fitting counterpart for Jackson. Both represent the working man, the self-made man, as well as the hero who is a bad boy and representative of the base power of sexuality.[31]

A California-based artist who displays his work through the art website deviantART.com using the name SharpWriter presents Jackson as a superhero in his work *"Iron" Andrew Jackson: Alien Slayer* (2011) (see www.sharpwriter.deviantart.com/art/Andrew-Jackson-Alien-Slayer-202767355). Superheroes became popular-culture icons during World War II, often por-

FIG. 8.5. Cover art by Jessica Disbrow Talley for the original cast recording of *Bloody, Bloody Andrew Jackson,* Ghostlight Records, 2010.

traying the ability of the everyday man or woman to transform himself or herself into a superhuman. The extra abilities of SharpWriter's superhero are used to rescue the rest of humanity from its plight. In *"Iron" Andrew Jackson,* Jackson appears clad in a military-inspired yet space-age metallic suit (the costume does reference earlier military portraiture); his physique appears muscular. From the center of his breastplate, or blue military coat, shines a light like that of the popular American superhero Iron Man, whose mortal name is Tony Stark. Jackson's right arm appears to have been replaced with a super-space-age laser gun; in his right hand is the head of a slain alien. Over his back he carries what appears to be an enormous sheathed sword. Fire rages behind Jackson. Says the artist of his work:

In the year 2055 the world was invaded, humanity sat on the brink of destruction the work governments united and sent agents back in time to get the best general we'd ever known . . . Andrew Jackson and throughout his life he did a lot of cool shit, dueled people . . . a lot of which is how he ended up with a musket ball in his chest pretty much like exactly Tony Stark. Went to war, gambled, etc. etc. This is a war portrait as he stands victorious in yet another battle.[32]

SharpWriter's admirers reply to him with comments like the following: "Were Andrew Jackson president right now, I thoroughly believe that this is the image he would pick to be his official presidential portrait"; "Andrew Jackson might . . . I say might actually have been more of a ass than George Washington"; and, "He was literally one of the worst humans to ever live, but nice pic anyway man."[33]

Youthfulness is still a mighty draw for audiences today, and it is likely to remain so. Television, print, and web ads still emphasize the importance of youth. Youth represents perfection, strength, energy, vitality, and sexuality today as much as it did in antiquity. The public is inundated with images that re-create celebrities—who are another form of hero—to make them look younger than their actual chronological age. Jackson was subjected to this in his own early days of celebrity. Many artists portrayed the general as more youthful than he really was. Often portraits of Jackson showed fewer gray hairs, healthier skin, and perhaps a plumper face. This sort of treatment was not unusual in portrait painting of the day. The subject should look his or her best, and sometimes that involved a little fudging. Interestingly, Jackson has received a similar treatment recently. In a redesign of US currency to make it more difficult to counterfeit, Jackson's image on the twenty-dollar bill has received a facelift, as have images of several other Founding Fathers and notable statesmen. The New York surgeon David Hidalgo commented in *Newsweek* magazine that the aged Jackson looked younger and more feminine: "President Jackson has been treated with injectables to fill his temple hollows and laugh lines (nasolabial fold). His lower-eyelid fat bags have been removed to make him less tired looking, but he has acquired an overall 'surgical look' in the process."[34] Although Americans have shaped and reshaped him into a perfect, youthful celebrity, the image remains that of a heroic figure, if seemingly vain.

Whether beloved or maligned, Andrew Jackson and the image he helped curate in his own time are pivotal to American perception of the hero and whom we perceive as heroic. From the perpetuation of ideals from early antiquity to express his importance to more contemporary interpretations that emphasize new archetypes, Jackson has continually been heroic.

NOTES

1. James G. Barber, *Andrew Jackson: A Portrait Study* (Washington, DC, and Seattle: National Portrait Gallery, Smithsonian Institution, and Tennessee State Museum, Nashville, in association with the University of Washington Press, 1991), 36.

2. Ibid., 28.

3. Ibid., 37.

4. Aloys Senefelder, *The Invention of Lithography,* trans. J. W. Muller (New York: Fuchs & Lang, 1911), 12, Project Gutenberg e-book, www.gutenberg.org/files/40924/40924-h/40924-h.htm.

5. "The History of Currier & Ives," The Currier & Ives Foundation, 1997–2011, accessed 22 December 2014, www.currierandives.com.

6. "Star-Spangled Banner and the War of 1812," The Star-Spangled Banner Project, National Museum of American History, Behring Center, in cooperation with Public Inquiry Services, Smithsonian Institution, accessed 22 December 2014, www.si.edu/Encyclopedia_SI/nmah/starflag.htm#pageTop.

7. Penelope J. E. Davies, Walter B. Denny, Frima Fox Hofrichter, Joseph Jacobs, Ann M. Roberts, and David L. Simon, *Janson's History of Art: The Western Tradition,* 8th ed. (Upper Saddle River, NJ: Prentice Hall, 2012), 154.

8. "Andrew Jackson by Thomas Sully," Office of the Senate Curator, accessed 22 December 2014, www.senate.gov/artandhistory/art/artifact/Painting_32_00018.htm.

9. Barber, *Andrew Jackson,* 43.

10. Ibid., 42.

11. Rachel Elizabeth Stephens, "America's Portraitist: Ralph E. W. Earl and the Imaging of the Jacksonian Era" (PhD diss., University of Iowa, 2010), 15, accessed 24 December 2014, ir.uiowa.edu/etd/3538.

12. Barber, *Andrew Jackson,* 43.

13. Ibid., 44.

14. Ibid., 135.

15. Stephens, "America's Portraitist," 31.

16. Ibid., 199.

17. Davies et al., *Jansen's History of Art,* 206.

18. Frederick Hartt and David G. Wilkins, *History of Italian Renaissance Art,* 6th ed. (Upper Saddle River, NJ: Prentice Hall, 2006), 19.

19. James M. Goode, "Four Salutes to a Nation: The Equestrian Statues of General Andrew Jackson," *White House History,* no. 27 (110): 1–18, www.whitehousehistory.org/whha_publications/publications_documents/whitehousehistory_27-goode.pdf.

20. Lorado Taft and Charles Rufus Morey, quoted in Andrew S. Keck, "A Toast to the Union: Clark Mills' Equestrian Statue of Andrew Jackson in Lafayette Square," *Records of the Columbia Historical Society, Washington, D.C.,* 1971–72, 292–93, www.jstor.org/stable/40067778.

21. Ibid., 297, 299 (quotation).

22. Barber, *Andrew Jackson,* 143.

23. Akin's 1834 lithograph *Office Hunters for the Year 1834* is in the Peters Collection, National Museum of American History, Smithsonian Institution, Washington, DC.

24. Fred S. Kleiner, *Gardner's Art through the Ages: A Global History,* 14th ed. (Boston: Wadsworth, 2013), 728 (quotation), 745.

25. Barber, *Andrew Jackson,* 156.

26. Ibid., 157.

27. Robert Hughes, *American Visions: The Epic History of Art in America* (New York: Knopf, 1997), 147. Thomas Cole's series *The Course of the Empire* (1834–36) is at the New-York Historical Society, New York.

28. Hughes, *American Visions,* 149.

29. Ibid.

30. Ibid., 150.

31. *Bloody, Bloody Andrew Jackson,* original cast recording, Ghostlight Records, 2010, compact disc, music and lyrics by Michael Friedman and Alex Timber, cover art by Jessica Disbrow Talley.

32. SharpWriter, *"Iron" Andrew Jackson: Alien Slayer,* deviantArt.com., 29 March 2011, accessed 22 December 2014, sharpwriter.deviantart.com/art/Andrew-Jackson-Alien-Slayer-202767355.

33. Ibid.

34. David Hidalgo, quoted in Daniel Stone, "Did Founding Fathers on Currency Get Facelifts?" Newsweek.com, Newsweek LLC, 6 April 2011, accessed 23 February 2014, www.newsweek.com/did-founding-fathers-currency-get-facelifts-70365.

9

The Battle of New Orleans in Popular Music and Culture

TRACEY E. W. LAIRD

In 1959, Johnny Horton's version of "The Battle of New Orleans" reached the top of Billboard's Hot 100 singles chart, and it remains among the top US popular songs of the twentieth century.[1] While many of the battle's historical details fall away, the lyrics communicate the gusto and attitude of a band of American underdogs whose strategy and skill sent their foes "runnin' on down the Mississippi to the Gulf of Mexico." Horton's catchy version still circulates at camps for Scouts and remains a well-known singalong, especially the refrain. At the same time, the song invites questions as to how this recording, along with other music and culture about the Battle of New Orleans, reflects its time, its purpose, and its audiences, as well as how and why those elements have changed over the years.

Horton's cover was based on a song written in 1936. An Arkansas school principal with a love for both music and history aimed to reinvigorate the story for his teenaged students by giving it a melody. James Morris Corbitt, better known as Jimmy Driftwood, composed "The Battle of New Orleans" as a contrafactum based on the fiddle tune "Eighth of January," which had been recorded by both black and white fiddlers in the early twentieth century.[2] The longstanding practice of writing contrafacta, or adding new words to already existing melodies, dates from a time when the printed page was far less common. In general, contrafacta allow a text to be learned and remembered easily whether for religious purposes, entertainment, or to memorialize an important historic event.

FIG. 9.1. Transcription for fiddle melody for "Eighth of January." Courtesy of *Bluegrass Unlimited.*

Driftwood's particular choice of music, titled "Eighth of January" for the battle date in 1815, bears a typical fiddle-tune structure: two contrasting eight-measure lines (A and B) based on simple, straightforward harmonies, each of which can be repeated and varied multiple times to keep the dancers' feet moving. Driftwood retained the two-part melodic structure but slowed down the tempo, inserted extra beats in between certain lines, and added lyrics that include many highlights of the battle, told from a soldier's perspective with a sense of both distance and humor:

> Well, in eighteen and fourteen we took a little trip
> along with Colonel Jackson down the mighty Mississip.
> We took a little bacon and we took a little beans,
> And we caught the bloody British near the town of New Orleans.[3]

Driftwood's original version includes a verse that mentions Jean Lafitte meeting with the future president "Mars Jackson," emphasizing an attitude of defiance in the face of the British threat:

Well, I seeʼd Mars Jackson walkin down the street
talkin' to a pirate by the name of Jean Lafitte
He gave Jean a drink that he brung from Tennessee
and the pirate said heʼd help us drive the British in the sea.

He follows this with a verse about Jackson's determination to "whup the britches" off the British. The action builds slowly in Driftwood's song, depicting the British advancing with great pomp and show and the Americans waiting quietly behind their cotton bales, squirrel guns in hand. These narrative portions correspond to the more harmonically active of the two fiddle lines, while the more static second line corresponds to the refrain. In short, the refrain interrupts the forward progress of the narrative to remind the listener of the ultimate British defeat:

We fired our guns and the British kept aʼcomin';
there wasn't nigh as many as there was a while ago.
We fired once more and they began to runnin'
on down the Mississippi to the Gulf of Mexico.

More than two decades after Driftwood composed the song, Horton's cover distilled the material to its essence, boiling ten verses down to four. From the original lyrics his version culls only the most critical stanzas and thus speeds up the narrative action. He skips, for example, references to Lafitte and a verse like the one below, reflecting on the importance of this military victory for Jackson's future presidential bid:

We'll march back home but we'll never be content
till we make Old Hickory the people's President.
And every time we think about the bacon and the beans,
we'll think about the fun we had way down in New Orleans.

Horton does, however, retain the funniest verse:

Well, we fired our cannon til the barrel melted down,
so we grabbed an alligator and we fought another round.

We filled his head with cannon balls and powdered his behind,
and when they tetched the powder off, the gator lost his mind.[4]

In the Horton arrangement the refrain occupies a more central position, appearing after every verse. This move further highlights the refrain variation that marks the musical height of the song:

Yeah, they ran through the briars and they ran through the brambles
and they ran through the places where a rabbit couldn't go.
They ran so hard that the hounds couldn't catch'em,
On down the Mississippi to the Gulf of Mexico.[5]

Horton's timing for the variation creates a satisfying sense of dramatic apex (occurring approximately at the "golden ratio") that is effective enough that he repeats it at the end. Musically speaking, the production choices in Horton's recording take full advantage of the song's potential drama. Its military theme is emphasized by the insertion of snare-drum licks and marching syllables ("hut, two, three, four" in the background). In addition to military evocations, Horton infuses greater rhythmic drive and momentum through his hard-edged vocal delivery, interspersed with growls and upturned ornaments to punctuate some of the lines.

Driftwood's contrafactum and Horton's interpretation of it connect to a musical history of fascination with the War of 1812 in general and the Battle of New Orleans in particular that dates back to the event itself. Two of the United States' most enduring patriotic songs in fact come from the War of 1812. "Hail to the Chief," written in honor of President James Madison, still accompanies appearances by US presidents, although its words are largely forgotten.[6] The song destined to become the nation's official anthem was penned after a dramatic conflict at a critical eastern seaport. After burning Washington, DC, the British had moved toward the Chesapeake Bay in the first of three strategic attacks. The British plan had been to follow the Chesapeake Bay offensive by securing Lake Champlain and therefore their claims to territories in the Northeast by attacking from New York; the final assault would secure the mouth of the Mississippi River at New Orleans, again strangulating trade, and therefore American independence, via the country's main economic artery. America's success in the battle for Baltimore inspired Francis Scott Key to write "The Star-Spangled Banner." His 1814 poem recounted his view of the "rockets' red glare," "the bombs bursting in air," and the relief and exaltation that when the smoke cleared, "our flag was still there," a sight he beheld from the British ship to which he had been sent as an emissary and detained during the combat.[7] He set these words as a contrafactum based on the British drinking song "To Anacreon in Heaven."[8]

Yet of all the battles fought, it was the final confrontation in the War of 1812, already noteworthy for its enduring cultural artifacts, that inspired the most copious responses from writers, artists, and musicians. January 8, 1815, was two weeks after the Treaty of Ghent, an official ending to the hostilities unbeknownst to both Andrew Jackson and Edward Pakenham, who commanded the British troops. Yet the incongruity of dates does not diminish the significance of the Battle of New Orleans both real and remembered. Politically speaking, the battle effectively stifled any lingering aspirations on Great Britain's part to reclaim its former territories. More importantly, it sealed America's confidence regarding its own preeminence in the Western Hemisphere, which would become official US policy with the Monroe Doctrine in 1823. Johnny Horton aside, time has tempered the battle's significance. We no longer celebrate January 8 with the fervor of our nineteenth-century ancestors, distant as we are from the idea that a different outcome would have positioned the British to reclaim some of what they had lost during the American Revolution. For those living closer to the time of the battle, that significance was worth dwelling upon.

The years immediately following the Battle of New Orleans saw a number of creative responses, including musical, theatrical, literary, and visual remembrances. The New Orleans pianist and composer Philip Laroque, for example, published a programmatic piece in 1818 titled "Battle of the Memorable 8th of January," which depicted cannon fire and other scenes from the conflict.[9] Writers and artists would commemorate the event as well. An author named C. E. Grice published a play in 1816 titled *The Battle of New Orleans, or Glory, Love and Loyalty; an Historical and National Drama, in Five Acts.*[10] That same year a Philadelphia engraver named Joseph Yeager created *The Battle of New Orleans and death of Major General Packenham*

FIG. 9.2. Etching by George Willig, used as title page of sheet music for Philip Laroque's programmatic piano piece titled "Battle of the Memorable 8th of January." Prints and Photographs Division, Library of Congress, LC-USZ62-55789.

[sic] on the 8th of January, 1815. Memorials continued in the decades to follow. Examples include the 871-line epic poem *General Jackson's Victory at New Orleans,* published in 1827 by Richard Emmons; an 1840 lithograph by John Landis; an 1862 piano piece by Charles Grobe; a nostalgic Civil War–era song sheet by Eug. T. Johnston titled "Old Hickory's Days"; and other works.[11]

In short, the Battle of New Orleans resonated longer in popular culture than any other War of 1812 confrontation, partly because its details constituted the raw potential ingredients for a good story. Indeed, some of the legendary aspects of the fighting exceed the confines of verifiable fact, yet they remain no less powerful in popular memory. Outnumbered by the British foes, the resistance forces comprised an unlikely mishmash of regular soldiers and volunteers: Haitian refugees, riflemen from the Tennessee and Kentucky backwoods, and pirates led by Lafitte. The alligator-filled swamps, the cotton bales doubling as American barricades, the hodgepodge of weaponry from proper cannons to squirrel guns, and the unexpectedly rapid quashing of the British foes were colorful enough to spark the imagination. More than any other individual participant, the bold and audacious General Andrew Jackson proved an irresistible character, and his success secured a reputation that would eventually sweep him into the presidency on a tide of populism fueled at least in part by musical and other artistic tributes.[12]

Among the musical commemorations of the resounding British defeat was a song written soon after the fighting ended that was also titled "The Battle of New Orleans."[13] Likely written shortly after the fray, the song con-

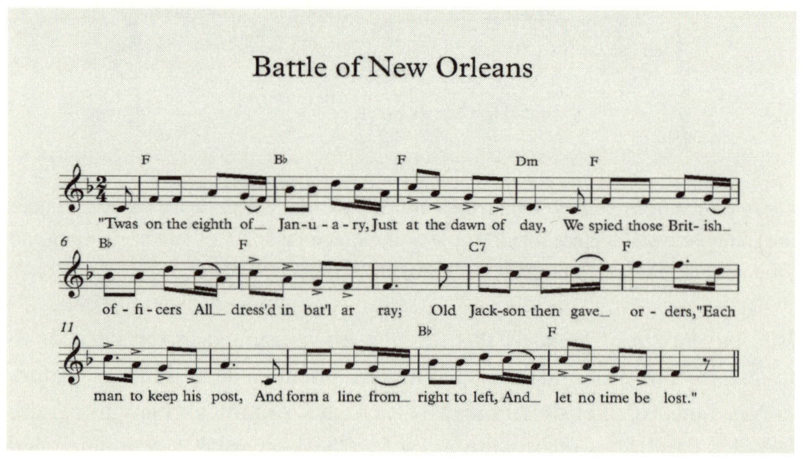

FIG. 9.3. Musical notation for 1815 song titled "The Battle of New Orleans." Reprinted from Silber, *Songs of Independence*, 213.

veys a more direct point of view than does the twentieth-century song. Its simple, four-line structure—AA'BA—proceeds economically in only four stanzas. The first stanza sets the scene from the perspective of an American soldier, who likely composed it, establishing date and time and then recounting sights of the advancing British soldiers and sounds of Jackson booming orders.[14]

The two inner verses describe battle images of rockets and bombs and reckon the suffering and loss of life on both sides. This sense of immediacy and horror of the war experience comes through at the end of each inner stanza. The second ends, "While many a brave commander lay withering in his gore." The third paints the scene in still more gruesome terms: "Great heaps of human pyramids lay strewn before our eyes; we blew the horns and rang the bells to drown their dying cries." The final stanza shifts to an attitude of riposte, a message to the British and the closest in mind-set this song gets to its twentieth-century successor.

> With rockets and with bombshells, like comets we let fly;
> Like lions they advanced us, the fate of war to try;
> Large streams of fiery vengeance upon them we let pour,
> While many a brave commander lay withering in his gore.
>
> Thrice they marched up to the charge, and thrice they gave the ground;
> We fought them full three hours, then bugle horns did sound.
> Great heaps of human pyramids lay strewn before our eyes;
> We blew the horns and rang the bells to drown their dying cries.
>
> Come all you British noblemen and listen unto me;
> Our Frontiersman has proved to you America is free.
> But tell your royal master when you return back home,
> That out of thirty thousand men, but few of you returned.

Despite the mild swagger in the final stanza's lyrics, the melody as a whole is mellow, almost wistful in character. In musical terms, the tune alternates gently between the tonic and subdominant chords, with a notable submediant (deceptive cadence) at the end of each stanza's first line.

The contrasting B melody line (B in each AA'BA stanza) stands out against the overall even keel: it begins with the only appearance of the dominant harmony; it dwells on the highest note of the melody (F5) for nearly a full measure; and it employs the song's only dotted-eighth-note rhythms.

The relative contrast of each B line draws attention and emphasis to it in a way that marries the lyrical and musical momentum. The third lines include the peak poetic phrases, a Cliffs Notes–type summary for the entire song: "Old Jackson then gave orders, 'Each man to keep his post'"; "Large streams of fiery vengeance upon them we let pour"; "Great heaps of human pyramids lay strewn before our eyes"; "But tell your royal master when you return back home."

During the nineteenth century, the extent to which a song or its performance moved the listeners' passions was often the measure of its success. As one contemporary observer wrote, "Music is to be understood as a powerful assistant to sentimental expression (I speak here of vocal music) which, by the power of its charms, enforces our attention to some natural passion of mankind."[15] Images of gore, human pyramids, and the cries of the dying wounded evoked and aroused emotions through the lyrics and, when performed by a soloist, presumably through the musical interpretation. In that way the song typifies its era.[16]

Even a little distance from the fighting engendered songs with less emphasis on the grim reality of battle and more on the conflict's more colorful elements, including boasting rights of the American victors. "The Hunters of Kentucky" recounts the triumph of Jackson's troops over British forces with a focus on the role played by Kentucky sharpshooters with long rifles.[17] The lyrics were from a poem written by Samuel Wordsworth and published in a New York newspaper called the *Mirror.*[18] In 1822, an actor and singer named Noah Ludlow was in New Orleans preparing for a run of performances and looking for a new song with which to kick off his show. He had come across Wordsworth's poem and experienced a moment of inspiration.

He set the poem as a contrafactum on the melody of an older song, "Miss Bailey,"[19] which tells the bawdy story of a girl who hangs herself after being seduced by a captain and then haunts the captain because the local parson refuses to bury her in consecrated ground; when the captain offers to bribe the parson to "bury her properly," her shade happily departs.[20]

Ludlow's new song retains the narrative AABB' ballad structure of the original, along with its mostly tonic-dominant harmonies dressed up by one secondary dominant in the initial B line. Each four-line stanza is interrupted by a refrain half as long: "Oh Miss Bailey, unfortunate Miss Bailey" in the original became "O Kentucky, the hunters of Kentucky" in Ludlow's song. Meanwhile, the stanzas celebrate a battle that would have been fresh in the minds of the performer's New Orleans audience.

On the night of its first performance, Ludlow decked himself out in buckskin and rifle, a sight that brought him "heavy applause, the thunder of stomping feet, and prolonged whoops" even before the song began.[21] He performed it as an "in-character song," a convention familiar to nineteenth-century audiences in which the singer, often with props and costume, acted out the lyrics to increase its emotional impact.[22] The first verse calls attention to "ye gentlemen and ladies fair, who grace this famous city," and announces that they are about to enjoy a rare opportunity to "see a hunter from Kentucky." The proceeding verses alternate several themes. Some reflect on the bravery and derring-do of Kentucky hunters ("We are a hardy free born race, each man to fear a stranger; / whate'er the game, we join in chase, despising toil and danger"). Others dwell on the threat to New Orleans represented by Pakenham:

> I s'pose you've heard how New Orleans is fam'd for wealth and beauty.
> There's gals of ev'ry hue, it seems, from snowy white to sooty;
> So, Pakenham he made his brags, if he in fight was lucky,
> He'd have their gals and cotton bags in spite of old Kentucky.

Throughout the song, verses emphasize the wherewithal and alertness of General Jackson, as well as his reliance on his Kentucky volunteers: "Behind it [a raised bank] our little force; none wish'd it to be greater; / For ev'ry man was half a horse, and half an alligator."[23]

The song went over so well that the audience demanded to hear it three times that first night, and the touring Ludlow performed it frequently for years to come. It also became a campaign song for future president Andrew Jackson, who took office in 1828. In an era characterized by a populist shift of public sentiment, "The Hunters of Kentucky" celebrated the type

FIG. 9.4. Two-page piano score from c. 1824 for "The Hunters of Kentucky." Courtesy of Baylor University Libraries Digital Collections, Baylor University, Waco, TX.

2nd We are a hardy free born race, each man to fear a stranger;
Whate'er the game, we join in chase, despising toil and danger;
And if a daring foe annoys, what e'er his strength or force is,
We'll show him that Kentucky boys are alligators, horses.
O Kentucky &c.

3rd I s'pose you've read it in the prints, how Packenham attempted
To make Old Hickory Jackson wince, but soon his schemes repented:
For we with rifles ready cock'd, thought such occasion lucky,
And soon around the general flock'd the hunters of Kentucky.
O Kentucky, &c.

4th I s'pose you've heard how New Orleans is fam'd for wealth and beauty,
There's gals of ev'ry hue, it seems, from snowy white to sooty;
So Packenham he made his brags, if he in fight was lucky,
He'd have their gals and cotton bags in spite of old Kentucky.
O Kentucky, &c

5th But Jackson he was wide awake, and wasn't scar'd at trifles,
For well he knew what aim we take with our Kentucky rifles;
So he led us down to Cypress Swamp, the ground was low and mucky;
There stood John Bull in martial pomp; but here was old Kentucky.
O Kentucky, &c.

6th We rais'd a bank to hide our breasts, not that we thought of dying,
But then we always like to rest, unless the game is flying;
Behind it stood our little force: none wish'd it to be greater;
For ev'ry man was half a horse, and half an alligator.
O Kentucky, &c.

7th They didn't let our patients fire before they show'd their faces;
We didn't choose to waste our fire, but snugly kept our places,
And when so near we saw them wink, we thought it time to stop'em;
It would have done you good, I think, to see Kentucky drop'em.
O Kentucky, &c.

8th They found at length 'twas vain to fight where lead was all their booty,
And so they wisely took to flight, and left us all the beauty.
And now if danger e'er annoys, remember what our trade is;
Just send for us Kentucky boys, and we'll protect you, Ladies.
O Kentucky, &c

THE HUNTERS OF KENTUCKY.

of common man whose moxie won the day on January 8, 1815. Jackson's own "common man" quality contrasted with the patrician identity of predecessors like Jefferson, Madison, and Monroe and represented a new era in American politics.[24] Likewise, as a piece of music, "The Hunters of Kentucky" represented a renewed and growing appreciation for more folklike, American-rather-than-European-centered cultural expressions.

Among the three nineteenth-century musical examples, only "Eighth of January" remained in popular circulation beyond its time. Yet, the Battle of New Orleans has continued to fascinate poets, musicians, and artists up to the present day. Perhaps Johnny Horton's distillation of the event to a raw sense of energy and pride in the underdog victory of Americans resonated at a time of post–World War II history—between the Korean War and the Vietnam War—when Americans began to grapple with the country's role as an imperial power in conflicts far from home. If popular culture about the Battle of New Orleans mirrors its day and time, then more recent examples reflect an era more inclined to explore the nuances, ambiguities, dark corners, and tragedies of our own history—in other words, the ups and the downs, the good and the bad. Andrew Jackson today holds a dual reputation based on two extremes: the competent, skilled military strategist who won the Battle of New Orleans and saved the United States from being retaken by the British, and the ruthless ethnocentrist who forced an entire civilization of people to leave their homeland for a doomed Trail of Tears.

A recent musical takes on this dichotomy of personality and historical understanding. Titled *Bloody, Bloody Andrew Jackson,* the work positions its central figure as a presage of our current political climate, in which presidential politicians in particular are treated like rock-star figures. National leaders today are subject to close scrutiny of aspects of their lives outside their political leadership and subject to a kind of fandom based more on emotions than on thoughtful articulations of policy. American society in this musical comes across as adolescent—a teenaged mass looking for the next idol. An acerbic review of the production in 2011 points out that "Old Hickory" is the nickname not only for Jackson but also for Mephistopheles.[25] The reviewer sums him up thus: "Andrew Jackson was a skilled guerrilla fighter from the frontier, whose rise to power was largely based on his reputation as a bloodspiller, borne upon the resentment of backward hinterland folk who felt no kinship with the metropolitan regime in the distant capital, which could provide neither basic public services nor defend them with the military."[26] The theater work includes a punk-rock version of "The Hunters of Kentucky," which becomes a nuanced musical interrogation of how popular culture about historical events reflects the concerns and preoccupations of its day, then and now, real, remembered, and imagined.

Examples of contemporary artists still grappling with the significance of the Battle of New Orleans extend beyond music. In 2008 the Beat poet Ed Sanders published his collection *Poems for New Orleans,* which opens with a poem titled "Battle of New Orleans." The poem connects the victory of Jackson, referred to as "Andy," with the experiences of that city's residents following Hurricane Katrina. Specifically, it focuses on "Lemoine Lebage, a Haitian émigré schooled in the ideals of the French Revolution" and one of six hundred black soldiers who participated in the Battle of New Orleans.[27] Lebage was likely among the more than ten thousand Haitian refugees who fled to New Orleans because of war in 1809; about a third of them were free people of color, some of whom formed a unit to help Jackson fight in early 1815.[28] According to the poem,

> Lemoine Lebage was one of those Haitian republican soldiers
> who'd gone to Texas about a year ago
> to help the Mexican revolutionaries.

In the poem, the soldier Lebage is treated for battle wounds by Marie Leveau. The text then turns to his descendant Grace Lebage, who is desperately trying to recover from the devastation Katrina wrought on the home built by her ancestor sometime around 1830. The poem recounts the response from the insurance company paid by her for fifty years, and by her parents before her, and by their parents before them:

> I'm sorry, Miss Lebage
> you did have some wind and fire insurance
> but this was from Poseidon

The company offers her $623 and promises that it will be available "in about four months." Grace Lebage invokes Andy and Marie Laveau and all the historical inequalities and imbalances that stand in tension with the equally powerful beauty and richness of New Orleans. The Battle of New Orleans becomes a metaphor for an ongoing struggle for socioeconomic equality and the way Katrina put that city's gaping imbalances on nationwide display. The Battle of New Orleans becomes at once a metaphor for both the best and worst of American character: the proud battle scars that represent a uniquely American combination of individualism and communal sacrifice, alongside the shameful scars that represent the horror and injustices of the nation's history of race-based slavery. Near the end of the poem the narrator declares:

> And the Battle of New Orleans
> is never over, Andy!
>
> It's never over![29]

NOTES

Thanks to Amanda Bryant and Jimmy Bryant at the University of Central Arkansas Archives; Tim Gahr at Stackpole Books; Sarah Serafimidis at North Atlantic Books; Don Warden of Warden Music Company; Eric S. Ames, Curator of Digital Collections, Digital Project Group, Baylor University; and Briana Robinson at Agnes Scott College.

1. One list released by the Recording Industry Association of America and the National Endowment for the Arts places Johnny Horton's version of "The Battle of New Orleans" at number 333. See The Recording Industry Association of America: Top 365 Songs of the Twentieth Century, accessed 7 November 2014, www.theassociation.net/txt-music5.html.

2. Among the recordings of the tune, a version performed by Nathan Frazier and Frank Patterson appears on the 1999 collection *From Where I Stand: The Black Experience in Country Music,* Warner Brothers, 9 46248-2, 1998, compact disc box set. Several other versions appear on the Library of Congress website, including one recorded by Tommy Rhoades (guitar) and J. D. Allen (fiddle) on 6 August 1940; it is part of "Voices from the Dust Bowl: The Charles L. Todd and Robert Sonkin Migrant Worker Collection, 1940–1941," *American Memory,* Library of Congress, accessed 10 November 2014, memory.loc.gov/cgi-bin/query/D?toddbib:5:./temp/~ammem_xAYq.

3. In the recording Driftwood released in 1958, he inserts two extra beats between lines 2 and 3 of the verse. The recording can also be heard online at "Jimmie Driftwood Original Battle of New Orleans," YouTube, accessed 11 November 2014, www.youtube.com/watch?v=nE4yTfawEH8.

4. Unfortunately, Horton omits the verse that follows: "They lost their pants and their pretty shiny coats / And their tails was all a-showin' like a bunch of billy goats. / They ran down the river with their tongues a-hanging out / And they said they got a lickin', which there wasn't any doubt."

5. In Driftwood's original, this variation appears twice, once in the middle and once at the end. In a later live recording, Driftwood removes the extra beats, seeming to accommodate the sing-along handclaps of the live audience; in that live version, the refrain variation appears only once, at the song's end. See Jimmy Driftwood, "The Battle of New Orleans," *Kerrville Folk Festival: The Early Years 1972–1981,* Silverwolf Records 1009, 1998, compact disc box set.

6. Irwin Silber, *Songs of Independence* (Harrison, PA: Stackpole Books, 1973), 204. Also mentioned in Jerome Rodnitsky, "War and Music," in *Music in American Life: An Encyclopedia of the Songs, Styles, Stars, and Stories That Shaped Our Culture,* ed. Jacqueline Edmondson, vol. 4 (Santa Barbara, CA: Greenwood, 2013), 1206.

7. Silber, *Songs of Independence,* 206; also covered in Rodnitsky, "War and Music," 1206. Other songs inspired by the war include three Canadian songs that mark historical events of the era: "Come All You Bold Canadians," about the Battle of Fort Detroit (3–16 August 1812, two months after the US declaration of war); "The Battle of Queenston Heights," written in October 1812 and memorializing the death of Brock; and "The 'Chesapeake' and the 'Shannon,'" about the Battle in Boston Harbor on 1 June 1813. See Lorne Brown, "The War of 1812, Brock, and Queenston Heights," *Canadian Folk Music* 46, no. 3 (2012): 14.

8. Brown, "War of 1812, Brock, and Queenston Heights," 14.

9. Mariana Whitmer, "Music and War," in *Encyclopedia of War and American Society,* ed. Peter Karsten (Thousand Oaks, CA: Sage, 2005), 541.

10. C. E. Grice, *The Battle of New Orleans, or Glory, Love and Loyalty; an Historical and National Drama, in Five Acts* (New York: printed for the author by John Low, 1816). A facsimile of the original is found on the Hathi Trust Digital Library website, hdl.handle.net/2027/loc.ark:/13960/t2j67j686, accessed 12 September 2014.

11. Images of the Yeager engraving and the Landis lithograph can be found at The Historic New Orleans Collection, accessed 14 November 2014, www.hnoc.org/. Emmons, Grobe, and Johnston examples can be found at the online collections for the Library of Congress: accessed 12 November 2014 at, respectively, lccn.loc.gov/16019564; www.loc.gov/item/ihas.200000192; and www.loc.gov/item/amss002387/.

12. The use of music in presidential campaigns predates Andrew Jackson but still resonates with the US political landscape today. See www.traxonthetrail.com.

13. The song is found in Silber, *Songs of Independence,* 213. See also Paul G. Brewster, "The Battle of New Orleans," *Southern Folklore Quarterly* 1, no. 3 (1937): 26; and Mariana Whitmer, "Using Music to Teach American History," *OAH Magazine of History* 19, no. 4 (July 2005): 5.

14. Unlike Brewster, Silber believes the song was likely written by "an anonymous soldier bard in Jackson's army." Silber, *Songs of Independence,* 228n24.

15. Nicholas E. Tawa, "Ballad Singers and Their Performances," liner notes to *Popular Music in Jacksonian America,* Musical Heritage Society 834561, 1982, LP box set, originally released in 1978. The quotation is from a "Mr. 'Chiron,'" in an essay titled "The Use and Abuse of Music," which appeared in a Boston paper called *Euterpeiad.*

16. Tawa elaborates on the relative excess of emotion, as viewed from a more contemporary perspective, that typified nineteenth-century musical performance throughout the book from which the previously cited liner notes were excerpted: Nicholas E. Tawa, *Sweet Songs for Gentle Americans* (Bowling Green, OH: Bowling Green University Popular Press, 1980).

17. For the full lyrics, see "'The Hunters of Kentucky': A Popular Song Celebrates the Victory of Jackson and his Frontier Fighters over the British, 1824," on History Matters: the U.S. Survey Course on the Web, accessed 4 September 2014, historymatters.gmu.edu/d/6522.

18. Tawa, "Ballad Singers and Their Performances."

19. Tawa, *Sweet Songs for Gentle Americans,* 84. Tawa gives the original song title as "Miss Baily," but evidence elsewhere confirms the spelling I use here, "Bailey." See Robert B. Waltz and David G. Engle, "Unfortunate Miss Bailey," The Traditional Ballad Index: An Annotated Bibliography of the Folk Songs of the English-Speaking World, version 3.4, accessed 3 November 2014, www.csufresno.edu/folklore/BalladIndexTOC.html.

20. Waltz and Engle, "Unfortunate Miss Bailey." The song had been included in a comic opera, *Love Laughs at Locksmiths,* written by G. Colman and premiered in London in 1803. See also Whitmer, "Music and War," 541.

21. Tawa, *Sweet Songs for Gentle Americans,* 84, also in excerpted liner notes.

22. Ibid., 83–85.

23. Lyrics printed from a digitization of the original sheet music, possibly dated 1824. See "The Hunters of Kentucky," Baylor University Libraries Digital Collections, Frances G. Spencer Collection of American Popular Sheet Music, accessed 31 October 2014, digitalcollections.baylor.edu/cdm/fullbrowser/collection/fa-spnc/id/21138/rv/compoundobject/cpd/21140. The full lyrics also appear in "'The Hunters of Kentucky': A Popular Song Celebrates the Victory of Jackson and his Frontier Fighters over the British, 1824."

24. David Pivar, "A Preface to the Popular Music of Jacksonian America," liner notes to *Popular Music in Jacksonian America.*

25. Kevin D. Williamson, "The Devil and Mr. Jackson," *New Criterion* 29, no. 5 (January 2011): 44.

26. Ibid., 43.

27. The figure six hundred comes from the poem itself. See Ed Sanders, *Poems for New Orleans* (Berkeley, CA: North Atlantic Books, 2008), 13–23. The quoted description of Lebage is from Bill Lavender, "The Battle of New Orleans," review of *Poems for New Orleans,* by Ed Sanders, in *Offbeat: America's Roots Magazine from New Orleans and Louisiana* 20, no. 11 (November 2007): 55.

28. Jason Berry, "Marching Bands, New Orleans," in *The New Encyclopedia of Southern Culture,* vol. 14, *Folklife,* ed. Glenn Hinson and William Ferris (Chapel Hill: University of North Carolina Press, 2009), 323.

29. Excerpted from "The Battle of New Orleans," from *Poems for New Orleans by Edward Sanders,* published by North Atlantic Books, copyright © 2008 by Edward Sanders. Reprinted by permission of publisher.

Bibliography

BOOKS AND CHAPTERS

Abernethy, Thomas P. *The Burr Conspiracy.* 1911. Reprint, Gloucester, MA: P. Smith, 1968.

Acceptance and Unveiling of the Statue of Andrew Jackson, Seventh President of the United States. Washington, DC: GPO, 1929.

Adams, Henry. *History of the United States during the Administrations of Thomas Jefferson and Madison.* Edited by Earl N. Harbert. 2 vols. New York: Viking, 1986.

———. *The Life of Albert Gallatin.* Philadelphia: J. B. Lippincott, 1879.

Altoff, Gerard T. *Amongst My Best Men: African Americans and the War of 1812.* Put-in-Bay, OH: Perry Group, 1996.

———. *Deep Water Sailors and Shallow Water Soldiers: Manning the United States Fleet on Lake Erie.* Put-in-Bay, OH: Perry Group, 1993.

———. *Oliver Hazard Perry and the Battle of Lake Erie.* Put-in-Bay, OH: Perry Group, 1999.

Appleby, Joyce O., and Arthur M. Schlessinger. *Thomas Jefferson.* New York: Time Books, 2003.

Ball, Charles. *Slavery in the United States: A Narrative of the Life and Adventures of Charles Ball, a Black Man, Who Lived Forty Years in Maryland, South Carolina and Georgia, as a Slave Under Various Masters, and was One Year in the Navy with Commodore Barney, During the Late War.* New York: John S. Taylor, 1837.

Barber, James G. *Andrew Jackson: A Portrait Study.* Washington, DC, and Seattle: National Portrait Gallery, Smithsonian Institution, and Tennessee State Museum, Nashville, in association with the University of Washington Press, 1991.

Belohlavek, John M. *"Let the Eagle Soar!": The Foreign Policy of Andrew Jackson.* Lincoln: University of Nebraska Press, 1985.

Berry, Jason. "Marching Bands, New Orleans." In *The New Encyclopedia of Southern Culture,* vol. 14, *Folklife,* edited by Glenn Hinson and William Ferris. Chapel Hill: University of North Carolina Press, 2009.

Blythe, Robert W. *Administrative History of Jean Laffite National Historical Park and Preserve.* Atlanta: Cultural Resources Division, Southeast Regional Office, National Park Service, 2013.

Booraem, Hendrik. *Young Hickory: The Making of Andrew Jackson.* Dallas: Taylor, 2001.

Brady, Cyrus Townsend. *The True Andrew Jackson.* Philadelphia: J. B. Lippincott, 1906.

Brady, Patricia. *A Being So Gentle: The Frontier Love Story of Rachel and Andrew Jackson.* New York: Palgrave Macmillan, 2011.

Brands, H. W. *Andrew Jackson: His Life and Times.* New York: Doubleday, 2005.

Browning, Charles H. *American Historical Register and Monthly Gazette of the Patriotic-Hereditary Societies of the United States of America.* Vol. 3. Philadelphia: Historical Register, September 1895–February 1896.

Buel, Richard, Jr. *America on the Brink: How the Political Struggle over the War of 1812 Almost Destroyed the Young Republic.* New York: Palgrave Macmillan, 2005.

Buell, Augustus C. *History of Andrew Jackson, Pioneer, Patriot, Soldier, Politician, President.* 2 vols. New York: C. Scribner's Sons, 1904.

Buenger, Walter L., and Robert A. Calvert, eds. *Texas through Time: Evolving Interpretations.* College Station: Texas A&M University Press, 1991.

Bullard, Mary R. *Black Liberation on Cumberland Island in 1815.* DeLeon Springs, FL: E. O. Painter, 1983.

———. *Cumberland Island: A History.* Athens: University of Georgia Press, 2003.

Burke, Pauline Wilcox. *Emily Donelson of Tennessee.* 2 vols. Richmond, VA: Garrett & Massie, 1941.

Butcher-Younghans, Sherry. *Historic House Museums: A Practical Handbook for Their Care, Preservation, and Management.* New York: Oxford University Press, 1993.

Byrd, Max. *Jackson.* New York: Bantam, 1997.

Cain, Joshua. "'We Will Strike at the Head and Demolish the Monster': The Impact of Joel R. Poinsett's Correspondence on President Andrew Jackson during the Nullification Crisis, 1832–1833." In *Proceedings of the South Carolina Historical Association, 2011,* http://www.palmettohistory.org/scha/proceedings/proceedings2011.pdf.

Casey, Powell A. Foreword to *Biographical Sketches of the Veterans of the Battalion of Orleans,* by Ronald Morazán. Baton Rouge: Legacy, 1979.

———. *Louisiana in the War of 1812.* Baton Rouge, 1963.

Cerami, Charles A. *Jefferson's Great Gamble: The Remarkable Story of Jefferson, Napoleon, and the Men behind the Louisiana Purchase.* Naperville, IL: Sourcebooks, 2003.

Chernow, Ron. *Alexander Hamilton.* New York: Penguin, 2004.

Christian, Marcus. *Negro Soldiers at the Battle of New Orleans.* New Orleans: Battle of New Orleans 150th Anniversary Committee, 1965.

City of New Orleans. *A History of the Proceedings in the City of New Orleans, on the Occasion of the Funeral Ceremonies in Honor of James Abram Garfield, Late President of the United States.* New Orleans, 1881.

Clowes, William Laird. *The Royal Navy: A History.* 7 vols. London: S. Lowe Marston, 1897–1903.

Cole, Donald B. *A Jackson Man: Amos Kendall and the Rise of American Democracy.* Baton Rouge: Louisiana State University Press, 2004.

Commager, H. S. *The Search for a Usable Past, and Other Essays in Historiography.* New York: Knopf, 1967.

Cox, Karen L. *Dixie's Daughters: The United Daughters of the Confederacy and the Preservation of Confederate Culture.* Gainesville: University Press of Florida, 2003.

Cress, Lawrence Delbert. *Citizens in Arms: The Army and Militia in American Society to the War of 1812.* Chapel Hill: University of North Carolina Press, 1982.

———. "A Well-Regulated Militia: The Origins and Meaning of the Second Amendment." In *The Bill of Rights: A Lively Heritage,* edited by Jon Kukla, 55–65. Richmond: Virginia State Library and Archives, 1987.

Curtis, James C. *Andrew Jackson and the Search for Vindication.* Boston: HarperCollins, 1976.

Dargo, George. *Jefferson's Louisiana: Politics and the Clash of Traditions.* Cambridge, MA: Harvard University Press, 1975.

Daughan, George C. *If By Sea: The Forging of the American Navy from the Revolution to the War of 1812.* New York: Basic Books, 2008.

Davies, Penelope J. E., Walter B. Denny, Frima Fox Hofrichter, Joseph Jacobs, Ann M. Roberts, and David L. Simon. *Janson's History of Art: The Western Tradition.* 8th ed. Upper Saddle River, NJ: Prentice Hall, 2012.

Davies, Wallace Evan. *Patriotism on Parade: The Story of Veterans' and Hereditary Organizations in America, 1783–1900.* Cambridge, MA: Harvard University Press, 1955.

Desdunnes, Rodolphe L. *Nos Hommes et Notre Histoire.* Montreal: Arbor et Dupont, 1911.

DeToy, Brian. "The Impressment of American Seamen during the Napoleonic Wars." In *Consortium on Revolutionary Europe, 1750–1815: Selected Papers,*

492–501. Tallahassee: Institute on Napoleon and the French Revolution, Florida State University, 1998.

Dillon, Richard. *We Have Met the Enemy: Oliver Hazard Perry; Wilderness Commodore.* New York: McGraw-Hill, 1978.

Dorris, Mary C. *Preservation of the Hermitage, 1889–1915: Annals, History, and Stories; The Acquisition, Restoration, and Care of the Home of General Andrew Jackson by the Ladies Hermitage Association for Over a Quarter of a Century.* Nashville, 1915.

Douglas, Frank J., Robert Bachman, George Lynn Woodruff, and LeRoy Habenight. *National Society of United States Daughters of 1812, 1892–1989: History.* Metairie, LA: National Society of United States Daughters of 1812, 1989.

Dunnavent, R. Blake. *Brown Water Warfare: The U.S. Navy in Riverine Warfare and the Emergence of a Tactical Doctrine, 1775–1970.* Gainesville: University Press of Florida, 2003.

Elkins, Stanley, and Eric McKitrick. *The Age of Federalism.* New York: Oxford University Press, 1993.

Ellis, Joseph. *Founding Brothers: The Revolutionary Generation.* New York: Knopf, 2000.

Emerson, W. Eric. *Sons of Privilege: The Charleston Light Dragoons in the Civil War.* Columbia: University of South Carolina Press, 2005.

Folk, Reau E. *Battle of New Orleans: Its Real Meaning; Exposure of Untruth Being Taught Young America Concerning the Second Most Important Military Event in the Life of the Republic.* Nashville: Ladies Hermitage Association, 1935.

Fortier, Alcée. *A History of Louisiana.* Paris: Manzi, Joyant, 1905.

Gelpi, Paul. "Slave Rebellion, Territory of Orleans." In *The Encyclopedia of the Wars of the Early Republic: A Political, Social, and Military History,* edited by Spencer C. Tucker. Santa Barbara, CA: ABC-CLIO, 2014.

George, Christopher T. *Terror on the Chesapeake: The War of 1812 on the Bay.* Shippenburg, PA: White Mane Books, 2000.

Gerson, Noel B. *Old Hickory.* New York: Doubleday, 1964.

Gilje, Paul A. *Free Trade and Sailors' Rights in the War of 1812.* New York: Cambridge University Press, 2013.

Grenville, William Wyndham, Baron, et al. *Report on the Manuscripts of J. B. Fortescue, Esq. preserved at Dropmore. . . .* 10 vols. London: Eyre & Spottiswoode for HMSO, 1892–1927.

Groom, Winston. *Patriotic Fire: Andrew Jackson and Jean Lafitte at the Battle of New Orleans.* New York: Knopf, 2006.

Hanger, Kimberly S. *Bounded Lives, Bounded Places: Free Black Society in Colonial New Orleans.* Durham, NC: Duke University Press, 1997.

Harper, John Lamberton. *American Machiavelli: Alexander Hamilton and the Origins of the U.S. Foreign Policy.* Cambridge: Cambridge University Press, 2004.

Harrison, William Henry. *Messages and Letters of William Henry Harrison.* Edited by Logan Esarey. 2 vols. Indianapolis: Indiana Historical Commission, 1922.

Hartt, Frederick, and David G. Wilkins. *History of Italian Renaissance Art.* Upper Saddle River, NJ: Prentice Hall, 2006.

Hatfield, Joseph T. *William Claiborne: Jeffersonian Centurion in the American Southwest.* Lafayette: University of Southwestern Louisiana, 1976.

Hattendorf, John B., and Bruce E. Elleman, eds. *Nineteen Gun Salute: Case Studies of Operational, Strategic, and Diplomatic Naval Leadership during the 20th and Early 21st Centuries.* Newport, RI: Naval War College Press, 2010.

Haynes, Sam. *Unfinished Revolution: The Early American Republic in a British World.* Charlottesville: University of Virginia Press, 2010.

Heidler, David S., and Jeanne T. Heidler, eds. *Encyclopedia of the War of 1812.* Santa Barbara, CA: ABC-CLIO, 1997.

Hickey, Donald R. *Don't Give Up the Ship! Myths of the War of 1812.* Toronto: Robin Brass Studio; Urbana: University of Illinois Press, 2006.

———. *The War of 1812: A Forgotten Conflict.* Urbana: University of Illinois Press, 1989. Bicentennial ed., 2012.

Hill, Daniel G. *The Freedom-Seekers: Blacks in Early Canada.* Agincourt, ON: Book Society of Canada, 1981.

Hirsch, Arnold R., and Joseph Logsdon, eds. *Creole New Orleans: Race and Americanization.* Baton Rouge: Louisiana State University Press, 1992.

Home, David Milne. *Report on the Manuscripts of Colonel David Milne Home of Wedderburn Castle, N.B.* London, Mackiefor HMSO, 1902.

Horsman, Reginald. *The New Republic: The United States of America, 1789–1815.* Harlow, UK, and New York: Longman, 2000.

———. *The War of 1812.* New York: Knopf, 1969.

Howe, Daniel Walker. *What Hath God Wrought: The Transformation of America, 1815–1848.* New York: Oxford University Press, 2007.

Hubbs, G. Ward. *Guarding Greensboro: A Confederate Company in the Making of a Southern Community.* Athens: University of Georgia Press, 2003.

Hughes, Robert. *American Visions: The Epic History of Art in America.* New York: Knopf, 1997.

Index to the Andrew Jackson Papers. Washington, DC: Library of Congress, 1967.

Interstate Board of the Perry's Victory Centennial Commissioners: Watterson, Henry, 1840–1921; The Perry memorial and centennial celebration under the auspices of the national government and the states of Ohio, Pennsylvania, Michigan, Illinois, Wisconsin, New York, Rhode Island, Kentucky, Minnesota and Indiana. Cleveland, OH: The Board, 1912.

James, Marquis. *Andrew Jackson, the Border Captain.* Indianapolis: Bobbs-Merrill, 1933.

———. *The Life of Andrew Jackson.* 2 vols. Indianapolis: Bobbs-Merrill, 1938.

James, William. *A Full and Correct Account of the Chief Naval Occurrences of the Late War between Great Britain and the United States of America.* London: T. Egerton, 1817.

———. *The Naval History of Great Britain, From the Declaration of War by France in 1793 to the Accession of George IV.* Rev. ed. 6 vols. London, 1822–26.

Jones, Howard. *Crucible of Power: A History of American Foreign Relations to 1913.* Wilmington, DE: SR Books, 2002.

Kaplan, Lawrence S. *Thomas Jefferson: Westward the Course of Empire.* Wilmington, DE: SR Books, 1999.

Kastor, Peter, and Francois Weil. *Empires of the Imagination: Transatlantic Histories of the Louisiana Purchase.* Charlottesville: University of Virginia Press, 2008.

Kendall, Amos. *Life of Andrew Jackson: Private, Military, and Civil.* New York: Harper & Bros., 1843.

King, Grace. *New Orleans: The Place and the People.* New York: Macmillan, 1895.

———. *Stories from Louisiana History.* New Orleans: L. Graham, 1905.

Kleiner, Fred S. *Gardner's Art through the Ages: A Global History.* 14th ed. Boston: Wadsworth, 2013.

Lambert, John. *Travels through Lower Canada and the United States of North America in the Years of 1806, 1807 and 1808, to Which are Added, Biographical Notices and Anecdotes of Some of the Leading Characters in the United States.* 2 vols. London: Richard Phillips, 1810.

Larrie, Reginald R. *Makin' Free: African-Americans in the Northwest Territory.* Detroit: Etheridge Books, 1981.

Latour, Arsène Lacarrière. *Historical Memoir of the War in West Florida and Louisiana in 1814–15, with an Atlas.* Edited by Gene Allen Smith. Rev. ed. Gainesville: University Press of Florida and Historic New Orleans Collection, 2008.

Lee, Henry. *A Biography of Andrew Jackson, Late Major-General of the Army of the United States.* Edited by Mark A. Mastromarino. Knoxville: Tennessee Presidents Trust, 1992.

Lewis, James E. *The Louisiana Purchase: Jefferson's Noble Bargain?* Chapel Hill: University of North Carolina Press, 2003.

Lossing, Benson J. *The Pictorial Field-Book of the Revolution.* 2 vols. New York: Harper & Bros., 1851–52.

———. *The Pictorial Field-Book of the War of 1812.* New York: Harper & Bros., 1868.

Maclay, Edgar Stanton. *A History of American Privateers.* New York: D. Appleton, 1899.

Mahon, John K. "Oliver Hazard Perry." In *Command under Sail: Makers of the American Naval Tradition, 1775–1850,* edited by James C. Bradford, 126–41. Annapolis, MD: Naval Institute Press, 1985.

———. *The War of 1812.* New York: Da Capo, 1972.

Marszalek, John F. *The Petticoat Affair: Manners, Mutiny, and Sex in Andrew Jackson's White House.* New York: Free Press, 1997.

Martin, François-Xavier. *The History of Louisiana, From the Earliest Period.* 1827–29. Reprint, 2 vols. in 1, Gretna, LA: Pelican, 1975.

———. *Louisiana Term Reports, or Cases Argued and Determined in the Supreme Court of that State.* Vol. 3. New Orleans, 1815.

Matloff, Maurice, ed. *American Military History.* Washington, DC: Center of Military History, 1988.

McConnell, Roland C. *Negro Troops of Antebellum Louisiana: A History of the Battalion of Freemen of Color.* Baton Rouge: Louisiana State University Press, 1968.

McDonough, James L., and Thomas Lawrence Connelly. *Five Tragic Hours: The Battle of Franklin.* Knoxville: University of Tennessee Press, 1983.

McDonough, John. Introduction to *Index to the Andrew Jackson Papers.* Washington, DC: Library of Congress, 1967.

Meacham, Jon. *American Lion: Andrew Jackson in the White House.* New York: Random House, 2008.

Mikaberidze, Alexander, ed. *Russian Eyewitness Accounts of the Campaign of 1812.* London: Frontline Books, 2012.

Montero de Pedro, José, Marqués de Casa Mena. *The Spanish in New Orleans and Louisiana.* Translated by Richard E. Chandler. Gretna, LA: Pelican, 2000.

Moore, Frank, ed. *Anecdotes, Poetry and Incidents of the Civil War: North and South, 1860–1865.* New York: Publications Office, Bible House, 1867.

Moore, John Preston. *Revolt in Louisiana: The Spanish Occupation, 1766–1770.* Baton Rouge: Louisiana State University Press, 1976.

Morazán, Ronald. *Biographical Sketches of the Veterans of the Battalion of Orleans.* Baton Rouge: Legacy, 1979.

Nolan, Jeanette Covert. *Andrew Jackson.* New York: Julian Messner, 1949.

Nolte, Vincent. *Fifty Years in Both Hemispheres: or, Reminiscences of the Life of a Former Merchant.* New York: Redfield, 1854.

Ogg, Frederic A. *The Reign of Andrew Jackson: A Chronicle of the Frontier in Politics.* New Haven, CT: Yale University Press, 1919.

Owsley, Frank Lawrence, Jr., and Gene A. Smith. *Filibusters and Expansionists: Jeffersonian Manifest Destiny.* Tuscaloosa: University of Alabama Press, 1997.

Papenfuse, Eric Robert. *The Evils of Necessity: Robert Goodloe Harper and the Moral Dilemma of Slavery.* Philadelphia: American Philosophical Society, 1997.

Parsons, Lynn Hudson. *The Birth of Modern Politics: Andrew Jackson, John Quincy Adams, and the Election of 1828.* New York: Oxford University Press, 2009.

Parton, James. *Life of Andrew Jackson.* 3 vols. New York: Mason Brothers, 1860.

Perkins, Bradford. *Prologue to War: England and the United States, 1805–1812.* Berkeley: University of California Press, 1968.

Phillips, Christopher. *Freedom's Port: The African American Community of Baltimore, 1790–1860.* Urbana: University of Illinois Press, 1997.

Piecuch, Jim, and Jason Lutz. "Charles Bankhead." In *Encyclopedia of the Mexican-American War: A Political, Social, and Military History,* edited by Spencer C. Tucker. 2 vols. Santa Barbara, CA: ABC-CLIO, 2013.

Quarles, Benjamin. *The Negro in the American Revolution.* Chapel Hill: University of North Carolina Press, 1961.

Quimby, Robert S. *The U.S. Army in the War of 1812: An Operational and Command Study.* East Lansing: Michigan State University Press, 1997.

Reid, John, and John Henry Eaton. *The Life of Andrew Jackson.* Edited by Frank L. Owsley Jr. Tuscaloosa: University of Alabama Press, 1974.

Reilly, Robin. *The British at the Gates: The New Orleans Campaign in the War of 1812.* New York: G. P. Putnam's Sons, 1974.

Remini, Robert V. *Andrew Jackson.* 3 vols. New York: Harper & Row, 1977–84.

———. *The Battle of New Orleans: Andrew Jackson and America's First Military Victory.* New York: Viking, 1999.

Rightor, Ella. "Military." In *Standard History of New Orleans, Louisiana,* edited by Henry Rightor, 129–70. Chicago: Lewis, 1900.

Rightor, Henry, ed. *Standard History of New Orleans, Louisiana.* Chicago: Lewis, 1900.

Roberts, Aline Gray, ed. *Celebrating One Hundred Years of the TN State Society United States Daughters of 1812.* N.p., 2009.

Robertson, James Alexander. *Louisiana under the Rule of Spain, France, and the United States, 1785–1807: Social, economic, and political conditions of the territory represented in the Louisiana Purchase, as portrayed in hitherto unpublished contemporary account by Dr. Paul Alliot and various Spanish, French, English, and American officials.* 2 vols. 1911. Reprint, Freeport, NY: Books for Libraries Press, 1969.

Rodnitsky, Jerome. "War and Music," In *Music in American Life: An Encyclopedia of the Songs, Styles, Stars, and Stories That Shaped Our Culture,* edited by Jacqueline Edmondson, vol. 4. Santa Barbara, CA: Greenwood, 2013.

Rogin, Michael Paul. *Fathers and Children: Andrew Jackson and the Subjugation of the America Indian.* New Brunswick, NJ: Transaction, 1991. First published 1975 by Knopf.

Rush, Richard. *A Residence at the Court of London: Comprising Incidents, Official and Personal, from 1819 to 1825; Amongst the Former, Negotiations on the Oregon Territory, and Other Unsettled Questions Between the United States and Great Britain.* 2 vols. London: Richard Bentley, 1845.

Sanders, Ed. *Poems for New Orleans.* Berkeley, CA: North Atlantic Books, 2008.

Savage, Kirk. *Standing Soldiers, Kneeling Slaves: Race, War, and Monument in Nineteenth-Century America.* Princeton, NJ: Princeton University Press, 1997.

Senefelder, Alois. *The Invention of Lithography.* Translated by J. W. Muller. New York: Fuchs and Lang Manufacturing, 1911. Project Gutenberg e-book. www.gutenberg.org/files/40924/40924-h/40924-h.htm.

Silber, Irwin. *Songs of Independence.* Harrison, PA: Stackpole Books, 1973.

Simpson, John A. *Edith D. Pope and Her Nashville Friends: Guardians of the Lost Cause in the Confederate Veteran.* Knoxville: University of Tennessee Press, 2003.

Skeen, C. Edward. *Citizen Soldiers in the War of 1812.* Lexington: University Press of Kentucky, 1999.

Smalley, Ruth. *An Interview with Andrew Jackson.* Johnson City, TN: Overmountain, 2001.

Smith, Gene Allen. *The Slaves' Gamble: Choosing Sides in the War of 1812.* New York: Palgrave Macmillan, 2013.

Smith, Elbert B. *Francis P. Blair.* New York: Free Press, 1980.

Sprout, Harold, and Margaret Sprout. *The Rise of American Naval Power, 1776–1918.* Princeton, NJ: Princeton University Press, 1944.

Stagg, J. C. A. *Mr. Madison's War: Politics, Diplomacy, and Warfare in the Early American Republic, 1783–1830.* Princeton, NJ: Princeton University Press, 1983.

Sumner, William Graham. *Andrew Jackson as a Public Man: What He Was, What Chances He Had, and What He Did with Them.* New York: Houghton, Mifflin, 1895.

Sweet Songs for Gentle Americans. Bowling Green, OH: Bowling Green University Popular Press, 1980.

Tawa, Nicholas E. "Ballad Singers and Their Performances." Liner notes to *Popular Music in Jacksonian America.* Musical Heritage Society 834561. 1982. LP box set. Originally released in 1978.

Thomas, C. M. *American Neutrality in 1793: A Study in Cabinet Government.* New York: Columbia University Press, 1931.

Thompson, Charles L. *United States Supreme Court Reports, Lawyers' Edition.* Rochester, NY: Lawyers Co-operative, 1917.

Tregle, Joseph G., Jr. "Creole and Americans." In *Creole New Orleans: Race and Americanization,* edited by Arnold R. Hirsch and Joseph Logsdon, 131–85. Baton Rouge: Louisiana State University Press, 1992.

Tucker, Spencer C., and Frank T. Reuter. *Injured Honor: The Chesapeake-Leopard Affair, June 22, 1807.* Annapolis, MD: Naval Institute Press, 1996.

Uttridge, Sarah, and Charles Catton, eds. *The Encyclopedia of Warfare.* London: Amber Books, 2013.

Waltz, Robert B., and David G. Engle. "Unfortunate Miss Bailey." In *The Traditional Ballad Index: An Annotated Bibliography of the Folk Songs of the English-Speaking World,* version 3.4, last modified 25 July 2014. www.csufresno.edu/folklore/Ballad IndexTOC.html.

Watson, Harry L. *Andrew Jackson vs. Henry Clay: Democracy and Development in Antebellum America.* Boston: Bedford / St. Martin's, 1998.

Watson, Samuel J. *Jackson's Sword: The Army Officer Corps on the American Frontier, 1810–1821.* Lawrence: University Press of Kansas, 2012.

Weigley, Russell F. *The American Way of War: A History of United States Military Strategy and Policy.* Bloomington: Indiana University Press, 1973.

———. *History of the United States Army.* London: B. T. Batsford, 1967.

West, Patricia. *Domesticating History: The Political Origins of America's House Museums.* Washington, DC: Smithsonian Institution Press, 1999.

Whitmer, Mariana. "Music and War." In *Encyclopedia of War and American Society,* edited by Peter Karsten. Thousand Oaks, CA: Sage, 2005.

Wilcox, Shirley, Mary Lou Little, and Wendy Barry. *Register of St. John's Church of England at Sandwich, 1802–1827.* Chatham, ON: Kent and Essex Branch, Ontario Genealogical Society, 1990.

Wilentz, Sean. *Andrew Jackson.* New York: Henry Holt, 2005.

———. *The Rise of American Democracy: Jefferson to Lincoln.* New York: Norton, 2005.

———. *The Rise of American Democracy: Jefferson to Lincoln.* Abr. ed. New York: Norton, 2009.

Williams, Patrick G., S. Charles Bolton, and Jeanne M. Whayne. *A Whole Country in Commotion: The Louisiana Purchase and the American Southwest.* Fayetteville: University of Arkansas Press, 2005.

Wills, Garry. *Henry Adams and the Making of America.* Boston: Houghton Mifflin, 2005.

Wood, William C. H., ed. *Select British Documents of the Canadian War of 1812*. 3 vols. New York: Champlain Society, 1968.

Wright, Evan. *Generation Kill: Devil Dogs, Iceman, Captain America, and the New Face of American War.* New York: G. P. Putnam's Sons, 2004.

Wright, Frances Fitzpatrick. *Andrew Jackson: Fighting Frontiersman.* New York: Abingdon, 1958.

ARTICLES

Bennis, Warren, and Robert J. Thomas. "Crucibles of Leadership." *Harvard Business Review* 80, no. 9 (September 2002): para. 1. hbr.org/2002/09/crucibles-of-leader ship. Brewster, Paul G. "The Battle of New Orleans." *Southern Folklore Quarterly* 1, no. 3 (1937).

Brown, Lorne. "The War of 1812, Brock, and Queenston Heights." *Canadian Folk Music* 46, no. 3 (2012): 8–14.

Bullard, Mary R. "Ned Simmons, American Slave: The Role of Imagination in Narrative History." *African Diaspora Archaeology Network Newsletter,* June 2007, 20–21. www.diaspora.uiuc.edu/news0607/news0607-7.pdf.

Cantrell, Gregg. "The Bones of Stephen F. Austin: History and Memory in Progressive-Era Texas." *Southwestern Historical Quarterly* 108, no. 2 (October 2004): 145–78.

"The Celebration of Jackson Day, January 8, 1915." *Tennessee Historical Magazine* 1 (March 1915).

Chiorazzi, Michael. "Francois-Xavier Martin: Printer, Lawyer, Jurist." *Law Library Journal* 80 (1988): 63–97.

Cray, Robert E., Jr. "Remember the USS *Chesapeake:* The Politics of Maritime Death and Impressment." *Journal of the Early Republic* 25, no. 3 (Fall 2005): 464–66.

Cress, Lawrence Delbert. "An Armed Community: The Origins and Meaning of the Right to Bear Arms." *Journal of American History* 71, no. 1 (June 1984): 22–42.

———. "Radical Whiggery on the Role of the Military: The Ideological Roots of the American Revolutionary Militia." *Journal of the History of Ideas* 40, no. 1 (January–March 1979): 43–60.

———."Republican Liberty and National Security: American Military Policy as an Ideological Problem, 1783–1789." *William and Mary Quarterly* 38, no. 1 (January 1981): 73–96.

Cusick, James G. "Some Thoughts on Spanish East and West Florida as Borderlands." *Florida Historical Quarterly* 90, no. 2 (Fall 2011): 133–56.

Evans, Freddie Williams. "Jordan B. Noble: The Drummer of Chalmette." *Preserva-*

tion in Print 27, no. 10 (24 February 2001): 24–25. www.prcno.org/programs/preservationinprint/piparchives/2001%20PIP/February%202001/25.html.

Everett, Donald E. "Émigrés and Militiamen: Free Persons of Color in New Orleans, 1803–1815." *Journal of Negro History* 38, no. 4 (October 1953): 377–402.

Fabel, Robin F. A. "Self-Help in Dartmoor: Black and White Prisoners in the War of 1812." *Journal of the Early Republic* 9, no. 2 (Summer 1989): 165–90.

Furber, Holden, ed. "How William James Came to Be a Naval Historian." *American Historical Review* 38, no. 1 (October 1932): 74–85.

Galpin, W. Freeman. "The American Grain Trade to the Spanish Peninsula, 1810–1814." *American Historical Review* 28, no. 1 (1923): 24–44.

Gelpi, Paul. "Mr. Jefferson's Creoles: The Battalion d'Orleans and the Americanization of Creole Louisiana, 1803–1815." *Louisiana History: The Journal of the Louisiana Historical Association* 48, no. 3 (Summer 2007): 295–316.

George, Christopher T. "Mirage of Freedom: African Americans in the War of 1812." *Maryland Historical Magazine* 91, no. 4 (Winter 1996): 427–50.

Goode, James M. "Four Salutes to a Nation: The Equestrian Statues of General Andrew Jackson." *White House History*, no. 27 (2010): 1–18. www.whitehousehistory.org/four-salutes-to-the-nation.

Gough, Robert J. "Black Men and the Early New Jersey Militia." *New Jersey Militia* 88 (Winter 1970): 227–83.

Hamilton, Milton W. "Augustus C. Buell: Fraudulent Historian." *Pennsylvania Magazine of History and Biography* 80, no. 4 (October 1956): 478–92.

Hutton, Patrick. "Recent Scholarship on Memory and History." *History Teacher* 33, no. 4 (August 2000): 533–48.

Kanon, Tom. "Forging the 'Hero of New Orleans: Tennessee Looks at the Centennial of the War of 1812." *Tennessee Historical Quarterly* 71, no. 2 (Summer 2012): 128–61.

Keck, Andrew S. "A Toast to the Union: Clark Mills' Equestrian Statue of Andrew Jackson in Lafayette Square." *Records of the Columbia Historical Society, Washington, D.C.*, 1971–72, 292–93. www.jstor.org/stable/40067778.

Lavender, Bill. "The Battle of New Orleans." Review of *Poems for New Orleans*, by Ed Sanders. *Offbeat: America's Roots Magazine from New Orleans and Louisiana* 20, no. 11 (November 2007): 55.

Levesque, George A. "Interpreting Early Black Ideology: A Reappraisal of Historical Consensus." *Journal of the Early Republic* 1, no. 3 (Fall 1981): 269–87.

Mercer, Keith. "Northern Exposure: Resistance to Naval Impressment in British North America, 1775–1815." *Canadian Historical Review* 91, no. 2 (June 2010): 199–232.

Moore, John Trotwood. "Historic Highways of the South." *Taylor-Trotwood Magazine* 5 (May 1907): 143.

Olick, Jeffrey K., and Joyce Robbins. "Social Memory Studies: From 'Collective Memory' to the Historical Sociology of Mnemonic Practices." *Annual Review of Sociology* 24 (1998): 105–40.

Owsley, Frank L., Jr. "Ambrister and Arbuthnot: Adventurers or Martyrs for British Honor?" *Journal of the Early Republic* 5 (Fall 1985): 289–308.

———. "British and Spanish Activities in West Florida during the War of 1812." *Florida Historical Quarterly* 46, no. 1 (October 1967): 111–23.

Riddell, William Renwick. "A Negro Slave in Detroit when Detroit was Canadian." *Michigan History Magazine* 18 (1934): 49–50.

Rosen, Deborah A. "Wartime Prisoners and the Rule of Law." *Journal of the Early Republic* 28 (Winter 2008): 559–95.

Shaw, Peter. "Blood Is Thicker than Irony: Henry Adams' *History*." *New England Quarterly* 40, no. 2 (June 1967): 163–87.

———. "The War of 1812 Could Not Take Place: Henry Adams's *History*." *Yale Review* 62, no. 4 (June 1973): 544–56.

Sheads, Scott S., and Anna Von Lunz. "Defenders' Day, 1815–1898: A Brief History." *Maryland Historical Magazine* 93, no. 3 (Fall 1998): 301–16.

Skelton, William B. "High Army Leadership in the Era of the War of 1812: The Making and Remaking of the Officer Corps." *William and Mary Quarterly* 51, no. 2 (April 1994): 253–74.

Stagg, J. C. A. "Enlisted Men in the United States Army, 1812–1815: A Preliminary Survey." *William and Mary Quarterly* 43, no. 4 (October 1986): 615–45.

Stone, Daniel. "Did Founding Fathers on Currency Get Facelifts?" Newsweek.com, 6 April 2011. www.newsweek.com/did-founding-fathers-currency-get-facelifts-70365.

Tregle, Joseph G., Jr. "Andrew Jackson and the Continuing Battle of New Orleans." *Journal of the Early Republic* 1, no. 4 (Winter 1981): 373–93.

———. "Early New Orleans Society: A Reappraisal." *Journal of Southern History* 18, no. 1 (February 1952): 20–36.

Vogel, Robert C. "Jean Laffitte, the Baratarians, and the Battle of New Orleans, A Reappraisal." *Louisiana History* 41, no. 3 (Summer 2000): 261–76.

Whitmer, Mariana. "Using Music to Teach American History." *OAH Magazine of History* 19, no. 4 (July 2005): 4–5.

Williamson, Kevin D. "The Devil and Mr. Jackson." *New Criterion* 29, no. 5 (January 2011): 42–46.

PRIMARY SOURCES

Acts Passed at the First Session of the Legislative Council of the Territory of Orleans. . . . New Orleans: James M. Bradford, 1805.

Acts Passed at the Second Session of the First Legislature of the Territory of Orleans. New Orleans: Bradford & Anderson, 1807.

Acts Passed at the Second Session of the Second Legislature of the Territory of Orleans. New Orleans: Bradford & Anderson, 1808.

American State Papers: Documents, Legislative and Executive, of the Congress of the United States. Edited by Walter Lowrie and Matthew St. Clair Clarke. Washington, DC: Gales & Seaton, 1833.

The Battle of New Orleans, Official Programme. New Orleans: Louisiana Historical Society, 1915.

Battle of New Orleans Scrapbook, 1815–1940. Louisiana Historical Center, Louisiana State Museum, New Orleans.

Carter, Clarence Edwin, ed. *Territorial Papers of the United States.* 28 vols. Washington, DC: GPO, 1934–75.

Claiborne, W. C. C. *Official Letter Books of W. C. C. Claiborne, 1801–1816.* Edited by Dunbar Rowland. 6 vols. Jackson, MS: State Department of Archives and History, 1917.

Clay, Henry. *The Papers of Henry Clay.* Edited by James F. Hopkins and Mary W. M. Hargreaves. 11 vols. Lexington: University Press of Kentucky, 1959–92.

Cockburn, George, Papers. Library of Congress. Washington, DC.

Fraser, Alexander David, Papers. Burton Historical Collection, Detroit Public Library.

House Report No. 81 to accompany House Resolution 2232, An Act in Reference to a National Military Park on the Plains of Chalmette, November 19, 1921.

Jackson, Andrew. *Correspondence of Andrew Jackson.* Edited by John Spencer Bassett and J. Franklin Jameson. 7 vols. Washington, DC: Carnegie Institute of Washington, 1926–35.

———. *The Papers of Andrew Jackson.* Edited by Dan Feller, Sam B. Smith, Harriet Fason Chappell Owsley, and Harold D. Moser. 9 vols. to date. Knoxville: University of Tennessee Press, 1980–.

Jefferson, Thomas. *The Papers of Thomas Jefferson.* Edited by Julian P. Boyd, Lyman H. Butterfield, and Mina R. Brian. 41 vols. to date. Princeton, NJ: Princeton University Press, 1950–.

———. *Thomas Jefferson: Writings.* Edited by Merrill D. Peterson. New York: Library of America, 1984.

———. The Thomas Jefferson Papers at the Library of Congress: Series 1: General Correspondence, 1651–1827, Manuscript Division.

Ladies Hermitage Association Board of Directors. Meeting Minutes, January 1906–September 1914. Collections at the Hermitage. Nashville.

Louisiana Act No. 8 (17 January 1894); An Act Providing for the Completion by the Secretary of War of a Monument to the Memory of the American Soldiers who fell in the Battle of New Orleans at Chalmette, Louisiana, and Making the Necessary Appropriation Thereof. 59th Cong., 2nd sess. (4 March 1907).

Michigan Historical Collections. Vol. 40, *Documents Relating to Detroit and Vicinity, 1805–1813.* Lansing: Michigan Historical Commission, 1929.

"The Negro in the Military Service of the United States, 1639–1886." M858, roll 1, vols. 1–2, 1639–1862. RG 94, National Archives.

Parton, James, Papers. Houghton Library, Harvard University.

Register of Blacks in Ohio Counties, 1804–1861. Ohio Historical Society Papers. Ohio Historical Society, Columbus.

The Revised Code of the Laws of Virginia. Richmond: Thomas Ritchie, 1819.

Richardson, James D., ed. *A Compilation of the Messages and Papers of the Presidents.* 10 vols. Washington, DC: Library of Congress, 1902.

United States Daughters of 1812, Chalmette Chapter, Papers. Tulane University Special Collections, New Orleans.

US Congress. *Debates and Proceedings in the Congress of the United States, 1789–1824.* 42 vols. Washington, DC: Gales & Seaton, 1834–56.

———. *State Papers and Public Documents of the United States, from the accession of George Washington to the Presidency, exhibiting a complete view of our foreign relations since that time.* Boston: T. B. Wait and Sons, 1817.

Wellesley, Arthur, Duke of Wellington. *The Dispatches of Field Marshal, the Duke of Wellington, K.G. During his Various Campaigns in India, Denmark, Portugal, Spain, the Low Countries, and France. From 1799 to 1818.* Edited by John Gurwood. 13 vols. London: John Murray, 1834–39.

Woodward, Augustus B., Papers. Burton Historical Collection, Detroit Public Library.

NEWSPAPERS

Baltimore Sun

Commercial Bulletin (New Orleans)

Nashville American

Nashville Banner
Nashville Tennessean
New Orleans Daily Picayune
New Orleans Times-Picayune
Niles' Weekly Register (Baltimore)

THESES AND DISSERTATIONS

McRae, Norman. "Blacks in Detroit, 1736–1833: The Search for Freedom and Community and its Implications for Education." PhD diss., University of Michigan, 1982.

Stephens, Rachel Elizabeth. "America's Portraitist: Ralph E. W. Earl and the Imaging of the Jacksonian Era." PhD diss., University of Iowa, 2010. ir.uiowa.edu/etd/3538.

Stoltz, Joseph F., III. "'An Ardent Military Spirit': William C. C. Claiborne and the Creation of the Orleans Territorial Militia, 1803–1805." MA thesis, University of New Orleans, 2009.

Toups, Gerard. "The Provincial, Territorial, and State Administrations of William C. C. Claiborne, Governor of Louisiana, 1803–1816." PhD diss., University of Southwestern Louisiana, 1979.

INTERVIEWS

Stratton, Jay (Director of Air Warfare/SPEAR, Office of Naval Intelligence). Telephone interview by author, 25 October 2014.

PRESENTATIONS

Howard, Michelle (Vice Admiral). "Battle of Lake Erie 200 Years Later: Lessons Learned." Paper presented at Naval History and Heritage Command's National Museum of the U.S. Navy, Washington, DC, September 2013. navylive.dodlive.mil/2013/09/10/battle-of-lake-erie-200-years-later-lessons-learned/.

MEDIA

Andrew Jackson. A&E Television, 2006. DVD.

Andrew Jackson: A Man for the People. A&E Television, 1995. DVD.

Andrew Jackson: Conqueror of Florida. A&E Television, 2005. DVD.

Andrew Jackson: Good, Evil, and the Presidency. KCET/Los Angeles & Red Hill Productions, 2007. DVD.

Bloody, Bloody Andrew Jackson. Original cast recording. Ghostlight Records, 2010, compact disc. Music and lyrics by Michael Friedman and Alex Timber. Cover art by Jessica Disbrow Talley.

Driftwood, Jimmy. "The Battle of New Orleans." *Kerrville Folk Festival: The Early Years 1972–1981.* Westminster, VT: Silverwolf Records 1009, 1998.

From Where I Stand: The Black Experience in Country Music. Warner Brothers, 9 46248-2, 1998, 3 compact discs.

WEBSITES

"Andrew Jackson by Thomas Sully." Office of the Senate Curator. Accessed 22 December 2014. www.senate.gov/artandhistory/art/artifact/Painting_32_00018.htm.

The Avalon Project. Yale Law School. avalon.law.yale.edu/subject_menus/jaymenu.asp.

Grice, C. E. *The Battle of New Orleans, Or Glory, Love And Loyalty: an Historical And National Drama, In Five Acts.* New York: printed for the author by John Low, 1816. Hathi Trust Digital Library. hdl.handle.net/2027/loc.ark:/13960/t2j67j686.

"The History of Currier & Ives." Currier & Ives Foundation, 1997–2011. Accessed 22 December 2014. www.currierandives.com.

"The Hunters of Kentucky." Baylor University Libraries Digital Collections, Frances G. Spencer Collection of American Popular Sheet Music. Accessed 31 October 2014. digitalcollections.baylor.edu/cdm/fullbrowser/collection/faspnc/id/21138/rv/compoundobject/cpd/21140.

"'The Hunters of Kentucky': A Popular Song Celebrates the Victory of Jackson and his Frontier Fighters over the British, 1824." *History Matters: The U.S. Survey Course on the Web.* Accessed 4 September 2014. historymatters.gmu.edu/d/6522.

"Jimmy Driftwood Original Battle of New Orleans." YouTube. Accessed 11 November 2014. www.youtube.com/watch?v=nE4yTfawEH8.

Oliver Hazard Perry Rhode Island. "Commodore Oliver Hazard Perry." Accessed 30 October 2015. www.ohpri.org/history-details/commodore-oliver-hazard-perry.

"Proclamation 4—Neutrality of the United States in the War Involving Austria, Prussia, Sardinia, Great Britain, and the United Netherlands Against France." 22 April 1793. The American Presidency Project. www.presidency.ucsb.edu/ws/index.php?pid=65475&st=&stl=.

SharpWriter. *"Iron" Andrew Jackson Alien Slayer.* deviantArt.com. 29 March 2011. www.sharpwriter.deviantart.com/art/Andrew-Jackson-Alien-Slayer-202767355.

"Star-Spangled Banner and the War of 1812." The Star-Spangled Banner Project. National Museum of American History, Behring Center, in cooperation with Public Inquiry Services, Smithsonian Institution, Washington, DC. Accessed 22 December 2014. www.si.edu/Encyclopedia_SI/nmah/starflag.htm#pageTop.

"Voices from the Dust Bowl: The Charles L. Todd and Robert Sonkin Migrant Worker Collection, 1940–1941." *American Memory.* Library of Congress. Accessed 10 November 2014. memory.loc.gov/cgi-bin/query/D?toddbib:5:./temp/~ammem_xAYq.

Contributors

MARK R. CHEATHEM is professor of history at Cumberland University in Lebanon, Tennessee. He is the author or editor of five books, including, most recently, *Andrew Jackson and the Rise of the Democrats* and *Andrew Jackson, Southerner,* which won the 2013 Tennessee History Book Award. He is currently completing a new book entitled *The Log Cabin and Hard Cider Campaign of 1840: Politics as Entertainment in Antebellum America.* He is also project director for the new presidential-papers project, The Papers of Martin Van Buren, located at Cumberland University.

BLAKE DUNNAVENT is an associate professor of history at Louisiana State University in Shreveport. He is the coauthor of *Combat at Close Quarters: Combat on the Rivers and Canals of Vietnam* (2015) and *Brown Water Warfare: The U.S. Navy in Riverine Warfare and the Emergence of a Tactical Doctrine, 1775–1970* (2003). He is also the author of the chapters "Maverick: Elmo Russell Zumwalt, Jr. (1920–2000)," in *Nineteen Gun Salute: Case Studies of Strategic and Operational Naval Leadership during the 20th Century* (2010), and "Battle for the Mekong: The River War in Vietnam," in *Rolling Thunder in a Gentle Land* (2006). Dunnavent spoke at the United States Naval Institute's Applied Naval History Conference "Riverine Warfare: Back to the Future," 6–7 April 2006, and at Camp Lejeune on the historical antecedents of riverine warfare as it applies to contemporary operations. He earned a BA from Abilene Christian University and a MA and PhD from Texas Tech University.

PAUL GELPI is a professor of military history at the Command and Staff College, Marine Corps University. He received his PhD in history from the

University of Alabama and his MA and BA from the University of New Orleans. He is a contributor to several encyclopedias of military and US history, as well as academic journals. He is the author of a forthcoming book on General Otto P. Weyland and national security issues in the Eisenhower administration.

LESLIE GREGORY GRUESBECK is an associate professor of art and the gallery coordinator at the Northwestern State University of Louisiana's Dear School of Creative and Performing Arts, where she teaches courses in art fundamentals to majors and minors as well as fiber-art courses. She has twice held the Donald F. Derby Endowed Professorship. She has studied at the Penland School of Crafts in Penland, North Carolina, and in the summer of 2015 she began coursework at the Royal School of Needlework in London.

DONALD R. HICKEY is a professor of history at Wayne State College in Nebraska. Called "the dean of 1812 scholarship" by the *New Yorker,* he is an award-winning author who has written seven books and nearly a hundred articles on the War of 1812. He is best known for *The War of 1812: A Forgotten Conflict* (Bicentennial edition, 2012) and *Don't Give Up the Ship! Myths of the War of 1812* (2006). He is the series editor for the Johns Hopkins Books on the War of 1812, has done extensive consulting work in connection with the Bicentennial commemoration of the conflict, and manages an e-mail list for those interested in the war. For promoting public understanding of the War of 1812, he received the Samuel Eliot Morison Award from the USS Constitution Museum in 2013.

TRACEY E. W. LAIRD is the author or editor of four books, including *Austin City Limits: A History* (Oxford University Press, 2014) and *Austin City Limits: A Monument to Music* (Insight Editions, September 2015), the latter coauthored with her spouse, Brandon Laird. She has also written about the famous radio barn dance that propelled both Hank Williams and Elvis Presley into the national spotlight in *Louisiana Hayride: Radio and Roots Music Along the Red River* (Oxford University Press, 2004), released in paperback in 2015. She is professor of music and chair at Agnes Scott College in Decatur, Georgia.

ALEXANDER MIKABERIDZE is associate professor of history and holds the Sybil T. And J. Frederick Patten Endowed Professorship for Excellence in Teaching at Louisiana State University Shreveport. He has written extensively on the Revolutionary and Napoleonic era, and his latest published book, *Napoleon's Trial by Fire* (London, 2014), completed his trilogy on the Franco-Russian conflict during the Napoleonic Wars. He is currently completing a book on the global history of the Revolutionary and Napoleonic Wars.

GENE ALLEN SMITH is professor of history at Texas Christian University in Fort Worth. During the 2013–14 academic year he held the Class of 1957 Distinguished Chair in Naval Heritage at the United States Naval Academy. He is the author or editor of books, articles, reviews on the War of 1812, naval and maritime history, and territorial expansion along the Gulf of Mexico, his most recent book being *The Slaves' Gamble: Choosing Sides in the War of 1812* (2013). Since 2002 he has served as director of the Center for Texas Studies at TCU.

JOSEPH F. STOLTZ III is the digital scholarship librarian at the Fred W. Smith National Library for the Study of George Washington at Mount Vernon. Prior to his recent move to Mount Vernon, he was assistant editor of the *West Point History of Warfare* at the United States Military Academy at West Point. He was also an instructor and senior thesis adviser in the history department. A New Orleans native, he received his PhD in history from Texas Christian University and his MA and BA from the University of New Orleans.

Index

Note: page numbers in *italics* refer to illustrations; those followed by "n" indicate endnotes.